SO-BMT-766

Welcome the Antichrist

Not quite asleep, Al turned on his back and opened his eyes, thinking that perhaps he was experiencing some negative side effect of having had too much beer. That, however, was not the case.

When he opened his eyes, he expected to see the ceiling, but instead, the spinning and dancing lights that seemed to draw nearer and nearer did not go away. Even with his eyes open, he saw them against a deep-black backdrop—not against the ceiling that he knew was above him.

As he watched in awe, the lights drew closer and closer together, slowly forming a figure . . . a very familiar figure . . . one that swept rapidly toward his face . . . the figure of Christ on the cross . . . but this Christ was unlike any in the pictures . . . this one had a face that was horribly mutilated . . . eyes bulging from their sockets . . . swollen tongue protruding from the fat, cracked lips, which moved and began to speak.

Other Books by Ed and Lorraine Warren

Werewolf
Ghosthunters
The Haunted
The Devil in Connecticut
Deliver Us from Evil
Satan's Harvest
The Demonologist
Graveyard

Other Books by Ray Garton

Dark Channel
Crucifax Autumn
Live Girls
Seductions
Darklings
Invaders from Mars
Warlock
Trade Secrets
Lot Lizards
The New Neighbor
Methods of Madness (collection of stories)

QUANTITY SALES

Most Dell books are available at special quantity discounts when purchased in bulk by corporations, organizations, or groups. Special imprints, messages, and excerpts can be produced to meet your needs. For more information, write to: Dell Publishing, 1540 Broadway, New York, NY 10036. Attention: Director, Special Markets.

INDIVIDUAL SALES

Are there any Dell books you want but cannot find in your local stores? If so, you can order them directly from us. You can get any Dell book currently in print. For a complete up-to-date listing of our books and information on how to order, write to: Dell Readers Service, Box DR, 1540 Broadway, New York, NY 10036.

In a Dark Place

The Story of a True Haunting

Ed and Lorraine Warren
and Al and Carmen Snedeker

Written by Ray Garton

A DELL BOOK

Published by
Dell Publishing
a division of
Bantam Doubleday Dell Publishing Group, Inc.
1540 Broadway
New York, New York 10036

If you purchased this book without a cover you should be aware that this book is stolen property. It was reported as "unsold and destroyed" to the publisher and neither the author nor the publisher has received any payment for this "stripped book."

Copyright © 1992 by Ray Garton, Al Snedeker, Carmen Snedeker, Ed Warren, and Lorraine Warren

All rights reserved. No part of this book may be reproduced or transmitted in any form or by any means, electronic or mechanical, including photocopying, recording, or by any information storage and retrieval system, without the written permission of the Publisher, except where permitted by law. For information address: Villard Books, a division of Random House, Inc., New York, New York.

The trademark Dell® is registered in the U.S. Patent and Trademark Office.

ISBN: 0-440-21698-2

Reprinted by arrangement with Villard Books

Printed in the United States of America

Published simultaneously in Canada

October 1994

10 9 8 7 6 5 4 3 2 1
OPM

To my wife, Dawn,
who remained
patient through every page

—*Ray Garton*

Acknowledgments

A lot of people were generous with their editorial talents and moral support during the writing of this book, and I would like to thank them here:

My agent and friend, Lori Perkins; my wonderful editor, Emily Bestler, and her assistants, Tom Fiffer and Amelia Sheldon, who were patient and helpful throughout; my friends Scott Sandin, Paul Meredith, and Stephanie Terrazas; my parents, Ray and Pat Garton; Joe Citro and Jerry Sawyer, two fine writers who tell the truth; Dean R. Koontz, from whom all good advice flows; Rev. Cheri Scotch, High Priestess of the Temple of Diana, whose good sense—and sense of humor—are always a big help; and, of course, Dawn, without whom this book would not have been written.

—Ray Garton

Preface:
Demonic Possession

The study of demonic possession never has been, is not now, and very likely never *will* be, a science.

There are, however, many who have devoted their lives to that study, who have tried to determine the point at which possession begins so that it might be avoided.

Possession goes back to the time of Christ, who cast demons from a number of people, according to the New Testament. Today, it is little more than a subject for Hollywood horror films. But many Christian churches and sects still practice the rite of exorcism, foremost among them being the Catholic church.

There are two different kinds of possession: that of a person and that of a place, such as a house or other kind of building. It is believed by many in the Catholic church, however, that both come about in much the same way.

First there is the point at which the demon(s) enters the person or the occupied building or house. There are a number of different theories as to what brings about the initial entry. In one well-documented case of demon possession, the demon claimed to have chosen its victim before the victim's own birth. Some believe that even a passing interest in the occult can be an invitation to possession. Still others think it will remain a mystery, that it is not for us to know until we face our Creator and hear the explanation firsthand.

One thing is almost unanimously agreed upon, however: The initial entry is only made after the victim, or the resident of the targeted building, has made a choice —however subconscious, however tenuous—to allow it.

For example, the Snedekers did nothing to bring on the possession of their house—that had begun long before. As Lorraine was able to sense clairvoyantly, something awful had taken place in that house sometime during its years as a funeral home. Someone had been using the dead bodies for their own sick pleasure, and it was that person's acts of necrophilia that opened the door to possession; it was that person who made a choice—by indulging in such perverse activities—to give the forces of evil entry to that house long before the Snedekers ever moved in.

Once the initial entry has taken place, the possessing entity gradually begins to break down its host or the occupants of the building it has entered. This is usually accomplished with fear. Not only does the possessing entity feed on fear, but it knows that fear will weaken its victim, thus bringing the entity closer to total control, closer to complete possession.

In the case of the Snedekers, the forces in the house, determined to gain entry to the Snedekers themselves, used fear to weaken them, to try to turn them against one another, all the while waiting for the third stage of demonic possession: Weakened and vulnerable, confused and terrified, the victim inevitably reaches a turning point and surrenders voluntarily to the forces of darkness.

An official exorcism cannot be held without proper investigation to determine whether or not the reported demonic activity is real. Sometimes, a person with mental problems or a substance addiction, or even a whole family suffering through domestic crises, can take the smallest of coincidences and turn them into a series of frightening events that lead to the conclusion that the house is possessed by demons. Mental illnesses have been mistaken for possession throughout history—illnesses such as schizophrenia, Tourette's snydrome, Huntington's chorea, Parkinson's disease, and even dyslexia—and even though medicine has advanced considerably over the years, such conditions must be ruled out by a priest before an exorcism is considered.

A priest with a medical or psychiatric background—sometimes both—begins the investigation by first trying to rule out all other possibilities; then, when satisfied, continues by testing the possibility of a demonic presence. Once he is able to prove demonic activity to his satisfaction, the priest then approaches the church. After the case has been reviewed and found to be thorough, the decision is made to go through with an exorcism.

According to those who have witnessed them, no two exorcisms are alike, although they all have two things in common, one of which is unforgettable to all those involved, whether it is an exorcism of a person or a building: the *presence.*

It is invisible, ethereal, and yet felt so deeply by everyone involved that it seems almost tangible. It is a presence neither male nor female . . . neither human being nor animal . . . neither a single entity nor a crowd of them . . . but it is distinct and, as the exorcism continues, usually becomes stronger. If and when it speaks, it sometimes refers to itself as "I," sometimes as "we." It moves around those present like an ice-cold breeze, a draft from the depths of the deepest cave in the earth, until the exorcism is over . . . until the possessing entity has been cast out in the name of God.

The second thing all exorcisms have in common is the most threatening: danger.

Those participating in an exorcism are in constant danger, and must antitipcate hearing the foulest insults and seeing the most frightening things they are likely to experience in their lives. Their faith must remain rock solid in the face of horrible, supernatural abuse. Demons will not uproot themselves without a powerful fight, and their chief weapon, as always, is fear. They feed on it, and will do anything they can to wring it out of those involved in the attempt to cast them out.

Not all such attempts are successful.

Demons wait for an invitation before their entry, but they don't always leave when told. . . .

In a Dark Place

1

Moving In

"Mom, we have to leave this house. There's something evil here."

Carmen Snedeker stood at the kitchen sink with foamy suds clinging to her forearms and hands as she washed a plate. Wadded clumps of newspaper and empty cardboard boxes were scattered on the floor around her and Willy, the Snedekers' pet ferret, played among them. The dishes that, shortly before, had been wrapped in newspapers and packed in boxes were on the counter to Carmen's right, grimy with newsprint and dusty from travel.

The laughing voices of the other children clattered off the bare walls as they ran in and out, breaking in their new home.

She heard the thunking and shifting of heavy furniture being moved in by Al and his brother.

Stephen, her fourteen-year-old son, had been wandering around the kitchen behind her, silent and restless, nudging boxes and papers with the toes of his sneakers as if he had something to say but didn't have the nerve. So she'd decided to wait until he was ready to speak.

"What'd you say, Stephen?" Carmen asked as she rinsed a plate.

He repeated himself: "I said there's something evil here, Mom, and we have to leave this house."

Putting the plate on the drainer to her left, Carmen turned to Stephen slowly, frowning. "Leave? We just got here, honey."

"I know, but we've gotta leave now."

"But where would we go?"

"Back to New York, back to our apartment. We have to, Mom. There's something . . ." He stopped a moment and squinted slightly, as if he were selecting his next word from a list of choices, then: ". . . wrong, there's something wrong with this house."

Carmen's frown deepened as she rinsed the suds off her hands and arms and dried them on a towel. She turned, leaned back against the edge of the counter, and folded her arms, facing her son.

He was so gaunt, so pale, with such dark gray half-moons beneath his eyes. She tried to get used to it—and, of course, she acted as if it were unnoticeable—but every time she looked at him, the physical changes in him clutched at her heart. It was as if the cobalt treatments he'd been receiving had sucked half of him away, had drained him down to a spindly porcelain doll that merely resembled her son. With those treatments had come a great deal of stress, and it was that stress to which Carmen attributed his claim about the house. That had to be it. He certainly couldn't know the truth about the house. Only Carmen and her husband, Al, knew about the house's past.

"What do you think's wrong with the house, Stephen?" she asked quietly.

His smooth forehead creased and he averted his eyes for a moment, then shrugged one shoulder and said, almost in a whisper, "I . . . don't know. It's just . . .

bad. It's"—he gave a jerky shake of his head, at once agitated and frustrated—"hard to explain. But it's bad. Evil. And if we don't leave here . . . something bad's gonna happen to us. Something really bad."

"Sweetheart, houses aren't evil. Only people are evil. Evil lives in their hearts, in the things they sometimes do and say to each other. But this house . . . well, it's just an old house. If it could talk, it could probably tell us some great stories, maybe even some *scary* stories. But it's not evil. It's just new to you, that's all," she added with a half-smile. "You'll get used to it after a while and you'll feel better about it, more comfortable with it. Did you see your room downstairs?"

Stephen bowed his head and stared at the floor, then nodded slightly. He said something, but it was too quiet for her to understand.

Carmen tucked a knuckle under his chin and tipped his head up slightly. "What?"

"That was the room that felt so bad. It felt . . . evil, Mom. I don't wanna sleep down there. It just doesn't feel . . . right."

Carmen tried to let nothing show on her face. Again, she reminded herself that Stephen knew nothing about the house, that he knew nothing about what kinds of things used to go on there. She took a deep breath and some of the tension in her chest relaxed.

"But that's your room," she said. "You've always wanted a room of your own."

He shook his head. "Well, I won't sleep down there alone."

"But Michael won't be back from Alabama for weeks. Where are you going to sleep till then?"

He shrugged as he leaned down to pet Willy. "I'll sleep on the couch. Or maybe on the living room floor, I don't know. But"—he began shaking his head again as he turned and headed back out to the kitchen, stepping around and over the empty boxes—"I won't sleep down there by myself."

Carmen remained with her back to the sink, arms folded, the towel dangling from one hand. She watched him walk away, then listened to his footsteps on the wood floor after he was out of sight, listening until she could no longer hear them.

Turning back to the sink, Carmen took another dish from the stack and began to wash it as she released a slow, quiet sigh.

In a short time, the Snedekers had traveled what seemed a very long and treacherous road. That road began in April of 1986.

Al and Carmen had met in 1977 in Plainville, Connecticut, in a bowling alley where Carmen was waitressing. Al had wholesome good looks, with a neatly trimmed mustache and short, dark brown hair. He stood a little over six feet in his socks and had a solid, muscular build from years of hard work. Carmen, on the other hand, was petite, with a broad, glowing smile and full, wavy blond hair. The two were immediately attracted to each other but Carmen preferred to take her time when making big changes in her life.

The middle of five children, Carmen was the daughter of a staff sergeant in the air force. Not long after her birth at Harris Air Force Base in Biloxi, Mississippi, Carmen, her two older sisters, and two younger brothers, were moved by their parents to another town. And another, and another . . . and they kept moving to wherever their father's work led them for five years, until he was disabled and subsequently discharged from service. Then they moved to Carmen's parents' hometown of Decatur, Alabama. But those years of constant uprooting, of never being able to settle, of always being on the move to someplace new and unfamiliar—even though she was very small at the time—had somehow stayed with Carmen, giving her a gnawing suspicion of changes in life, even the natural ones.

Later, when she was grown, Carmen made a drastic change in her life: marriage. With it came two more changes, her sons Stephen and Michael. But they were good changes, happy ones, changes that enriched her life rather than destabilizing it. Then came the worst change: divorce. Once again, Carmen found herself in unfamiliar territory, single with two sons. Carmen and the boys moved to Connecticut to stay with Carmen's parents, where, with little education and no work experience, Carmen went about the business of getting a job and making life as stable as possible for her children.

Al, on the other hand, had lived with his two brothers and three sisters in the same wood-frame house on the border of Plainville and New Britain, Connecticut, until he was grown. With no other children around but his brother and sisters, Al spent a lot of time with them playing in the woods around the house, and came to love the outdoors.

When he was grown, Al married in 1975, but the marriage lasted only nineteen months. Having led a life that was relatively smooth—except, of course, for the usual ups and downs, hurts and disappointments that everyone faces while growing up—Al was rocked by the bitter divorce and took his time getting into another relationship.

Then Al met Carmen in that bowling alley where she worked as a cocktail waitress, and everything changed. They were married in 1979, and began their new life full of hope.

In 1986, they were living in Hurleyville, New York, in the Catskill Mountains. During the summer months, New Yorkers came to the Catskills to spend their vacations. The Snedekers were never quite sure why because these big-city travelers seemed to have no appreciation at all for the beautiful green surroundings or the wildlife. During the summer months, in any store or shopping center, one could hear the vacationers complaining about the wild animals in the area that simply would *not* get out of the way of their cars. The number of dead animals on the roadside increased during the summer, too.

During that time, Al Snedeker worked in a stone quarry and Carmen babysat four children throughout the day, enabling her to stay home for her own. They were devout Catholics and went to church every Sunday. Carmen was involved in a number of church activities to which she devoted a good portion of what free time she had.

It was in April of that year that Stephen developed a dry, hacking cough. Al was the first to notice it and became concerned. But Carmen had seen the children come down with any number of combinations of coughs, sore throats, rashes, runny noses, and stuffed-up heads, so she was confident it would go away soon enough.

But the cough stayed.

"Mom, what's this?" Stephen asked one day, coming to Carmen frowning, with his fingertips pressed to the left side of his neck.

Carmen nudged his fingers away gently and replaced them with her own. Just beneath his jaw she found a pebble-sized lump.

Hormones, she thought with the slightest pinprick of worry piercing her chest, *that's all it is, just his hormones kicking in.*

Stephen pulled away as he broke into another fit of hoarse raspy coughs. Did the cough sound worse . . . or was it just her imagination?

Carmen thought, *It might just be hormones, but—*

"I think I'll make an appointment for you with Dr.

Ketchum," she said, putting her hands on his shoulders and giving them a squeeze.

Dr. Paul Ketchum was warm, pleasant, and usually smiling. None of the Snedeker children were ever afraid of seeing him. They trusted him; so did Al and Carmen. So when Dr. Ketchum said he wanted Stephen to spend a little time in the hospital for some tests, no one saw any reason to be overly concerned.

Carmen took the boy in to be admitted early the following Monday morning. It seemed odd to be hospitalizing Stephen when he seemed his usual healthy, upbeat self. Except for that cough. Except for that lump.

She admitted him and spent the morning with him in the pediatrics ward, but had to be back home when the younger children returned from school.

"Sorry I have to go, honey," she said, standing beside his bed.

Stephen held the control for the bed in his hand and was having fun moving it up and down. He looked up at her and gave her a big smile. It was such a *boy's* smile, so hungry for new experiences, so full of raw enthusiasm. "S'okay, Mom," he said. "I'll be fine."

After dinner that evening, Al and Carmen went to the hospital to visit Stephen. On their way to his room, they spotted Dr. Ketchum coming toward them down the corridor. They smiled at him, but his response was less than enthusiastic. His shoulders were slumped a bit and his walk was slower and less energetic than usual. He nodded once, greeting them with a silent hello.

"So, how's Stephen?" Al asked, holding his smile in place, although it threatened to fade.

"Stephen is just fine," Dr. Ketchum said quietly. "It's the tests I'm not too sure about."

Carmen took in a deep, steadying breath and exhaled, saying, "What do you mean?"

"Well, unfortunately they aren't really telling us anything conclusive about Stephen's condition. So, I think we're going to have to go a step further. I talked to Dr. Morley today. He's a surgeon, a very *good* surgeon."

Al took Carmen's hand and squeezed it.

"He agrees with me that we should do a biopsy and, as long as you agree, too, he'd like to do it tomorrow."

Al and Carmen exchanged a dark, worried glance.

His voice dry, Al said, "So, this . . . um, this just means that you and the surgeon want to get to the bottom of Stephen's problem. Right?"

Dr. Ketchum nodded and said encouragingly, "Yes, of course, that's *exactly* what we want to do."

They agreed to the biopsy, chatted with Dr. Ketchum a moment, their voices thin, their mouths dry, then went to Stephen's room. They did not speak on the way, just held hands.

Stephen was sitting up in bed watching television and chewing on the end of a drinking straw. He smiled at them as they went to his bedside. He looked a little tired, but still healthy as ever.

So why is he here? Carmen wondered.

"How was your day in the hospital, kiddo?" Al asked, slapping Stephen's knee beneath the blanket.

Stephen shrugged. "Okay, I guess. 'Cept for the vampires." He stretched out his arm to show them the Band-Aid on his inner elbow where blood had been drawn.

"We'll bring you some garlic," Carmen said smiling, "you can hold 'em off with that."

"I still don't know what's wrong with me," he said, frowning slightly. "I feel fine. Only time I feel sick is when I get sick of layin' around in here."

"The doctor's not sure what's wrong, either," Al said slowly, pulling a chair to the bed and sitting. "That's why he wants to do a biopsy tomorrow."

Stephen's eyes widened. "A *biopsy*? You mean where they cut you open and take out your *insides*?"

Al and Carmen laughed. "No, no," Al said, "that's an *autopsy*, and they only do that on dead people. No, a biopsy is where they take a tiny piece of your lump out and examine it."

The boy frowned. "Is it gonna hurt?"

"You won't feel a thing. Just before they do it, a nurse'll come in here with a great big mallet and bop you over the head with it. You'll be out like a light."

Stephen laughed and threw the straw at Al who, along with Carmen, hid his concern behind a smile.

The next day, Tuesday, was one of the longest of their lives. They waited outside the operating room listening to the doctors being paged over the P.A. system, to the hushed rubber-soled footsteps of the nurses bustling up and down the corridors, and breathing the antiseptic medicine-tinged hospital air as time passed at the speed of molasses oozing over a flat surface, until . . .

The double doors of the operating room opened and Dr. Morley, Stephen's surgeon, hurried out. He glanced at Al and Carmen, but seemed to look right through them as he walked on, hands slipped in the pockets of his white coat.

Al and Carmen looked at one another with wide-eyed surprise, then stood simultaneously and hurried after the doctor. Al called out, but got no response. Carmen moved ahead of her husband, closed in on the doctor and clutched his arm. Dr. Morley spun around, startled.

"We'd like to know how our son is," she said.

The doctor blinked a few times, then said, "Oh, yes, um, well . . . Dr. Ketchum will be in touch with you this afternoon. I think it would be best if you talked to him about the results. You can visit your son in a couple hours, after he gets out of recovery." Then he turned and headed down the corridor, blending in with all the other white coats and uniforms and white walls.

They had more time to kill, time filled with the restless ghosts of unanswered questions. Over lunch, Carmen said quietly, "It can't be too serious. I mean, he would've *said* something if it was serious, right?"

"Yeah," Al said, "I think so." Then he sighed, "I hope so."

After lunch, Carmen took Al home to be with the younger children when they got home from school, and she went to the store to buy Stephen a gift. When she got to the hospital, he was sound asleep, his neck bandaged and a thin tube trailing from the I.V. bottle hanging over his head to his inner elbow. She sat beside his bed holding on her lap the box of Lego blocks she'd bought for him—the advanced kind, far more sophisticated and complex than the kid stuff—and watched him sleep as she prayed silently, her rosary clicking gently as her fingers moved over it.

The only other time Stephen had been in the hospital was when he was born. The worst bout he'd ever had with illness was a cold or the flu, nothing more. Now this . . . whatever *this* was.

As she prayed, she heard her own words to Al echoing in her mind: *It can't be too serious . . . can't be too serious . . . too serious . . .*

Sometime toward dusk, Stephen opened his eyes long enough to smile. She stood quickly, put the box on the chair and whispered, "How you feeling, honey?" His eyes fluttered. "Stephen? Look what I brought you." She turned, got the Legos, but when she turned to him again, he was asleep.

An officious voice announced that visiting hours were over. She leaned forward, kissed her son's cheek, then left, feeling empty and cold, even though the evening was warm.

When she arrived home, Carmen could see Al through the big picture window in the front of the house. He was seated in his recliner watching television.

The familiarity of seeing him there doing what he did every evening at that time soothed Carmen somewhat, made her feel a little more normal and made her want to get inside to the comfort and safety of her family. She walked through the door, put down her purse, and went to Al's chair where he sat staring at the television through puffy red eyes, his cheeks glistening with streaks of tears. He looked up at her, his lips pressed together so tightly they were pale, then turned away, closing his eyes and spilling more tears.

Carmen was so stunned she could do no more than stare at him. Suddenly, her mind and heart began to compete in a dizzying race. Al was a very quiet man, spare with his words, speaking only when he had something specific to say, and, except for when he got angry enough, he held his emotions close to his chest, like a poker player hiding the cards in his hand. Something had to be *very* wrong for him to cry so openly. But what could it be? Not Stephen, it *couldn't* be Stephen, she'd just come from the hospital, after all, and Stephen was fine, just fine!

"What's wrong, Al?" she asked, her voice dry and hoarse.

He opened his mouth to respond but could only sob as he leaned forward and put his face in his hands.

Carmen knelt beside the chair and put a hand on his arm as her heartbeat thundered in her ears. "Al, please, will you tell me what's the matter?"

The telephone rang loudly, and when she picked up the receiver, she realized her palms were sweating. "Hello?"

"Oh, Carmen, I'm glad you're finally home. I've m-missed you wherever I've c-called." The voice was male and adult, but thick with tears and tremulous with emotion. "It's Dr. Ketchum," he said.

Dr. Ketchum? But he was crying. Why?

Because, she thought, *he's been our doctor for a long time, our friend, and he's a good man and he's crying now because something is wrong, terribly, terribly wrong . . .*

She tried to speak, had to clear her throat first, then asked, "What is it? What's the matter?"

"I'm very sorry, Carmen," he said after taking a deep breath, "but Dr. Morley said that Stephen's neck is filled with cancer."

That word was a drill that drove into her stomach and mangled her insides. It was an ugly word, glistening black and pulsating, that had a life all its own.

"I'm sorry," Dr. Ketchum said, clearing his throat, "but it . . . well, we're going to do everything we can, you know that, but . . . it doesn't look good."

She ended the conversation abruptly and dropped the receiver from her numb hand into the cradle. When she turned, Al was still in his chair staring at her with teary eyes.

They called both families to give them the news, and each call was worse than the last: voices crumbling into tears and sobs, grieving for Stephen almost as if the news had been that he'd already died.

Carmen saved her mother, Wanda Jean, for last. Wanda Jean had practically raised Stephen and Michael while Carmen worked, and Carmen knew she would find in her mother the support and strength she needed. But, like the others on the telephone before her, Wanda Jean fell apart.

Carmen felt her hands shake as she listened to her mother's tears. A few minutes later, when she hung up, she turned to Al who had been alternately sitting in his chair and pacing.

"Why is everyone doing this?" Carmen asked, her voice raspy. "Why is everyone acting like he's *dead* already, or something?"

"What do you mean, why is everybody doin' this?" Al

croaked. "He has *cancer*, Carmen. We're all *upset*, is why we're doin' this! I guess we can't all be strong like you. I guess we can't *all* be like one of those noble, long-suffering women Meryl Streep is always playing." He sat in his chair.

"I mean, am I gonna be the only one to hold up? *Somebody's* got to, otherwise we're gonna scare the hell out of Stephen."

But Al did not respond.

Carmen's eyes stung with tears as she sat silently by the telephone, trying to clean all the fear out of her mind.

The next morning, after the children had gone to school and Al had called in to get the day off work, Carmen said, "What a beautiful day to go fishing."

He stared at her, shocked. There were bags under his watery eyes and his face was drawn. "Are you *serious*?" When she didn't reply, he shook his head slowly. "No, I . . . I need to be with Stephen."

Gently as possible, placing her hand on his, she said, "Then you're gonna have to pull yourself together. Remember what I said last night? You'll only frighten him if he sees you like this."

"Yeah," he nodded, "I see your point."

Later that day, in the hospital corridor leading to Stephen's room, Carmen saw Al steeling himself. He rubbed a hand down his face once, as if to wipe off whatever anguish showed there. They pushed through the door smiling and found Stephen talking with Dr. Ketchum.

"You're just in time to see him off to X ray," the doctor said, and two young nurses came into the room behind Al and Carmen with a wheelchair.

"Time to hit the road," one of them said as Stephen slid off the bed and got into the chair.

"We'll be here when you get back, okay?" Carmen assured him.

"Boy, with all the attention you get around here, you're not gonna want to come home, kiddo," Al said with a weak smile.

As he was wheeled out of the room, Stephen said, "Oh, yes I will."

Once they were alone, Dr. Ketchum began to talk quietly to Al and Carmen about lymphatic cancer and the problems that could arise, and he suggested they tell Stephen soon. As he spoke, he kept glancing at Al, noticing the fists clenching and unclenching, the perspiration on his forehead, the fidgeting, and the way he turned his face away whenever someone looked at him.

"You don't look so good, Al," Dr. Ketchum said.

Al shrugged and began to pace the room.

The doctor said, "Listen, Al, I want you to sit down. I'm going to have a nurse come in and take your blood pressure." Once Al was seated in a chair, Dr. Ketchum stood in front of him and said quietly, "You're going to have to stay calm, Al. I know this is tough, but if you don't pull yourself together, you'll make yourself sick and you won't be any help to Stephen then. Understand?"

Al nodded. But in spite of his efforts to relax, his anxiety stayed with him, whispering in his ear the horrible things that *might* happen, things like death, a funeral, a gravestone. . . .

On Thursday, Stephen was released from the hospital to spend the weekend at home. On Monday, he was to go to John Dempsey Hospital in Connecticut for three weeks of tests. Over the weekend, Carmen managed to persuade Al to go fishing as much as possible. On Saturday, she and Stephen drove Al to the lake and dropped him off.

"Mom?" Stephen asked when they were alone in the

car. "What's wrong with me? I mean . . . exactly. Nobody will tell me."

O Lord, give me the right words, Carmen prayed silently. After a few moments of thought, she said, "You have . . . something called Hodgkin's disease. Well, it's . . . actually, it's lymphatic cancer, is what it is."

Stephen nodded very slowly, then said, almost in a whisper, "Cancer. I kinda thought it was something bad." He continued to nod slowly. "But I'm not gonna die."

Keeping her voice steady, she said, "Of course you're not, kiddo, 'cause we're gonna pray about it and fight it. But . . . you know it's not going to be easy, right?"

This time he whispered: "I'm not gonna die."

On Monday morning, Al drove Carmen and Stephen to the hospital in Connecticut. He had to drive straight back to Hurleyville to take care of the kids and he left right away, knowing he would be unable to hold up under the weight of a lingering good-bye.

The pediatrics ward at John Dempsey was like most others; the walls were decorated with cheerful cartoon figures and drawings by the children, mobiles of every sort hung from the high ceilings and, instead of the usual hospital whites, the ward was done in soft, soothing colors.

But it didn't help. The ward was still filled with sick children. Even dying children. And now Carmen's son was among them. All the cheerful colors in the world could not change that.

The tests began shortly after Stephen was admitted and they went on forever. There were blood tests, X rays, and scans, then he spent seven hours in surgery one day. After that, there were still more tests. The old saying that the cure is sometimes worse than the disease became very potent to Stephen and Carmen.

Doctors and nurses swarmed around Stephen's bed

like honeybees around a hive. But as Stephen began to grow pale and fragile, it was sometimes difficult for Carmen not to imagine them as circling vultures rather than swarming bees.

Al's family lived in Connecticut, so Carmen wasn't entirely alone. She spent the nights in a nearby motel and always called Al as soon as she got in. Since she'd seen him last, he'd begun having severe chest pains and, although she thought Stephen had drained every ounce of worry from her, she began worrying about Al as well. After a few tests at the hospital, however, it was determined that Al's chest pains were symptoms of extreme anxiety and were nothing serious.

Carmen knew that something would have to change at home to take some of the load off Al's shoulders, so she called her mother. Wanda Jean was in Italy at the time, but was happy to fly home and take care of the children for a while.

At the end of three weeks, Stephen was released from the hospital and allowed to return home to Hurleyville. He was thinner, pale, and there was a weariness in his every movement. It was as if a siphon had been attached to him for the past three weeks, slowly draining his youth. As if that wasn't enough, he had to return to Connecticut every day for cobalt treatments. His already weakened condition only grew worse under the strain of the grueling treatments and the 106-mile-a-day trips. In fact, that strain took a toll on the entire family.

Al and Carmen decided to look for an apartment closer to the hospital. With four children, they knew it would not be easy to find one big enough that they could afford—the medical bills were piling up quickly—but it would be easier than driving so far every day and spending so much money on gas.

Using every spare moment she could find, Carmen began the search. She encountered one disappointment after another: too small, too expensive, or both. Although wearing down, she continued looking, found another promising ad in the local classified section and made an appointment to see the apartment in Southington. On her way there, she drove by a beautiful three-story Colonial-style house with a sign in the front yard that read FOR RENT.

The apartment she'd arranged to see was very nice but, like so many others, simply too small. On the way back to the motel, however, she followed an impulse to stop at the Colonial house with the sign in front.

There were workmen all around the house and the sounds of hammering and drilling and sawing clashed in an ugly cacophony. Carmen approached one workman after another, asking whom she should talk to about renting the place, until one of them finally directed her around the corner of the house to a pleasant, soft-spoken man whose right arm was curled up in front of his chest, shriveled and useless.

"Help you?" he asked, raising his voice because of all the noise.

"I'm interested in looking at the house," she said, wincing slightly at the clatter.

"Oh. Well." He lifted his good arm and rubbed his hand back and forth over his kinky, graying hair. "The owner's not here right now and"—he chuckled, nodding toward the house—"you can see we're doing a lot of work right now, so I don't know if this'd be a good time, know what I'm sayin'?" He smiled around crooked teeth and the lines in his face deepened.

Carmen realized she was wringing her hands and stopped, not wanting to look *too* desperate. "I've been looking everywhere for days and I just can't find a place for my family. This one looks good and we need a place right away because my son has to—"

He began nodding and held up a hand to stop her.

"Tell you what. There's two apartments in there, one upstairs and one down. Why don't you go upstairs and look around and when you're done, I'll give you the name and phone number of the owner. Sound good?"

Relieved and excited, she went upstairs, hoping for the best. That was what she found. The living room was spacious with lots of windows that made it appear even larger. The kitchen was roomy, too, and had a built-in trestle table with benches. There were four large bedrooms and, upstairs, two more, one with built-in captain's beds paneled in solid pine.

It was beautiful. It was perfect. And it was probably way too expensive.

She hurried downstairs, got the owner's number and called him the second she got back to her motel room.

His name was Mr. Campbell and he sounded reluctant at first. Carmen didn't let that bother her once he'd quoted the monthly rate though; it was well within their price range. She told Mr. Campbell everything: about Stephen's illness, about how far they had to travel every day for his treatments, about how hard she'd been looking for a place.

He politely extended his sympathies, wished the best for Stephen, then fell silent, apparently thinking. Finally: "I can give you the downstairs apartment."

Carmen sat heavily on the edge of the bed and pressed a hand over her eyes. She hadn't *seen* the downstairs apartment. Was it as nice as the upstairs?

Who are you kidding? she thought. *If it's smaller, it can't be by much, and besides . . . we're desperate.* She decided that if it was anything like the upstairs apartment, she'd be thrilled.

"That sounds fine," she said. "We'll take it."

After she hung up, Carmen fell back on the bed with a long sigh. A tremendous weight had been lifted from her.

They began to prepare for the move immediately. Al would have to stay in Hurleyville for another six weeks or so until his transfer was complete. Michael managed to escape the chaos of moving; he decided to go with Wanda Jean to her home in Alabama for the summer.

Al and Carmen and the kids packed their belongings cheerfully and without a word of complaint, which was quite an achievement considering the fact that, along with all the work and organizing, Stephen still had to be taken to Connecticut every day for his cobalt treatment. They were anxious to move into their new apartment and return some stability to their lives. Of course, things wouldn't be completely stable until Stephen had recovered, but they had faith that he would.

Carmen told them over and over about the upstairs apartment, hoping theirs would be as nice, as perfect. But she spent a lot of time thinking about what the downstairs apartment *might* be like . . . a lot of time thinking the worst.

One night before they moved to Southington, Carmen slept restlessly. In spite of her worries about Stephen, she'd been falling asleep easily, exhausted from all the work. But on this night, sleep did not come quickly and when it did come, it brought a cold and muddy dream.

Caskets . . . lined up neatly . . . naked bodies with deathly pale skin . . . tools . . . equipment that looked old and sinister . . . hooks . . . chains . . . a faceless man wearing a white smock with dark brown stains caked on it . . . walking along one of the rows of caskets . . . zigzagging in and out between them . . . approaching one of the bodies . . . one of the dead bodies . . . carrying one of those tools . . . one of those old and ominous tools . . .

Carmen sat bolt upright in bed, unable to breathe for a moment, then sucking in a lungful of air. It was morning. Sunlight was shining through the windows, bright, safe sunlight. Her heart was hammering in her chest but she couldn't remember exactly why. A nightmare, yes, but that wasn't it . . . not exactly. It was something else, something she suddenly knew, just *knew* instinctively.

"I've rented a funeral home," she said, her voice thick with sleep.

Al lifted his head from the pillow. "Huh?"

"The apartment . . . that house . . . it's a funeral home. Or maybe . . . well, maybe it used to be."

"Did you have a nightmare?"

"No, no. I mean, yeah, I think maybe I did, but that's not it." She turned to him. "That house is a funeral home, Al."

He propped himself up on his elbows. "What're you talking about?" Then he sat up beside her with a squinty frown and said, "You're serious, aren't you?"

"Yes, I'm serious."

She leaned forward and hugged herself, closing her eyes.

Al put an arm around her. He was at a loss, but the look on her face was not one that came from a simple dream or nightmare; there was something much more real to it.

"We can back out of it, you know," he said. "I mean, if you really don't want to move into that apartment."

She shook her head slowly. How could they?

"We can't keep making that trip every day," she whispered. "It's too hard on all of us, especially Stephen. And I sure don't want to go out looking for another apartment."

They were silent a while, pressing close to one another, then Al said, "Look, even if this . . . well this dream or feeling or whatever . . . is true, and the place really is or was a funeral home . . . I mean, so what? The people died somewhere else, right? It's not like they died there in the house. And besides"—he kissed the top of her head—"you don't *know* it's true. I bet it's not. Just a dream. We'll get there, it'll be great, we'll move in, and we'll find out it's just a nice old house converted into two apartments."

They finally left Hurleyville on June 30, a hot summer day that was even hotter on the road. Al took Stephanie with him in the moving van they'd rented—she held Willy in his cage on her lap—and the two boys went with Carmen in the car. Every few miles, Peter, who was three at the time, asked with unfailing enthusiasm, "We there yet? We there yet?"

When they got to the house in Southington, most of Al's family was already there, ready to help them move in. Carmen got out of the car and Al got out of the van and, for a moment, they stared at one another, Carmen's face tight and apprehensive, Al's smiling reassuringly. When he came to her, she whispered, "Before we do anything, can we just . . . go inside and look around?"

"Sure we can." He took her hand and, after greeting everyone, they headed inside.

The ground floor was not finished yet and the carpenters were making plenty of noise. Inside, they found a lot of sawdust and pieces of wood and men with hammers and saws. But there was no one downstairs in the basement.

As Al and Carmen started down the stairs, the noise faded slightly behind and above them. It was musty down there and the thick air carried the smell of age. At the foot of the stairs was a spacious room that opened up to their left and, to their right, a pair of French doors that opened onto an even bigger room.

There were five rooms altogether, all musty. They walked around cautiously for a few moments, not quite sure what they were looking for . . . if anything at all. At the end of a hall, they found a room in which a number of shelves held tools. Alien, sinister tools. Frightening, unspeakable tools. Steel devices darkened with age. Tubes and hoses and blades. Across from the shelves was what appeared to be a fuel tank, old and grimy, and a small table beneath which were several sturdy boxes. Al and Carmen hunkered down to find the boxes filled with countless rectangular metal plaques. The plaques were blank, but Al and Carmen looked at one another silently, knowing full well what they were. The plaques had been waiting in the boxes for who knew how long . . . waiting to be put to use . . . waiting to be assigned names and placed over graves.

They left the room and stepped into a hall at the end of which was a ramp that sloped downward into the basement from a door on the side of the house. It resembled a handicapped entrance, or some sort of loading ramp.

Carmen reached out for Al's hand, more to steady herself emotionally than physically. The things they'd seen already were enough to tell her she'd been right . . . but there was more.

A heavy-looking metal cross hung over each doorway they passed through. The crosses looked like silver, but they were so tarnished with age it was difficult to tell. They looked up at one of the crosses for a moment, then turned to one another, but the silence was too heavy to break; neither of them spoke.

They turned right and entered a large room with another shelf, more stairs and—

"Oh, my God," Carmen breathed, "what's *that*?"

She pointed to something that looked like it had come off the set of an old black-and-white Frankenstein movie. A rectangular bedlike platform was hooked to chains that were attached to a large hoist. Al and Carmen looked up to see a rectangular trapdoor in the ceiling directly above the platform.

Al's shoes *scritched* on the concrete floor as he crossed the room to a piece of plywood about four feet square on the floor below the stairs. He bent down and lifted it up a few inches, peered beneath it, then lifted it higher. Carmen stood beside him and looked down the funneled sides to the bottom of the dark-stained concrete pit where woodchips were scattered around a circular drain.

Faint light seeped in through the two grimy window-panes above and to their left, casting misty shadows into the pits as Al and Carmen stared silently.

Al said, "I wonder what this—"

"I don't think I want to know," Carmen whispered, turning away and walking toward a doorway that opened onto another smaller room. She stood in the doorway and stared.

There was a sturdy rectangular table directly across from her, the kind one might find in a laboratory or hospital . . . or in a morgue. The wall to her left was stained reddish-brown. To the right, a large deep sink bore the same rusty stains.

A loud bang behind her made her gasp and spin around to see Al brushing his hands together as he walked toward her and away from the pit. The bang had been the plank crashing back into place when he let go of it.

"What's in here?" Al asked.

Carmen started to speak, started to say something about there being a big *mess* to clean up, *that* was what was in there, but her throat was too dry and when she realized her voice wouldn't work, she closed her mouth and just stared at the stains. Al did the same.

There was a different smell in that room, darker and more cloying than the odor permeating the rest of the basement. It was a thick, almost greasy smell, the kind that remains in the nostrils for a while after the source of the smell has been left behind.

Al walked over to the wall, pressed his fingertips to it tentatively, then turned to Carmen. His brow was creased; his upper lip was curled slightly. He opened his mouth to speak but, as Carmen had earlier, simply closed it again. It wasn't necessary to speak.

They both knew what the stains were.

"I'll just paint over it," Al said as they headed back upstairs. "Right away, I'll just paint over all of it."

"And we won't tell the kids," Carmen added.

" 'Course not. And we can . . . well, just get rid of all that stuff. Get it out of here. When we're through, it'll just be a big basement, is all."

At the top of the stairs, Carmen turned to him and said, "I can't bear the thought of looking for another place. I want us to settle down. We *need* to settle down so Stephen can get better."

"And we're going to. Don't worry, hon." He gave her a quick kiss and smiled, then put an arm around her shoulders as they went back upstairs.

They found that, even up there, crosses hung over every door leading down to the basement.

Outside, Mr. Campbell arrived and met them in front of the house. He was a paunchy fellow in unfaded jeans and a plaid shirt. While Al talked with his family, Carmen took Mr. Campbell aside.

"I'd like to ask you something," she said cautiously. "This house . . . in the past, was it . . . by any chance . . . a funeral home?" It still seemed so ridiculous to her —even in spite of what they'd found in the basement— that her vague feeling could actually be correct that she winced when she said the words *funeral home.*

One corner of Mr. Campbell's mouth twitched into a smirk. "How did you find out?" he asked.

She was annoyed by his smirk and her voice held the slightest hint of anger. "Well, I think there's plenty of evidence in the basement. Have you been down there?"

He closed his eyes and nodded, smiling. "Yes, I've seen the stuff that's down there. If you don't mind, I'd just like to leave it there. I don't want any of it destroyed, or anything. They make great conversation pieces, don't you think?"

She blinked several times. This was ridiculous, but she was in no position to argue.

He said, "Yeah, the original owner's in his nineties now. He's gone off to live with his son. When I bought the place, I intended to convert it into an office building, but"—he shrugged—"zoning problems. Couldn't do it. So, I figured it'd make valuable real estate, what with the hospital expanding. Plenty of people need a place nearby. People like yourself." He gave her a big close-lipped smile and joined his hands behind his back. When Carmen didn't return his smile, he said, "Oh, don't worry, Mrs. Snedeker. The place hasn't been in use full-time for . . . oh, two years or so. Since then, it's only been used a couple of times. Just for special occasions."

Carmen frowned. "What kind of special occasion?"

"I mean, for members of the previous owner's family, that sort of thing." He turned toward the house and put his hands on his hips. "Yeah, the funeral-home business is in the past for this old place. You've probably figured out by now that the downstairs apartment isn't finished yet. You might want to store your things in the garage and stay in a motel or with friends, or something like that."

Carmen was facing the house, too. She nodded and said, "Yeah, okay." But her voice was flat and expressionless; she wasn't sure if she was disappointed that they couldn't move in right away . . . or relieved.

Al had to return to Hurleyville for work, so Carmen and the children moved into a motel room. But like most motel rooms, this one was cramped, especially with three

children. After two days, Carmen decided that even an
unfinished apartment would be preferable.

They returned to the house on Meridian Road and
pulled some mattresses out of the garage. She and the
children pushed them together in the dining room,
where they decided they would sleep until the workmen
were finished. But it wasn't long before the sound of
Peter's unsettling wheeze began to echo off the bare
walls: an asthma attack brought on, no doubt, by the
sawdust in the air. They drove him to a local walk-in
clinic where he was treated, then returned to the motel
room. Peter was feeling much better the next day. They
returned to the house and began cleaning out the sawdust to give it another try.

By that weekend, the house was in a livable state, so
they began the tedious job of moving in. Al returned for
the weekend and, along with his brother, moved the furniture into the apartment while Carmen began to unpack
all the dishes and wash them. Stephen went downstairs
to see what would be the first room of his own that he'd
ever had. . . .

Carmen stopped washing dishes and stared out the window over the sink as she thought about what her son had
told her.

Yes, the house used to be a funeral home. But evil?
She did not believe that a *thing* could be evil. It was a
beautiful old house and their apartment was perfect. But
. . . what could have made Stephen say such a thing?
Why would he even *think* such a thing? Something had
to have triggered it.

She rinsed off her hands, dried them, and caught Al
on his way back out to the garage. She told him what
Stephen had said.

He frowned. "*I* didn't say anything to him about the
house," he said, a bit defensively. "Did you?"

"Of course not. We agreed."

"Then . . . what do you think?"

"Well"—she spread her arms—"I don't think the house is *evil*, if that's what you mean. How can a building be evil? Creepy, sure, I can understand that, but I don't even think it's that. At least . . . not *very* creepy. Nothing a little paint won't fix."

Al stuffed his hands in his back pockets, looking around. Stephen was nowhere in sight. "You've gotta figure," he said, "Stephen's been under a lot of strain with the treatments, and all. I don't think it's anything to worry about. He'll probably forget all about it. I wouldn't worry." Then he went out to the garage to bring in another piece of furniture.

Carmen stood in the unfinished living room and looked around. The apartment had a lot of windows, which was sort of a prerequisite with her. There were no curtains on them at the moment, though. Even so, there didn't seem to be much light coming through in spite of the sunny day outside, no shafts of sunlight spilling bright pools on the floor. She walked to one of the panes and ran two fingertips over it.

"Have to wash these," she muttered. "Have to wash these first thing."

But when she rubbed her thumb in tiny circles over her fingertips, they did not feel the least bit dirty.

2

What Stephen Heard

Carmen got up earlier than usual on Monday morning to fix breakfast for Al and see him off for the week. He ate quickly and was taking his last bites as she sat down to a breakfast of her own.

"Finished already?" she asked.

"Gotta go. I want to make sure I'm not late. I mean, in case something happens. I'm not used to driving this far to work in the morning, y'know. Gonna brush my teeth." He was gone in a flash. The bathroom door opened and closed; the hiss of the sink and the wet sounds of brushing were muffled behind it.

He was feeling anxious, Carmen was sure that was it. She knew he was apprehensive about leaving them there for the week, about being able to come home only on weekends until his transfer went through. But Al would never voice his concern; he would hold it in, *keep* it in by doing things like gobbling up his breakfast and taking off as soon as possible so he could dive into his work and try hard not to worry about Stephen.

Carmen didn't touch her breakfast for a while; she waited until she heard the bathroom door open, then got up and met Al in the hall. He wrapped his arms around her and rested his chin gently on top of her head.

"You guys gonna be okay?" he asked.

"Of course we are."

"You sure you don't mind the house?" He whispered because Stephen—still refusing to stay downstairs alone —was asleep on the living-room sofa and Al didn't want him to hear them talking about the house. The boy had enough to think about already.

Carmen started to say, "Of course I don't mind the house, it's a gorgeous house," but she knew exactly what he meant and decided the response would be lame.

"Well," she whispered, "I'd rather it *wasn't* an old funeral home, but . . . it'll be all right, you know that as well as I do."

"Oh, yeah, I know. I'm not worried about"—a small, breathy chuckle—"ghosts, or anything, but what about Stephen? He can't sleep on the sofa forever."

"Don't worry about him. Like you said, he's been under a lot of stress. Once he's been here a while, he'll get over it. And when Michael gets back, he'll forget all about it. I think he misses Michael. Must be kinda tough on him to see his brother go off to Grandma's for the summer while he has to stay behind and be sick."

Hearing a slight noise, Carmen pulled away and turned around to see Stephen standing just outside the living-room doorway rubbing his sleepy eyes. His tank top and boxers seemed too big for his bony frame and his dark-blond hair sprouted in every direction.

"You guys call me?" he asked, voice hoarse and thick with sleep.

Carmen went to him, smiling. "Uh-uh. I was just saying good-bye to your dad. He's on his way back to New York."

"When're you coming back?" Stephen asked through a yawn.

"I'll be back at the end of the week." He went to Stephen's side and gave his frail shoulder a squeeze. "Take care of your mom while I'm gone. And do what the doctors tell you, okay?"

Stephen nodded. "Drive safe."

"No other way, kiddo."

Al and Carmen said their good-byes, then Al was gone.

Stephen headed for the kitchen and Carmen followed, hoping she wouldn't be able to hear Al drive away in there. Stephen got a glass of water and Carmen sat down to her breakfast again. Suddenly, she was no longer hungry; in fact, she wasn't sure she'd been hungry in the first place.

"You want some breakfast, Stephen?" she asked. "I just made this for myself, but I don't really want it." She got up and Stephen took her seat, still looking as though he were half asleep. "You awake enough to eat?"

He shrugged.

Standing behind him, Carmen put her hands on his shoulders and said, "I'm gonna take a shower, okay?"

He nodded, staring at the food.

As she started out of the kitchen, Stephen said, "Were you talking about me, or something?"

Carmen turned to him. "Maybe. Why?"

"I thought I heard . . . well, somebody called me. Woke me up."

"You probably just heard me mention your name." *But*, she wondered, *what else did he hear*? She hoped he hadn't heard her talking with Al about the house. "Well, I'm hitting the showers. You can watch TV if you want, just don't wake Peter and Stephanie. It's still early yet."

Carmen went into the bathroom and closed the door, but didn't start the shower right away. She sat on the edge of the tub, frowning, hoping Stephen had not overheard them talking about the house's background. He didn't need *that* little tidbit for his imagination to chew on.

"He would've said something," she breathed to herself. "Yeah, he would've said something if he'd heard that."

She stood, turned on the shower, and began to undress.

Stephen stared down at the breakfast through bleary eyes. The sausages looked like bruised, swollen fingers and the sight of the fried eggs—although he usually loved eggs for breakfast—made him wince slightly. He pushed away from the table and stood with his glass of water. He put the glass on the kitchen counter, and looked out the window. It was another white Colonial, just like their house and the house on the other side of them. Their new house . . . with new neighbors . . . in a new town . . . even a new state . . . all because of him.

Stephen supposed it was easier on everyone to be close to the hospital so they wouldn't have to make such a long trip every day, but still . . . he felt as if he'd uprooted his entire family from New York and transplanted them here in Connecticut all by himself.

As if that weren't bad enough, he hated the house to which his illness had brought them. It was an attractive house, yes, with lots of space and a room all his own. But it was a room he did not want.

He knew Mom and Dad didn't believe him when he said the house was evil. He knew that, when he said he didn't want to sleep in that room downstairs, at least not alone, they humored him because he was sick. They didn't really *say* anything like that, of course, but he knew that was what they thought; he could tell by the way they'd talked to him and looked at him when he'd told them.

But that didn't change anything. He still felt—knew

—that there was something wrong with the house, that there was something bad about it, he just wasn't sure what that something was . . . and he wanted to find out.

He'd known the moment he went downstairs to see his room for the first time. He'd seen nothing, he'd smelled nothing other than a musty old basement odor, but something had been wrong enough down there to spontaneously raise goose bumps all over the upper half of his body. Something about the very air in his room had stiffened the fine hair on the back of his neck and had given him an odd queasy sensation, as if he were about to become nauseated. The room had a bad, dark feeling about it . . . a *secret* feeling.

And he'd had the unshakable feeling that he was not alone, that he was being watched, that if he were to spin around, he would find someone—or something—in the room with him, moving toward him silently, smoothly . . . rapidly. He *had* spun around . . . but nothing was there. The fact that he saw nothing did not comfort him, however. His heartbeat quickened, his palms grew clammy, and his breaths came quickly. He'd gone back upstairs, fighting the urge to run, and had told—or tried to tell—his mother.

Of course, she hadn't believed him. But that didn't mean it wasn't so.

There was something very bad in the house, something bad *about* it.

And Stephen's family had moved into it because of him.

He stared out the window wondering what kind of people the neighbors were, wondering if they had any kids his age . . . wondering if they knew there was something wrong with the house.

Early morning sunlight shone through the treetops and dappled the ground outside with a half-hearted brightness, as if it were still too early to turn the light on high.

Stephen turned from the window and left the kitchen with a long yawn, wondering if there was anything good on television so early in the morning. In the hall, he could hear the shower hissing from the bathroom, could hear his mother's voice briefly, talking to herself the way she sometimes did when she dropped the soap or grabbed the wrong shampoo. He walked along the staircase and had started into the living room when a strong male voice called, "Stephen?"

He jerked to a halt, frozen in place. The voice had not come from the bathroom, and certainly not from the shower. His mother's voice could never sound that deep, anyway.

It was a man's voice.

"Stephen?"

He turned around slowly. Waited.

"Stephen?"

The voice sounded impatient.

It wasn't very loud, but it was crystal clear.

"Come *here*, Stephen!"

Slowly, cautiously, he walked back along the staircase, a trembling hand on the banister, toward the bathroom.

"Stephen?"

He stopped and looked over the banister at the stairs that led down to the basement . . . down to his room.

The voice was coming from down there.

Insistent. Losing patience with him.

The shower continued to hiss.

"Stephen, come down here."

Mouth open, thin, white-knuckled hands clutching the banister, eyes widening slowly, he leaned a little farther over. His mouth became cotton-dry almost instantly.

"Stephen?" A laugh now, low and conspiratorial, a

secret laugh. "Come down here, Stephen, you've gotta see this."

He turned to the bathroom. He could still hear the shower.

"Come here, Stephen. I want to show you something."

Peter and Stephanie were sound asleep in their rooms, and neither of them could sound like that, anyway.

There was no one downstairs. At least, there wasn't *supposed* to be anyone downstairs.

He tried to move forward to the top of the stairs so he could look down to the landing below but he felt goose bumps rising on his skin and the vague churning in his stomach that he'd felt when he'd gone downstairs before and—

"Stephen?"

He thought of the feeling he'd had down there, the feeling of being watched, of not being alone and, wondering if he'd been right, wondering if whatever had been down there just a couple days ago had declined to speak up, he began to walk backward instead, stumbling as he turned around and went into the living room and sat on the sofa.

Fainter now with distance, but no less distinct. "Stephen, come down here."

He leaned forward and slapped his hands over his ears, but it didn't help; the voice was muffled, but still there. He stood, went to the television and turned it on, turned the volume up louder than he normally would, then returned to the sofa and curled up beneath the blankets, pulling them up over his ears.

On the television, Bugs Bunny was arguing with Daffy Duck about whether it was rabbit season or duck season . . . and downstairs, the voice continued to call him.

"*Rrrabbit* season!"

"Stephen?"

"Duck season."

"Stephen, come down here."

"*Rrrabbit* season!"

"I said come *here*, Stephen."

"Duck—"

"What're you *doing*?" A voice, in the room with him now. Stephen gasped and jerked the covers all the way over his head and clenched his eyes shut. The television was silenced suddenly and the voice said, "I told you not to wake the kids." Silence. "Stephen? What's the matter?"

He realized, through the pounding of his heart in his ears, that it wasn't the voice. Something was different. He pulled the covers down slowly and opened his eyes to see his mother standing over him in her blue terrycloth robe with her hair wrapped in a towel.

She was frowning, but the anger was gone from her voice when she spoke again: "You okay?"

He nodded.

"Why'd you have the television so loud?"

"It didn't wake them."

"I know, but *why*?"

He licked his lips, and tried to hide the trembling in his hands as he thought of something to say. He finally settled on the truth. "I heard, um . . . a voice."

"A voice? You mean, one of the kids?"

He shook his head. "A . . . man."

"Oh, it was probably me, hon, I was talking to myself in—"

He shook his head insistently and said, "No, it came from downstairs. And it was calling me down there. Calling my name."

She stared at him a moment, hands on her hips, then seated herself on the edge of the sofa. "Well, that's just silly. Isn't it?"

He didn't respond.

"Well, think about it, Stephen. There's nobody down there."

Again, no response.

"Right? I mean, I was in the shower and the kids're asleep . . . I think. Anyway, we know there's no one downstairs. Right?"

"It . . . wasn't a person. And it was t-trying to get me to"—his voice quaked for a moment and a chilly feeling crawled over his shoulders—"to go down there."

"What was?"

"Whatever's down there."

"There's nobody down there, Stephen."

"I *said* . . . it's *not* . . . a *person*."

Mom's frown deepened and she closed her eyes a moment, at a loss. Then: "I thought you said you heard a voice."

"Yeah, but . . . I know there's nobody down there. But I also know that there's something wrong with this house . . . something *evil*. I think there was a—"

"Oh, stop it, Stephen! We talked about this. Houses aren't evil. And there's no such thing as ghosts and voices don't come out of nowhere."

Stephen looked away from her, frustrated and still a little frightened . . . because what if no one *ever* believed what he knew to be true?

"*This* house is evil," he whispered, staring at the back of the sofa. "I don't know why, but it *is*."

His mother released a long quiet sigh, then said, "You know what I think's wrong here? I think you were lying in here a while ago, maybe half asleep, and you overheard your dad and me talking in the hall. Talking about the house."

Stephen looked at her again, curious. "What about the house?"

"Well . . . if I tell you, you have to promise you'll keep it to yourself. I do not want Peter and Stephanie to know. You're older, I think you can take it. In fact, it'd probably be best if you didn't tell Michael, either. Your dad and I wanted to keep quiet about it altogether, but I think it would explain your—"

"*What?*" Stephen asked impatiently, sitting up on the sofa.

"Well, this house . . . before we moved in . . . it used to be a funeral home."

Stephen's eyes widened.

A funeral home . . .

Somehow, it sounded right. Almost as if . . . well, it was impossible, of course, but it was almost as if Stephen had sort of known it all along, known it without actually *knowing* it. It sounded so right that Stephen found himself nodding slightly. "But it's not a funeral home anymore," his mother continued. "And, besides, no one actually died here, the bodies were just brought here to be prepared for burial. Nothing bad happened here, the bad things—I mean, the people dying—all happened somewhere else. So, see, there's nothing that—"

"What was downstairs?"

She blinked, stared at him. "What?"

"I mean, did they do it downstairs? All that stuff with the bodies?"

"Well, I'm not sure yet, but I think . . ." Her voice softened. "Yes. I think they did."

Another slight nod from Stephen.

"What I'm saying is that there's nothing *evil* here. Okay? You believe me?"

He looked at her again but said nothing, did nothing. He knew . . . he *knew* he was right. What his mother had told him had not reassured him. It had merely convinced him.

3

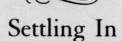

Settling In

As the first week passed, the house began to look orderly as well as occupied. Carmen spent a good deal of her time seeing to it that the furniture was arranged just so. She took great care in hanging pictures and paintings and unpacking delicate knickknacks, some much older than she, and placing them in all the right rooms on all the right shelves.

It began to look like a home, like *their* home. The only things missing were Al . . . and Stephen's health.

She talked to Al every evening, but it simply wasn't the same. She wanted him home, with her, where his mere presence would remove some of the weight from her shoulders.

Stephen was continuing with his cobalt treatments. She took him to the hospital every day and waited for him on one of those antiseptic vinyl-covered sofas. He was always drained after undergoing the radiation, and he complained that the smell and taste of it—harsh and metallic and dry—clung to him throughout the day.

One afternoon, Carmen decided she didn't like the old venetian blinds on the windows. They were keeping out the sunlight. At least, she thought it was the blinds.

The room seemed rather dim, although there was a lot of bright direct sunlight outside. But when she raised the blinds all the way, it made no difference. It would probably be a good idea to get rid of the blinds anyway. She'd have to talk to Mr. Campbell about it first. She remembered her promise to herself on the first day in the house: to wash the windows. So she put on her scrub clothes and went to work.

As she washed, Stephen came in with his friend Cody. She was happy to see Stephen make a friend so quickly. She'd been worried that the move would make him more introverted than the cancer already had, and she thought a new friend might help his spirits and—who knows?—maybe even his health. About the only time Stephen had gotten out of the house in the last few days was when she took him to the hospital for his treatment every morning. Now that he had a friend, she hoped he would stay out more, be a bit more active, and get plenty of fresh air.

Cody lived across the street. He was Stephen's age, a blond, stocky boy, full of nervous energy, but seldom smiling and with eyes as nervous as his fidgety hands and feet.

"What're you guys up to?" Carmen asked amiably as she knelt before the window, scrubbing up and down.

"We're going downstairs," Stephen replied from the hall.

Her hand stopped moving on the glass and she stood. "Uh, Stephen . . . you wanna come here a second?"

Their footsteps stopped on the oak floor and their voices whispered, then one set of footsteps started back and Stephen appeared in the living room.

"Yeah?" he said, his eyebrows rising high over his shadowy, deepset eyes.

"I thought you didn't like it downstairs," she whispered.

"I don't. But only when I'm alone."

"And you're going down there with Cody?"

He nodded. "I told him what the house used to be and"—Stephen grinned—"he thinks it's cool. So we're going downstairs to look around."

"I wish you wouldn't go around telling people about the house, Stephen. I know I said it wasn't evil, but . . . well, I don't think it's exactly *cool*, either."

"Don't worry, Mom, I won't."

He turned and left the room, and she heard their anxious voices and clattering footsteps fade down the stairs.

First it's evil and we have to leave, she thought. *Now it's cool and he's showing it off.*

Carmen smiled with relief as she went back to work. Stephen was already starting to get over his fear of the house.

Friday moved at an arduously slow crawl and Carmen thought the evening, when Al would come home for the weekend, would never arrive. She'd just finished making lunch for the kids—sandwiches and chips with milk and a variety of fruits—when Mr. Campbell dropped by.

"Just thought I'd stop by and see how you're coming along," he said with a smile after Carmen invited him in. Standing in the hall, he looked from the living room to the dining room and nodded. "Looks very nice. Looks like you've settled in."

"Not quite, but almost," Carmen said. She sounded a little distracted because she was thinking to herself that this would be a good time to get a few more questions answered.

"Well, is there anything you need?" he asked. "Anything I can do?"

"As a matter of fact, there is. Could you come downstairs with me?"

Mr. Campbell nodded and followed her down the hall,

down the stairs to the room that would be Michael's when he returned, through Stephen's room, across the concrete floored hall and into the room that contained the chain-and-pulley device and the funneled pit.

"Do you have any idea what that's for?" Carmen asked, nodding toward the pulley.

Mr. Campbell crossed his arms over his chest. "Yeah, that's the body lift."

Carmen flinched.

"See, the bodies were brought down that ramp out there"—he pointed into the hall—"and prepared in that room." He turned and pointed into the room with the blood-stained wall and sink. "That was the morgue, see. When they were ready, they were lifted up through that trap door with this chain hoist."

"Into our bedroom," Carmen murmured. Before Mr. Campbell could respond to her remark, she turned to the pit. "What about that?"

"Well, the way I understand it, that was the blood tank. The bodies were drained into that, which leads to a separate holding tank than, say, the septic tank. They needed a separate tank for the blood because . . . well, it would be unsanitary otherwise."

Carmen took a deep breath and let it out slowly. He was speaking so matter-of-factly. She supposed she should take it the same way, because it was, after all, in the past . . . but she couldn't.

"Well, I just wondered," she said quietly, nodding. Then she turned and led him out.

"Oh, by the way," he said, waving vaguely overhead. "You see the crosses over the doorways?"

"Yes, I noticed those the first time I came down here."

"I'd appreciate it if you didn't move any of those. Even if it's just to clean them. Just . . . leave them where they are."

Carmen gave him an odd look. "Any particular reason?"

He shrugged. "They're old. I'd like to keep them as they are."

"All right. We will."

In Stephen's room, Mr. Campbell stopped and asked, "Somebody sleep in these rooms down here?"

"Well . . . that room is for my son Michael, but he's staying with his grandma for a while. This is Stephen's room, but . . . he doesn't sleep down here."

"How come?"

"He doesn't like it."

A smirk twitched over his lips. "Any reason? I mean, did something happen down here? Something, um . . . odd? Strange?"

"Why?"

He shrugged again, still with the slightest hint of a smirk on his lips. "Just wondered."

"Well, he just doesn't like it, he says. And, uh . . . he says he's heard voices down here."

A nod . . . but it was a slow, thoughtful nod. "I see." He cocked a brow, said, "Kids," then moved on. He went through the French doors and stopped in what would be Michael's room when he returned. Mr. Campbell looked around the room, smiled and said, "You know, they used to call this the south coffin room." Then he led the way back upstairs.

Carmen was at the desk in the sun-room that branched off the living room, looking through the day's mail and wondering what to fix for dinner when Stephanie screamed. She dropped the mail and it scattered over the desktop as she hurried through the living room and down the short hall that led to Stephanie's room, from which the scream had come. She nearly ran into Stephanie, who dashed out of the room in a blind run and straight into Carmen's arms.

"What's the matter, honey?" Carmen asked, kneeling before Stephanie.

"There's a woman, Mommy, a woman in my room!"

"*What?*"

A furious nod. "A woman, it was a *woman*, and she was standing there with her arms open!" Her eyes were stretched open to their limit and her small fingers dug into Carmen's forearms as her words tumbled into one another in an excited jumble.

"Whoa-whoa-whoa, Stephy, c'mon, calm down a sec, okay?" When Stephanie was silent, Carmen took her hand and led her to the bedroom saying, "Okay, now, we're gonna go into your room so you can show me what you saw."

Stephanie pulled back and said, "It was a *woman!*"

"Well, then, let's go in and see her. She's probably still there, right?"

Timidly, Stephanie went into the bedroom with Carmen.

"Now, where was she?" Carmen asked.

Stephanie pointed to her dresser, which stood against the wall and had a large mirror over it. "Right there. She was standing right there, like this." Stephanie spread her arms as if to embrace Carmen and gave her an odd, dreamy smile.

"Where do you suppose she went, Steph?"

Stephanie looked around frantically, rigid with tension, then shrugged and muttered reluctantly, "I dunno."

Carmen went to Stephanie's bed and sat on the edge. She felt anger welling in her chest. Stephen had promised not to tell the kids about the house, but obviously he'd broken that promise. Yes, he was ill, and no, she could not expect him to be himself exactly, but there was no excuse for *this*.

"Has Stephen said anything to you lately, Steph? Anything that maybe . . . scared you?"

Stephanie shook her head.

"You're sure he hasn't been telling you any spooky stories?"

"Uh-uh."

"Where is Stephen right now?"

"Outside with Cody."

Carmen turned to the window that was directly across from the mirror over Stephanie's dresser. "Do you think he might've been playing a trick on you, honey?"

Her eyes widened and she shook her head insistently. "No! How *could* he? She was standing right there!"

"You know what I think happened, honey?" She motioned for Stephanie to come to her, put an arm around the girl and pointed to the window. "If somebody was standing outside that window, their reflection would be in that mirror. And if somebody—like Stephen, maybe —wanted to scare you by doing something creepy across from that mirror, you just might think you had another person in here with you."

Stephanie closed her eyes, pressed her lips together and shook her head again, shook it hard. "No. I *saw* her. She was *there*."

"But sweetheart, you know that can't be. How did she get in? How did she get out?"

The girl bowed her head slowly and said nothing.

"What's the matter?"

"You don't believe me."

"Oh, no, I believe you saw *something*. All I'm saying is that it couldn't have been a woman standing in your room, that's all. You saw something in the mirror that probably *looked* like a woman. But I *do* believe you saw something. Okay?"

Head still bowed, Stephanie gave a slight shrug and mumbled, "Guess so."

Carmen stood and kissed her on the head. "You want a glass of juice?"

She shook her head no.

"You wanna go outside and play?"

Another no.

"Well . . . okay." A hug, another kiss, then Carmen went to find Stephen.

"You promised me you wouldn't tell your brothers or sister about what you thought of the house," Carmen said to Stephen. She'd called him to the porch and they sat on the top step while Cody waited several yards away.

"Yeah, I know," Stephen said.

"So, why did you tell Stephanie?"

"I *didn't.*"

"Were you outside her bedroom window trying to scare her just now?"

"I was—no, *no*—I was with Cody and we were—"

"She said she saw a woman standing in front of her dresser, standing there with her arms open and a weird look on her face. The mirror on that dresser is right across from the window, so it wouldn't be hard for you to play a little trick on her."

Stephen's eyes widened and his back stiffened and Carmen saw what she thought, at first, to be guilt. Then she realized it more closely resembled fear.

"She did?" he whispered. "I mean, she . . . *saw* somebody in her room?"

Carmen nodded. "I don't want this going on, Stephen, do you understand? I want it to stop right now."

"But I didn't say anything to—"

"Then why would she say she saw—"

"Maybe because she *did*!"

Carmen blinked rapidly, then sighed. "Okay, listen, Stephen. Maybe she overheard you talking about it, or something, I don't know, but I know she was very scared

a little while ago. I don't want that to happen anymore,
do you hear me? Just keep it to yourself, okay? You can
talk to me in private about it if you want, but . . . just
keep it to yourself around the other kids. All right?"

"But I didn't say anything."

"Please, will you do that for me?" With his eyebrows
knit so tightly and his pale face so tense, he looked too
upset by her accusation for her to argue with him any
further.

Stephen nodded and Carmen gave him a quick kiss
before going back in the house.

She hoped that was the last of it.

"I think I'm gonna go inside for a while," Stephen said.

Cody asked, "You in trouble?"

"No. Why?"

"Because your mom wanted to talk to you privately
just now and she was pretty intense, and . . . well, you
look, um . . . I don't know, worried. Like something's
bothering you."

Stephen shook his head absently, said, "I'll see you
later," and walked slowly back to the house.

So Stephanie had seen someone in her room. Was it
the same someone he'd heard? Mom said it was a
woman, but even so . . . if it could come and go like
that woman apparently had, then it could probably do
any voice it wanted. So, he wasn't crazy, he wasn't imagining things. But he wasn't in any better shape than he
was before. Now Mom not only didn't believe him, she
didn't believe Stephanie, either.

No matter where Stephen went in the house, he could
not shake the vague feeling that there was something else
there, a presence other than his family's, something that
was watching them . . . perhaps waiting for something.
But he kept those feelings to himself mostly because it

was pretty obvious no one was going to believe him. It made him feel better to know that he was not alone now.

But it made him feel only a *little* better.

He climbed the front steps wearily and went inside, wondering if anyone else in his family would encounter the presence . . . and, if so, who would be next?

When Al arrived that night, Stephen, Stephanie, and Peter were in the living room watching television and Carmen was in the kitchen filling the apartment with the warm smell of baking chicken. She heard Al pull up, dropped what she was doing and hurried out to meet him on the front walk.

"Oh, I am *so* glad you're home," Carmen whispered into his neck as she wrapped her arms around him. He carried a brown paper bag in his left arm and she crushed it between them.

"Everything okay?"

"Oh, yeah. I just miss you, is all. We *all* miss you."

The children greeted him at the door, laughing, grinning, and hugging . . . all except Stephen, who stood back a few feet, pensive and unsmiling, thin arms folded over his chest.

In the living room, Al announced he'd brought surprises for everyone and reached into the bag. He removed a fuzzy, stuffed Opus the penguin for Peter, three coloring books and a box of crayons for Stephanie, and a brand-new fishing reel for Stephen, who barely reacted to the gift. Included with the reel were some new hooks and sinkers and a roll of fishing line. He gave a distant smile as he inspected the reel and thanked Al quietly.

Fishing was a passion Stephen shared with Al, but they hadn't gone in some time because Stephen's reel was broken. Now all he needed was a Connecticut license, a lake or river with some fish in it . . . and maybe some enthusiasm.

"So where's *my* surprise?" Carmen asked.

Al put an arm around her, squeezed her to him and whispered in her ear with a smirk, "You'll get yours later."

Dinner was festive, with utensils clattering against plates and voices chattering. After dinner, everyone retreated to the living room—Al with a beer; she'd stocked the fridge on her last trip to the supermarket—to look for something good to watch on television while Carmen began to clear the table. Without being asked and without saying a word, Stephen came into the dining room and began to help her.

"Well," she said with quiet surprise, "to what do I owe *this* honor?"

Stephen smiled, but said nothing for a while, not until the table was cleared and the dishes were ready to be washed.

"I'll help you wash 'em if you'll do me a favor," he said sheepishly.

"Oh? What's that?"

He bowed his head and thought about it a moment, then: "Would you, um . . . go downstairs and get my tacklebox out of my bedroom?"

She smiled, but held back the small laugh that was trying to escape. "Sure, honey," she said. "And you don't even have to help me with the dishes if you don't want."

When he got his tacklebox, Stephen put it on the dining-room table beside his reel, hooks, sinkers, and line, seated himself and opened the box slowly, almost reverently. As he was putting the new additions in the box, Al slid a chair over and sat down beside him after getting another beer from the fridge.

"Pretty neat, huh?"

"Yeah," Stephen said with a nod.

Al put something on the table, a small rectangular card. "Whatta you say we break it in tomorrow?"

Stephen smiled down at the license, then up at Al. "Really? That'd be great," he said, a little flatly.

They discussed fishing for a while, discussed where they might go, with Al doing most of the talking. Then they fell silent. The air between them changed, grew somewhat tense, until Stephen finally asked in a hoarse whisper, "Dad, do you think that if a person hears . . . um, voices, that he's crazy?"

Al took a sip of beer, then said, "No. No, lots of people hear voices. Some people see things. Sometimes, if a person's under enough stress, all *kinds* of weird things can happen to him. Especially if that person's been sick, you know what I mean?"

Stephen looked at him with suspicious curiosity.

Al nodded. "Your mom told me about it on the phone. And no, I don't think you're crazy. But listen, Stephen. You're gonna have to keep it to yourself, okay? You can't go around telling the other kids. You already scared the hell out of Stephanie."

Stephen closed his eyes and sighed quietly, thinking, *I didn't, dammit, I* didn't *tell them.*

"You need to relax, is all," Al continued. "And that's what we're gonna do tomorrow, just you and me. We're gonna relax and make some *fish* nervous, okay?"

Stephen nodded. "Okay."

"Come into the living room. There's an old Abbott and Costello movie on."

"In a minute."

Al returned to the living room and Stephen put everything in the tacklebox, then closed and latched it. He left it on the table as he got up and went down the hall to the bathroom. His hand froze two inches from the bathroom doorknob as a voice said, "Stephen, what are you doing?" Quiet, but clear.

His breath caught in his throat. He turned only with

great effort, slowly, stiffly. He looked down the stairs into the blackness below.

"Stephen? I really think you should come down here." Just quiet enough so the others couldn't hear over the sound of the television.

Stephen backed up a couple steps until his back was touching the bathroom door.

"Stephen?"

There was movement in the darkness below, a subtle shift of gray in the black.

Stephen's throat seemed to swell. His chest ached with the pounding of his heart.

"Come here, Stephen."

The dry shuffle of feet scraped over the concrete floor.

"Stephen?"

He peeled himself away from the bathroom door, hurried along the hall toward the living room and stopped in the foyer to catch his breath. He stood still a moment, eyes closed, arms clenched tightly over his chest, lips pressed together.

Then he went into the living room, sat on the sofa, and stared blindly at the black-and-white images on the television. He remained silent while the others laughed, trying not to think of what he'd heard, trying not to think of his full, aching bladder.

4

More Voices

During the next month, Carmen became friends with Fran, her next-door neighbor. Fran was a short woman with curly red hair and she was *very* pregnant. She and her husband, Marcus, had bought the house next door and moved in only a few months earlier, hoping to be completely settled before the baby decided to make his or her appearance, which would be any time now.

"Look, I wouldn't worry about it if I were you," Fran said over iced tea in Carmen's sun-room one afternoon. "Stephen's illness has really upset things for everybody and you're in a new house, a new town . . . makes sense that the kids aren't themselves. I can understand Stephen hearing things, Stephanie seeing things." She sipped. "Don't make a big deal of it and it'll pass."

"Well, I don't know. I could sort of understand Stephen thinking he'd heard things . . . y'know, voices, whatever. But when Stephanie said—"

"But you said yourself that Stephen probably said something to her about the voices he heard, maybe even about the house's ugly past. Besides, they miss their dad. You know how that is, *you* miss him. Don't you feel a little off-center because of that?"

"Yeah. You're right," Carmen said, smiling. "But it drives me nuts, you know?"

"If they stop doing things that drive you nuts, *then* you should worry."

Carmen laughed. "You talk like you've been a mother as long as I have and you haven't even had your baby yet."

Fran shrugged and grinned. "So, I'm practicing."

That evening, as the sunlight faded outside where Stephanie was keeping an eye on Peter, Carmen was sitting on the sofa talking to her mother on the telephone. The television was on with the volume low and Stephen was somewhere in the house. She was telling her mother how Stephen was coming along, talking about Stephanie and Peter, when Stephen hurried into the room buckling his belt, with eyes wide.

"Is . . . is Dad home?" he asked, looking around.

"No, course not, you know that. He's in New York until the weekend."

"I heard him call me."

"What?"

"I heard him call me just now. It . . . sounded like he was in the hall, like he'd just come in," he said as he looked back over his shoulder toward the front door.

"Mom, can I call you back in a little while?" Carmen said. After she said good-bye and hung up, she asked, "Now, what'd you say?"

"I thought . . . maybe Dad came home early, or something. I heard him call me just now."

"Well, you couldn't have heard him, hon. He's not here. But, you know what? Sometimes I miss him so much, I wouldn't be surprised if I thought I heard him, too. But it won't be long before he'll be here with us all the time and he'll come home from work every evening and when we think we hear him, it'll be because we *do*."

Stephen stared at her as if she'd just told him water was wet.

"I heard him," he said, calmly, flatly. Then he turned and headed for the front door.

Frustration and anger suddenly burned like bile in Carmen's throat. If he was going to go on insisting that he was hearing voices, then there obviously wasn't a damned thing she could do about it.

"Okay," Carmen snapped as she shot up from the sofa and followed him, her jaw set, "okay, fine, if you want to believe that, go right ahead. I mean, it's pretty obvious he's not here, right? Oh, but don't let that stop you. Just, for crying out loud, don't tell your sister."

He turned to her, his eyes weary, and said quietly, "I'm gonna go outside for a while."

After he'd gone out and closed the front door, Carmen stood in the living-room doorway for a few moments, just staring at nothing in particular.

It was going to have to stop. Stephen simply could not go on talking about voices he'd heard, voices that did not exist. He'd already upset Stephanie—what next? She would have to talk to Al. They would have to do something about it. Maybe they should speak with the doctor, see what he had to say. Maybe it *was* something they should be worried about.

Carmen was also starting to get annoyed. She didn't know what got on her nerves more: Stephen's insistence that he heard voices that she never heard, and Stephanie's insistence that she'd seen a woman in her bedroom who wasn't there, or the vague, gnawing curiosity deep inside Carmen that made her wonder if maybe . . . just *maybe* . . .

"Uh-uh," she said to herself, going back in the living room. "No way. Ridiculous."

* * *

That Saturday night, after Peter and Stephanie had gone to bed and Stephen was asleep on the sofa, Al and Carmen spoke in hushed tones at the dining-room table.

"So, what do you think we should do?" Al asked. "You think maybe they need some kind of therapy?"

"Oh, Lord, I hope it's nothing that drastic yet. I'm just worried that . . . well, that it might turn into something like that if it's not stopped now. What do you think?"

"I dunno. You're with them all week, you're the one who hears about all these . . . voices, or whatever. I think their life has just been a little too interrupted recently and they want some attention, wanna feel normal again. And Stephen . . . well, those cobalt treatments are no picnic. At least, that's what I think. Do you think they need therapy? Hell, do you think we could *afford* therapy?"

She thought it over a moment. "No. No, you're right. It's just . . . well, it's getting on my nerves."

"Let them know that. If they're just after attention, give it to them, but let them know you're fed up with the ghost stories. I think they'll stop."

"Yes," she said, nodding, staring at her tea, "that oughtta do it. Yes." She kept nodding, but that gnawing feeling of uncertainty, of mild confusion—the thing that had *really* been getting on her nerves lately—rose up inside her and would not go away.

Stephen waited for the silence that told him it was safe to get up. He hadn't meant to eavesdrop, but he'd been unable to sleep—in fact, he'd been unable to sleep a *lot* lately—and their voices had been clearly audible in the night's silence, so he'd heard everything Mom and Dad had said in the dining room. He'd felt his heart sink into his stomach as he listened and he'd thought over and

over, *They'll never believe me. Never. There's no way they'll
ever believe me.*

He threw back his covers, got off the sofa and flicked
on the lamp at one end of the sofa before going into the
kitchen for a drink of water. Because of the radiation
treatments, his saliva ducts had dried up completely, and
his mouth was constantly dry, so he drank more than he
ever had before. When he was finished, he went quietly
down the hall to Stephanie's room and tapped on the
door with one fingertip before opening it and stepping
inside cautiously.

"Stephanie? You awake?" He closed the door silently
and stared into the dark. "Steph? It's me." Squinting in
anticipation, Stephen reached out and turned on the
overhead light.

She was lying on her back in bed, tense and trembling,
the edge of the blankets pulled up just beneath her widened, terrified eyes. When she saw him, her body relaxed
and she closed her eyes as she sighed and pushed her
head back into the pillow.

"What's the matter?" Stephen whispered.

"I thought you were a ghost."

Stephen stared thoughtfully at her a moment.

"Is that what you think they are?" he asked, sitting on
the edge of the bed. "Ghosts?"

"I don't know." She shrugged. "What else?"

"Do you . . . feel them?"

She squinted, cocked her head to one side and thought
about it a moment. "Mmm . . . sometimes. I think."

"Me, too," he whispered. "Sometimes I feel like . . .
I don't know, like there's just something *there*. Even
though I can't see it."

"I wish Michael'd come home," she breathed.

Stephen felt the same way, but asked, "How come?"

"Well . . . I think *he'd* believe us. Don't you?"

Stephen watched her for a long time. Most of the time,

his little sister was an annoyance, a pain in the neck. Since he'd gotten sick, he'd been looking at everything a little differently—as he was looking at his little sister now. She had become an ally, a friend. He took her small hand in his and whispered, "Listen, Steph. If anything else happens, you can tell me. Come to me right away and let me know, okay? *I'll* believe you."

"Will you tell me if anything else happens to you?"

He nodded and squeezed her hand.

Carmen began to spend as much time with the kids as she could. With Peter, it was easy; he didn't wander far. But Stephanie was active, playing with other girls up and down the street, and Stephen spent a lot of time with Cody. They didn't seem to be in need of attention, but Carmen decided to keep trying.

As usual, she missed Al; having the house and the kids to herself all the time made her feel like she had more on her shoulders than she could handle. It helped to keep busy around the house and she visited with Fran a lot. She took Stephen to the hospital for his treatments and watched as he slowly grew more pale and brittle-looking. Sometimes she wanted to take him in her arms and hold him, to keep him away from that hospital, fearing that the treatments were only making him worse. But the doctors assured her that those treatments were Stephen's best chance.

Her weeks were speckled by stories from the kids, mostly from Stephen, stories of voices heard around the house.

One morning, Carmen got up to find every light in the living room on and Stephen sprawled on the sofa, as if he'd had an unusually restless night. She went around the room and turned off all the lights, then woke Stephen. He said he'd heard a voice in the dark, so he'd turned on the lamp beside the sofa. But the voice—a man's voice—continued, coming from the darkest corner of the room, so he got up and turned on another light, then another, until they were all on and he was able to sleep. He'd told her knowing full well that she would not believe him, and that didn't seem to bother him. But the fact that he didn't care whether she believed him or not bothered *her*. His attitude poked a hole in the attention-getting theory.

It happened again and again: Stephanie would hear a voice in the bathroom or Stephen would hear one in the hall and no matter how Carmen talked to them, they nodded and apologized for bothering her, but somehow managed to give the impression that they knew something she didn't. . . .

The incidents bothered Carmen enough for her to write about them a number of times in her journal. It had become a habit for her to write down her thoughts and experiences, if not every day then at least a few times a week, even when nothing particularly eventful had happened. It was comforting to put her feelings on paper with the knowledge that no one would read what she wrote, that it wouldn't be criticized or graded.

Early one Friday afternoon, she sat at the desk in the sun-room, writing in her journal as music played softly on the stereo in the living room. Stephanie and Stephen were outside and Peter was taking a nap. More than anything, Carmen was trying to pass time until Al arrived that evening.

She was writing in her journal about the latest voice—a man's voice that had called to Stephen from downstairs—when a man called, "Carm? You in here?"

She dropped her pen and stood, thinking, *Al's home early*, as she spun around and smiled and said, "Al? I'm in here."

Silence.

"Al?" She went into the living room and stopped,

staring at the empty doorway that opened onto the hall and the front entrance.

Her smile quivered, then fell away. She frowned as she stepped through the doorway.

"Al?" she asked again, but now her voice was quiet and just a bit unsteady.

She was alone.

Al had not come into the house.

She looked out the window to find that he had not even arrived yet.

Carmen released a long, breathy sigh, forced a smile, and muttered, "Well," thinking, *I must miss him, that's all, it's just that I miss him and was thinking about him and . . . yeah, that's all.*

She turned and went back into the sun-room to continue writing, but not before turning up the music on the stereo.

5

Summer into Fall I

It was a hot summer with day after day of endless blue skies and nights covered with brightly shining stars. The air was redolent with honeysuckle, and during the day, the neighborhood rang with the laughter of children.

Fran had a baby girl and named her Janine, and sometimes the sound of her crying was picked up by a summer breeze and carried next door to Carmen's. The sound made Carmen smile; somehow, it made the neighborhood complete, more comfortable.

So why does something not feel right? Carmen asked herself again and again. The question was asked by an inner voice so quiet it was almost inaudible . . . because Carmen was trying her best to silence it.

Stephen hated his treatments more every day and was becoming more resistant. He was rude to the doctors and nurses in the hospital and sometimes even snapped at Carmen. She tried to take it in stride, tried to tell herself that it was to be expected considering the strain the treatments put on the boy. But it worried her nevertheless. On top of that, he'd lost more weight and was looking more frail than ever before. Sometimes when she hugged him, she feared he would break.

Dr. Berry told her it was a good sign, though.

"If he's being cantankerous," the doctor said, "that means he's holding up. If he's fighting us, then he's fighting the cancer. It's encouraging."

So maybe it wasn't such a bad thing after all. According to the doctor, Stephen was doing very well and was likely to do even better.

That was good. So what didn't feel right?

Al was still working in New York, but came home every weekend like clockwork. The hard workweeks and long drives, not to mention his ongoing concern for Stephen, were wearing hard on him; he drank more when he was home on the weekends and was growing short-tempered. But, in spite of his grumbling, he was willing to help around the house. He painted the stained walls downstairs.

They went to church every Sunday; Carmen became involved in church activities, just as she had back home in New York, and had made some friends there, women with whom she was able to spend time during the week. Plus she saw Fran a lot and they took turns taking care of one another's kids so each of them could get away from the house once in a while.

So what was it?

The other children, Stephanie and Peter, were fine. Michael was still in Alabama, but called regularly. Everything was just fine.

Except for . . . something.

The feeling had started the day she'd mopped the kitchen floor.

Kitchens seemed to be the first casualty in a house full of children, and it hadn't taken long for the brick-red mosaic linoleum floor in the Snedekers' kitchen to lose its shine, despite regular, if hurried, moppings. So, one day a few weeks ago, Carmen had gotten the mop and bucket, taken off her shoes and rolled her pantlegs half-way up to her knees, and begun a real scrubbing.

The kids were all outside that afternoon and the house was quiet.

The mop sloshed back and forth over the linoleum, its soggy strands of cotton writhing like tentacles over Pepsi stains and water spots. Carmen had mopped enough kitchen floors to be able to do it with a certain detachment, so she'd dipped the mop into the bucket a few times before she finally noticed the smell.

It wasn't very strong, but the cloying, coppery smell was certainly unpleasant.

Then she noticed the water in the bucket.

It was a deep, dark red.

The mop's strands were a glistening crimson.

And Carmen's bare feet were smeared with red. In fact, the entire floor was smeared with red. She stared down at her feet with her lip curled up in a sickened grimace. The smell hung in the air like smoke.

Suddenly, Carmen thought of what Stephen had said their first day in the house—*Mom, we have to leave this house. There's something evil here*—and her heart began to thunder in her chest as she stared at the dark red fluid on the floor all around her, smelling that faint but awful smell.

"No, it can't be," she whispered to herself, "that can't be it, it's just . . . just the linoleum, that's all. That's *all*."

Deciding she couldn't let the kids see the mess, she quickly cleaned it up, using old kitchen towels and nearly half a roll of paper towels for the finishing touches. Then she'd given the room a couple of shots of air freshener.

"Just have Al rip that linoleum up, is all," she muttered. "That's what I'll do."

But it had bothered her that day, and in the days that followed.

Carmen hadn't told Al about it. She wasn't sure how. And what if he laughed it off? She just didn't look forward to mopping the floor again.

The kitchen floor was part of Carmen's off-center feeling. Another part was the fact that Stephen had stopped talking about the voices he'd been hearing in the house. He no longer made references to the house's being evil. In the space of just a few weeks, he'd simply stopped, as if it had never come up in the first place.

Carmen tried to tell herself that it was a good thing, that it was a sign Stephen was getting better. But whenever she told herself that, her inner voice whispered, *Is it?*

Sometimes, she walked into a room to find Stephen and Stephanie talking to one another with hushed, secretive voices. When they saw her, they would fall silent and pull away from one another, as if they had been caught doing something wrong. She'd thought nothing of it at first, but when it continued to happen—half a dozen times or so—she began to wonder if perhaps they were keeping something from her.

"So, what're you guys talking about?" she asked one day when she found them whispering on the sofa in the living room. She seated herself in Al's recliner and watched for their reaction.

Stephen shrugged and muttered, "Nothin'." He turned to the cartoons on television.

"We were wondering when Dad's coming home to stay," Stephanie said.

"It won't be long now," Carmen said. "It'll be a month, maybe a little less, till his transfer comes through."

Stephanie nodded, then she, too, turned her attention to the television.

It's just your imagination, Carmen told herself. *They aren't keeping any secrets and Stephen is getting better and everything is just fine!*

But, as it had so often recently, that tiny voice in the basement of her mind whispered, *So why does something not feel right?*

Stephen had stopped talking to his mom about the voices he heard because it didn't do any good. She didn't believe him. He didn't talk to Al about them, either; Al had become so cranky lately that if Stephen so much as hinted at the topic of disembodied voices, he snapped at him to knock it off and act his age.

The only person Stephen could talk to about voices was Stephanie. Although she still insisted she'd seen a woman appear in her bedroom, Stephanie did not hear voices. "But," she told Stephen one day as they whispered together on the sofa in the living room, "sometimes I . . . I . . . ." Her face was tense with thought, with frustration at not being able to find the right words. It was much too tense for a six-year-old. "I feel like I'm not alone when I really am. Nobody's with me, I don't see nobody, but . . . I feel like there *is* somebody there."

But she didn't hear the voices Stephen heard: the cold, sneaky voices . . . the angry, mocking voices . . .

Only Stephen heard those.

But Stephanie was always willing to listen to him talk about them and had promised not to mention them to Mom. Her responses were neither judgmental nor disbelieving, but were filled with little-girl concern. Stephen found their talks comforting; they made him feel less alone.

Even so, the voice was becoming more insistent, more demanding. It seemed to know when it was frightening him—and it seemed to enjoy his fear.

"Stephen?"

Stephen froze outside the bathroom late one night. Everyone had gone to bed long ago, but Stephen had awakened with a full bladder. The voice spoke to him on his way out of the bathroom.

"Stephen, come down here," it whispered.

Stephen headed down the hall, his body chilled with fear, legs stiff with tension. But he moved slowly because, in spite of his fear, he was drawn to the voice, compelled to stop and listen to what it had to say.

"We have things to talk about, Stephen," the voice went on. "There are things to be done. No time to waste, Stephen. Let's get started."

What things? he thought, moving a little faster now. *Get started on what?*

"Time to stop putting it off," the voice said, then chuckled. It was a sound like ice cubes clacking together.

Stephen rounded the corner and went into the dark living room.

"I have things to tell you, Stephen. We have things to do." The voice was still whispering and yet Stephen could still hear it clearly.

He turned on the lamp at one end of the sofa, then the other. Under his pillow, he had a Walkman with an AM/FM radio and a pair of tiny earplug-like headphones. He'd had his mom get them for him from downstairs. He fumbled the small disks into his ears, turned on the radio and turned up the volume.

Music pounded in his head from a local rock station and he felt his body begin to relax.

But through that music, through the throbbing beat and the shrieking voices, Stephen thought he heard, for a moment, the voice's hard, cold chuckle. . . .

It happened at different times and in different parts of the house, but no one else ever heard it. Stephen began to wonder if the voice was perhaps in his head; otherwise, why didn't anyone else hear it talking about the things it wanted to tell Stephen, about the things he needed to do? Why was he the only one?

He saw things, too . . . sort of. Sometimes, he would catch a glimpse of something moving quickly to his right or left, nothing more than a gray blur in his peripheral vision; when he turned toward it, there was nothing there. The first few times, it had happened so quickly that he thought he'd imagined it, or that perhaps it had been Willy darting through the room in that quick, wiggly way he had. Then he realized that, whatever it was, it was darting from behind one piece of furniture to another, as if to hide from him. Stephen told no one of what he'd seen—or at least *thought* he'd seen—not even Stephanie. It seemed too vague to talk about; he felt silly enough for what he'd said already.

But he also felt afraid. First the voice, which was becoming more ominous all the time, then the glimpses of something small and gray darting around him, hiding from him mockingly. What was next?

That was what frightened Stephen. He didn't know what was next, but somehow, deep in his gut, in his bones, he knew there would be more . . . and he wasn't looking forward to it.

With the summer winding down, it was time for Michael to come home and get ready to start another year of school. Around noon on Saturday, Al took the kids to the airport with him to get Michael while Carmen stayed home and prepared a big meal.

Carmen had been raised in a family that believed in celebrating things—big or small—with food. It was Labor Day weekend and she wanted to get it off to a good start, so she cooked up plenty of fried chicken and corn on the cob and hot rolls; she made a green salad, a potato salad, set out two kinds of chips and made plenty of iced tea. Then, when she knew they would be home anytime, she set all of it out buffet-style on the dining-room table.

She went to the kitchen, got a stack of plates from the cupboard and put it at the end of the table, then put the silverware beside it. She was about to set out some napkins when the telephone rang. Carmen went into the living room to answer it.

It was Wanda Jean.

"Has my boy got there yet?" Wanda Jean asked.

"Not yet, Mom. I expect them any minute."

"How's Stephen?"

"Oh, the same. His treatments end in another week, unless the doctor says otherwise."

"What then?"

"Then we pray a lot."

Carmen explained she was in the middle of fixing a big lunch and promised to call back later. She hung up and headed toward the dining room, but froze halfway down the hall, her feet coming to a halt on the wood floor as she stared at the dining room table.

The stack of plates was gone and so was the silverware.

Carmen closed her eyes a moment, then opened them, half hoping to find that they had only been playing tricks on her and the plates and silverware were still there after all.

But they were not.

Taking slow, almost cautious steps, she crossed the dining room and went into the kitchen where she opened the cupboard.

All the plates were stacked in their regular place.

Her mouth opened as she frowned and made a noise as if she were about to speak, but she didn't. Instead, she closed the cupboard and pulled the silverware drawer open.

The silverware she'd removed—or thought she'd removed—had been replaced.

She closed her mouth, pressed her lips tightly together and could hear her breaths coming rapidly through her nose. Slamming the drawer closed, she spun around, leaned back on the edge of the counter and murmured half her thoughts aloud.

That's all it was, I just—

"—thought I set them out, that's all, I just—"

—thought I did it, but I didn't, is all, because it's really—

"—hot today, and with the cooking and—"

—the stress, there's been a lot of stress around here, and—

"—yeah, yeah, that's all it was, just a little . . . mistake."

There was suddenly a burst of sound and movement in the house and Carmen started, clutching her chest with one hand and letting out a little yelp.

"Hey, Mom!" Michael called, stomping through the hall and into the dining room, grinning into the kitchen at her.

The others came in behind him, talking, laughing.

Carmen took a deep breath, held the tiny crucifix around her neck between thumb and forefinger and sent up a silent prayer.

6

Sleeping Downstairs

The air grew cooler as Stephen went down the stairs and it felt good against his skin. Carmen, Al, and Michael had been down there for a while and, on his way down, Stephen could hear an occasional exclamation from Michael: "Cool!" or "All right!" Obviously, he liked the basement in general and his room in particular.

Earlier, while the others were eating, Stephen had taken Mom aside and asked her to please not tell Michael about why he hadn't been sleeping downstairs.

"Okay, but why?" she'd asked. "He'll find out sooner or later anyway."

"Yeah, but I wanna tell him. Probably tonight. 'Cause I think I'd like to start sleeping down there. Tonight, I mean."

"Really?"

"Yeah, now that Michael's home. But . . . not alone."

"What do you mean, alone? He'll be—"

"I mean, not in my room."

"You want to share a room?" She'd frowned as she thought about that. "But you were each gonna have your own room."

"I know, Mom, but . . . please," he'd whispered. "I'll sleep down there. But not if I have to sleep in a room by myself."

"You're still that scared of the basement?" She'd cocked her head, as if she found it hard to believe.

He'd averted his eyes and just stood there without replying.

"Okay," she'd said. "I'll talk to Al about moving the bed. And he should probably ask Michael if *he* minds."

"He won't," Stephen had said.

And he'd been right. In fact, Michael liked the idea. They'd moved Stephen's bed into Michael's room and, although neither bed had been slept in yet, Carmen put fresh sheets on them.

Carmen and Al seemed pleased that Stephen had finally decided to sleep downstairs, even though he wanted to share a room with his brother. In fact, they seemed so pleased and relieved about it that Stephen was a little embarrassed.

"Well, what do you think?" Al asked as Stephen came down the stairs.

He looked around the room, at the beds, the dresser, the wood-panel shelf that ran along three walls. The room looked as if it had been made to be a bedroom for two boys from the beginning.

The problem was, of course, that Stephen knew that wasn't the case at all. It had been made to serve a much different, much darker, purpose.

"Looks great," he said, smiling as he entered the room.

"You two will have to fight over the beds," Carmen said. "And I figured I'd let you decide where you wanted to put all your stuff, so you'll have to bring it in from the other room."

"Thanks," Stephen said, nodding at Al.

"Sure, kiddo."

Carmen headed for the stairs. "Well, we're gonna leave you to it."

She and Al were halfway up the stairs when she called back, "Leftovers okay for dinner?"

"Yeah, Mom," Stephen said.

When they were gone, the room fell silent and the boys just stood there for a long moment.

"So how come you haven't been sleeping down here?" Michael asked.

Stephen licked his dry lips, jerked his head back toward the French doors that led into his old room and said, "I'll tell you while we're moving the stuff. But you've gotta promise," he added, holding up a rigid forefinger, "it's just between us, right?"

Michael shrugged. "Yeah, sure."

So, as they went into the next room and began moving Stephen's things, Stephen told his brother everything: that he'd been hearing some rather frightening voices since they'd moved in, that Stephanie said she'd seen a strange woman standing in her bedroom with arms open for an embrace, and, saving the most surprising fact for last, that the house used to be a funeral home.

"Really?" Michael said with a grin. "Cool!"

"I don't see what's so cool about it."

Michael's grin faltered a bit. "Well . . . I kinda think it is. Y'know?"

"That they used to bring dead people in here, you mean? You think it's cool that they used to embalm corpses in here? Maybe in this room, for all we know."

The grin disappeared entirely as Michael put down a box of things and faced Stephen. "I didn't think of that," he said quietly. "You think that's the reason for the voices you thought you heard?"

"I didn't *think* I heard them, Michael, I *did* hear them. Jeez." He turned and went back for another box of stuff, muttering, "Stephanie said you'd believe us, but I guess she was wrong."

"Oh, no, I didn't mean it that way," Michael insisted, hurrying after him. "I believe you. I just wondered if . . . well, you know, it's kind of . . . *weird*, is all, you know?"

They carried the last two boxes into the room, then sat on the floor and began to sort through the contents.

"You think this place is haunted? Is that what you mean?" Michael asked.

"All I meant was that I've been hearing this voice. And usually it's coming from down here. Calling up the stairs for me."

"What kind of voice is it? What does it say?"

"It's always a man's voice. Sometimes it sounds like Dad, but only when he's working in New York. Usually, it just calls my name." Stephen turned his attention from the box in front of him to the room around him. He looked around slowly, a frown growing darker and deeper on his face as he spoke in nervous spurts. "It keeps saying it wants me to come down here and . . . I don't know, it says I have something to do and that we have to get to work, but it . . . well, it never says what."

Michael's smiles were gone; he didn't even look like he was enjoying the conversation now. He, too, had developed a frown as he listened to Stephen speak.

"Then . . . maybe we shouldn't live here," Michael said after a long silence, his voice hushed.

"Mom and Dad can't afford to move again. After all the medical bills I've made for them, they could probably barely afford to move in here."

"How is your . . . um, I mean, how're you feeling, anyway? You never said anything earlier."

Stephen shrugged. "I'm feelin' the same, I guess. And

Mom told me it was cancer a long time ago, so you don't have to be afraid to say the word."

There was a silence between them then; it was such a curiously tense silence in which their eyes did not meet that Stephen wondered if he'd made a mistake in telling Michael about the voices, if his brother thought that he was crazy, that he'd been affected by his illness or by the treatments.

Then: "So what're we gonna do, Stephen? I mean about the house? About the voices, and the woman that Steph saw?"

Michael tried to appear no more than curious, but Stephen could see a spark of fear in his eyes.

"I don't know," Stephen said casually, not wanting to frighten his brother any more than he had already. "Just wait and see what happens, I guess."

Michael nodded slowly and said, "Wait. Yeah. Okay, we'll wait and see," smiling slightly, as if they'd been talking about what kind of turn the weather might or might not take, and not about strange voices calling out of the darkness.

As the evening grew darker outside, Stephen became more and more anxious. He found himself fidgeting, unable to concentrate even on the silliest television programs and unable to stop looking at the clock.

How late was it?

How much longer before everyone would begin making their way to bed?

Stephen decided he wouldn't go down until Michael was ready to go to bed. As stupid as it sounded, he didn't want to go down there to sleep alone, not yet; maybe later, after he'd been sleeping down there for a while, he'd be able to do it, but not yet.

After watching a couple hours of television, during which he told everyone about things he'd done at

Grandma's, Michael stood from where he'd been sitting on the floor and said, "I'm gonna go to bed. I'm kinda tired."

For an instant, Stephen's mind raced: *Would it look weird if I went down with him? Should I wait a while and then go down? But then he might be asleep and I just might as well be alone. I'm not even* tired *yet.*

"Yeah, me too," Stephen said, standing from the sofa slowly, as if he were weary and ready to sleep.

After all the goodnights were exchanged, Stephen followed Michael downstairs.

"You never said which bed you wanted," Stephen said on the way down.

"Whichever one you don't want."

"Well, I want whichever one *you* don't want. I mean, it's your room."

Michael laughed and said, "Okay, I'll take the one by the wall."

At the bottom of the stairs, Stephen reached out to close the French doors without even giving it a thought. He wasn't quite successful, though, and they remained open just a few inches. He decided it was silly for him to feel that they needed to be closed, though, so he left them alone.

Stephen started to undress right away, looking forward to lying down in a bed again. It had been a while. Once he was down to his shorts, he pulled back the covers, sat on the edge of the bed and then saw Michael heading back up the stairs.

"Where you going?" Stephen asked, trying not to sound panicky.

"Brush my teeth. Be right back."

Stephen's fingers dug into the mattress until his knuckles turned a yellowish white as he watched Michael go up the stairs, disappearing a bit at a time: first his head and shoulders, then his arms, torso, legs, feet . . .

And Stephen was alone.

"You think he's gonna do okay?" Carmen asked. She was sitting at the end of the sofa. Al was in his recliner; he was watching television and didn't respond.

Peter was asleep on the floor and Stephanie was involved in the television program along with Al. They were watching an old Sinbad the Sailor movie.

Carmen tried again. "Al, do you think Stephen's gonna be okay about the house now?"

Still no response; he just took a few swallows of his beer.

"Al!"

He turned to her suddenly, startled. "What?" he said, quietly at first, then snapped, "*What*!"

"I've been talking to you over here."

"I'm watching the movie, okay? What did you say?"

"I asked you if you think Stephen's gonna be okay about the house now that he's moved downstairs with Michael."

He finished off the beer, then said, "He'd better be. It'd be nice not to hear any more of that crap about voices."

"He hasn't said much about it lately."

"Not outright, but somehow he manages to make a remark now and then, something that just *suggests* there's weird things going on in the house. Well, it's time he gets okay about the house, I think." He yawned, then held out the empty beer bottle. "You wanna get me another one, hon?"

Stephen looked down at his hands, still clutching the mattress's edge, and relaxed them. It seemed silly to just sit there and wait for Michael to get back. He'd only gone to brush his teeth. How long could that take? Not long enough for anything to happen. Besides, the lights were still on, so what *could* happen? The only darkness was on the other side of the French doors, pressing against the square panes of glass.

He opened the drawer of the nightstand and got his Walkman, then lay back on the bed, pulling the sheet over him. After putting the small disks in his ears, he turned on his side and propped himself up on one elbow to browse through the radio stations and see what was playing. He watched the red needle move along the dial from station to station, until he caught some movement with his peripheral vision, just a shadowlike hint of it, but enough to make him raise his head and look across the room at the French doors.

The Walkman slipped from his hand and toppled off the edge of the bed to the floor where it broke with a crack of plastic, jerking the earphones from his ears.

He didn't move. For a while, Stephen *couldn't* move. He could only stare at the French doors—at the face that stared at him through the small opening between them.

It was a young man's face, maybe in his early twenties, but pale, so pale it looked unreal, like the face of a white-painted mannequin. It was a long, gaunt face with deep, hollow cheeks and sunken, corpselike eyes. It held no expression, just stared.

The young man's hair was black and stringy and fell past his shoulders. Pale arms hung from the short sleeves of his dark shirt and long bony fingers twitched against his blue jeans. His colorless lips began to move slightly, silently, as if he were murmuring to himself.

But worst of all, the thing that made Stephen feel as though he was losing his mind, was the fact that the young man shimmered now and then, became transparent and almost disappeared before taking shape again, like a mirage, a vapor.

Stephen stopped breathing for a long moment and felt his throat begin to close, as if it were swelling slowly, growing thicker and thicker, until he was sure he soon would be unable to breathe if he tried.

To get up the stairs, he would have to pass within inches of the sickly young man behind the French doors.

The white lips began to move a little faster, though the face remained expressionless, the eyes empty. One twitching, bony hand began to move upward, outward, to open one of the doors further. Stephen kicked at the sheet to get it off him but his feet became tangled in it and he struggled to get free, as long, skeletal fingers curled around the edge of one of the doors. Stephen broke free of the sheet, tumbled off the bed, clambered to his feet and shot for the stairs, hearing, for just a moment as he passed the young man, the dry, insectlike whispering sound coming from the thin lips. Then he ran up the stairs, taking them two at a time. When he reached the landing, he nearly collided with Michael, whose eyes widened with shock and concern as he watched Stephen run by.

Stephen thumped down the hall and stumbled into the living room.

"Stephen!" Carmen cried as he tripped and fell to his knees. She hurried to his side and put an arm around his shoulders. "What's wrong, what's the matter? Stephen?"

He couldn't reply. His mouth had become dry and gummy and words sounded like nothing more than senseless noises.

When Michael came in behind him, Carmen asked, "What happened to him?"

"I don't know! I was coming out of the bathroom and he just—"

"Get him a glass of water."

By the time Michael returned with the water, everyone had gathered around Stephen, except for Peter, who was still sound asleep on the floor.

"There was a man," Stephen gasped, breathless, once he'd taken a few swallows of water. "He was on the other side of the F-French d-doors. Pale. Really white. Tall. With long black hair. Staring at me."

Al turned and hurried out of the living room. They heard him going downstairs. They were silent as they waited . . . for something, for anything that might tell them what was downstairs.

Stephen drank some more water.

Carmen chewed a thumbnail.

Michael cracked his knuckles.

All of them watched the doorway.

Al's footsteps started back up the stairs. When he appeared in the doorway, his eyes looked tired, heavy.

"There's nobody down there," he said.

Stephen's eyes widened. "But he was there. I *saw* him. A guy with long black hair, really pale and . . . and he was, like, transparent."

"There was nobody there." Al's voice was suddenly firm, hard. "I went through the whole basement, Stephen. Now . . . transparent?" Al squinted at him, curious. "You mean, like a ghost?"

Stephen nodded.

"Oh, c'mon, Stephen, you've gotta stop this. I think we've all had enough. I mean, transparent people hanging around in doorways is *enough*, okay?"

Although it didn't seem possible, Stephen's eyes grew even wider as he stared at Al. "B-but I-I-I *saw* him! He was starting to come through the doors as I—"

"Stop it, Stephen!" Al said, and it was not a request. Al's eyes hardened slightly. "There's nobody down there now and there wasn't before. Okay? You understand me?"

Slowly, Stephen nodded, jaw slack, eyes still wide beneath raised eyebrows.

"Now, why don't you go to bed," Al said quietly.

"I . . . I think I'd rather sleep on the sofa."

Al exhaled slowly. "This is a living room, Stephen, not a bedroom. It's time you started sleeping down there. With Michael. You've got a bed waiting for you, you've got all your stuff in the room. C'mon, okay? Go back downstairs and go to bed."

Stephen suddenly looked a bit more pale than usual. "Really, I'd . . . I'd rather sleep up here on the—"

"Dammit, Stephen, will you *stop* it," Al snapped, closing his eyes for a moment. "Just stop it. Act your age."

Stephen stared at Al for a moment, then stood slowly. He took the glass of water, turned and left the room. The others listened as his footsteps retreated down the stairs.

"I think maybe you were a little rough on him, Al," Carmen said quietly. "What would it hurt if he slept up here another night?"

"Yeah, and another night and another night. Jeez, it's like having overnight company night after night with him out here. Whatever he thought he saw in the basement, there was nobody down there."

"I don't know," Michael said quietly, almost timidly. "Stephen says he's been hearing voices in the house. Maybe he really did see—"

"He told you that?" Al interrupted.

Michael nodded.

"Dammit," Al growled, spinning around and heading out of the room.

"Oh, come on, Al, leave him alone," Carmen said, but he ignored her. She and Michael followed him downstairs and entered the bedroom as he began to speak.

"Listen to me, Stephen," Al said, his voice low but quivering slightly with controlled anger. "Whatever you think you see around here, whatever you think you hear, you just keep it to yourself from now on, all right?"

Stephen was lying in bed with a sheet over him, wearing his Walkman earphones. He stared at the ceiling and did not acknowledge Al's presence.

"You hear me?" Al continued. "You don't need to scare the other kids with your stories. And if you do, you're gonna wish you hadn't, you understand?"

After a while, Stephen nodded slightly.

As Al went back upstairs, Carmen went to Stephen's side and bent down to give him a kiss. "Sorry about that, hon. He's kind of tense tonight."

"He's kinda drunk, you mean," Stephen whispered.

"He's not drunk, Stephen. He just doesn't want you to panic the kids, is all. Go to sleep now, okay? Sleep well."

Michael went to his bed and sat on the edge after Carmen left.

"They don't believe you?" he asked. "I mean, they don't believe *any* of it?"

Stephen turned to him without expression and said flatly, "Welcome home."

7

More Visitors

During the next few days, Carmen found herself feeling very tense. Al had seemed angry all weekend, and he'd allowed it to come out Saturday night with Stephen. She was sure that living in a motel and driving all that way every weekend was taking its toll on him, but she thought he'd been a little rough on Stephen, and she felt it was her duty to make it up to the boy.

Al's mood over the weekend had left a bad taste in her mouth and, after he'd gone, she did not feel rested or relaxed, as the weekend usually left her. She'd planned for this weekend to be especially fun, but it had been less enjoyable than most.

Unfortunately, Stephen's claim that he'd seen a pale young man with long black hair down in the basement didn't make her feel any better. In fact, she suspected— although she tried not to admit it to herself—that Stephen's story was the biggest cause of her discomfort.

Why? she'd asked herself several times. *Why would a silly story like that make you so jumpy?*

But every time she asked herself that question, she remembered the plates and silverware returning to the cupboard and drawer from which she'd taken them. She tried, again and again, to tell herself that it had been a mistake, that she hadn't actually taken the plates from the cupboard or the silverware from the drawer, that she'd only thought she had, but she was never quite able to convince herself. She knew she'd gotten the plates and silverware, could still feel them in her hands when she thought about it, but somehow, they had returned to the cupboard, to the drawer.

Unable to dismiss it, she brought it up with Fran as they drank iced tea on Fran's front porch while the baby slept just inside.

"Yeah, I do that all the time," Fran said. "It's like going all the way across the house for something, and then forgetting what you were after once you get there. It's distraction, is all it is. When you have stuff on your mind, you do stupid, embarrassing things like that. Don't worry about it. We all do it."

"But I was so sure that I—"

"Yeah, I know, I always feel that way. But I've gotten so used to it happening that I don't even think about it anymore."

Rather than talking about it any longer, Carmen felt it was time to change the subject. But although she didn't say as much, she did not agree with Fran.

That night—Monday night—Stephen and Michael went to bed early. They'd both been tired since Saturday night because neither of them had gotten much sleep. They spent much of their time Saturday and Sunday nights talking to one another in the dark. They talked about nothing in particular—music, movies, what Michael had done at Grandma's—just anything that might get their minds off what Stephen had seen. So, come Monday night, they were exhausted. They knew they had only a week of summer left before they would have to go back to school and they wanted to stay up late and watch television, but they couldn't stay awake.

And yet, once they got into bed, they couldn't quite get to sleep. They lay on their backs and stared into the darkness, talking now and then in soft tones about the coming school year and about the new Schwarzenegger movie when there was a sound in the room and both boys lifted their heads from their pillows. Michael drew in a ragged, frightened gasp of breath. . . .

Carmen was in the kitchen fixing herself a cup of cocoa. She'd put Peter to bed and told Stephanie to go, and now she just wanted to relax and, eventually, get to sleep.

She returned to the living room with her steaming cup and found Stephanie still on the floor scraping a crayon over a page in a coloring book.

"I thought I told you to go to bed," Carmen said.

"Can't I stay up a little longer? I'm not tired."

"You'll be tired in the morning when you have to go to school, and then I'll have to listen to you whine, so go. Now." She softened her tone. "Okay, hon?"

"Oh, awright, Mom." Stephanie stood and gave Carmen a kiss, then went to her bedroom with her coloring book tucked under one arm.

Carmen sat in Al's recliner and turned the television to *Murder, She Wrote*, leaning back in the recliner to relax. . . .

Stephen and Michael stared at the dresser against the wall across the room from their beds. On top of the dresser was a toy robot that belonged to Michael.

Staring at the robot, touching it, examining it, were three men. They stood in the dark tilting their heads this way and that, looking at the robot from different angles.

One man, the tallest, wore a pin-striped suit and a

fedora. The other two wore dark clothes that blended with the darkness in an indistinguishable, shadowy mass.

Their voices hissed in the silence as the man in the suit picked up the robot and examined it. He turned and faced the boys.

Neither Stephen nor Michael could move.

The man holding the robot looked at them for a long time, and the other two, standing on either side of him, turned and did the same.

They whispered, gesturing toward the boys, their words indistinguishable, but their voices sibilant, secretive.

Suddenly, the man in the suit spun around, raised the robot high above his head and held it there, turning his eyes to Stephen. "Toys," he hissed, smiling around teeth that looked grimy and broken. "Mere toys." Then he brought his arm down hard and smashed the robot on the top of the dresser.

Stephen stared wildly as the man smashed the robot down again and bits of its body scattered in the darkness, chittering against the walls and floor.

One of the men laughed, a low, throaty chuckle, and Stephen blurted, "Run!" as he bounded from his bed and headed up the stairs, followed closely by Michael.

The boys took two steps at a time, both of them screaming, "Mom! *Maawwwm*!"

Carmen spilled a drop of cocoa on her shirt and muttered, "Oh, damn," as she leaned forward in the recliner, grimacing at the boys' screaming.

"Okay," she said, setting her mug on the coffee table, "okay, *okay*!"

The boys stumbled into the living room in their underwear, out of breath, saucered eyes frantic, both of them talking at once.

"Mom, men, there are men, down in the room, right now, *right now*!" Stephen screamed.

"My robot," Michael gasped, "they broke my robot, they came outta nowhere and—"

"Stop it this instant!" Carmen shouted.

The boys fell silent, their shoulders heaving as they tried to catch their breath.

"Now, what the hell are you talking—*screaming*—about? And please talk slowly and quietly and one at a time."

The boys glanced at one another and Stephen said, "There are three men down in our room, Mom. They were standing around the dresser fooling with Michael's Robby the Robot and—"

"Wait, just wait a minute," Carmen said, holding up a hand. "How did they get in?"

"They were just *there*," Michael said.

"But the windows are locked and nobody came through the front door, so how—"

"Mom, they were talking about us," Stephen said, "whispering to each other about us, laughing."

"Okay, okay, c'mon." She walked between the boys, out of the living room and down the stairs. At the bottom, she flicked on the bedroom light and looked back up the stairs at the boys who stood at the top, huddled close together.

She walked away from the stairs, then froze in the center of the room.

What if there really was someone in the basement? She'd come down unarmed, unprepared, automatically assuming the boys had just scared each other. She felt her heartbeat speed up, felt her palms become moist and sticky.

Moving slowly, cautiously, she looked around the room. The more she looked, the more she relaxed, and a little smile curled the corners of her mouth.

"There's nobody down here, you guys," she called

over her shoulder, her relief disguised by her firm tone of voice.

She heard their footsteps hurrying down the stairs.

Her anger returned and she said, "Now exactly what the hell were you trying to—"

She stopped when her eyes fell on Michael's robot on the dresser. It lay on its side; an arm and a leg were missing, and the transparent plastic cover that had been over the face was gone. Fragmented bits of black plastic were scattered over the top of the dresser and on the floor below.

"Did one of you do this?" Carmen asked angrily as the boys came into the room.

"No, Mom, *they* did," Michael insisted.

"There was no one in this room but you two, so stop saying that."

"Mom," Michael said deliberately, as if he were speaking to a small child, "the guy picked up the robot and—"

"Okay, hold it, just hold it a second," Carmen said, holding up both palms. She studied the boys a moment. They not only looked sincere, they looked terrified. But it would have been impossible for anyone to get into the basement. She looked at the French doors; they were shut, with only darkness beyond them. All the windows were locked, she was certain of that.

Well . . . pretty certain.

No, they had to be making it up. At the very most, it was probably just the result of Stephen's telling Michael about all the voices he claimed to have heard. He probably scared the hell out of Michael and, before they knew it, *both* their imaginations were running away with them.

And Carmen was pretty sure she could prove it.

"Go upstairs a minute, Stephen," she said.

"What?"

"Just go upstairs and leave me with Michael. We won't be long."

Reluctantly, Stephen climbed the stairs, puzzled and a little angry.

"Okay, Michael," Carmen said, sitting on the edge of Stephen's bed and patting the mattress beside her, "sit down and tell me about it. Tell me everything you saw."

"Well, there were these three guys. They were standing over there by the dresser foolin' around with Robby the Robot and whispering to each other."

"What did they look like? What were they wearing?"

"Well, two of 'em were hard to see because they wore dark clothes and, well, the room was dark, so . . . but the one guy was wearing this suit. It was striped . . . thin little stripes, kind of old-fashioned."

"Pinstripes?"

"Yeah. And he wore a hat. An old-fashioned hat, the kind men wore in the old movies all the time."

"What did they do?"

"They looked at the robot and whispered, then they looked at us and whispered. One of 'em laughed. Then, the guy in the suit said something about . . . about toys, and picked up the robot and smashed it down on the dresser."

"Where'd they go?"

Michael shrugged. "I dunno. We ran."

"And they just stood here and let you run after you'd seen them standing in your room busting up a toy? Doesn't that seem odd to you?"

"Maybe it's odd, but . . . you wanted me to tell you what happened. That's what happened."

Carmen studied Michael's face, looking for some sign of guilt, for one of the familiar clues that he was lying. He was a lousy liar, always had been. Stephen could get away with it, but she'd only seen him use his poker face to pull pranks on her and Al, harmless jokes that required a straight face until the payoff, never anything as pointless as this.

But she saw nothing in Michael's face that told her he was lying, so either he'd picked up his big brother's talent for keeping a straight face, or . . .

Or he was telling the truth.

"Okay, stay here," she said as she stood and started up the stairs.

"You don't believe us, do you?" Michael asked softly.

Carmen stopped and turned to him. "Just stay here, hon. I'll be back in a minute."

Upstairs, she found Stephen slumped on the sofa with his arms folded over his thin chest looking dejected as he whispered to Stephanie, who sat beside him, leaning close. Stephen stopped and Stephanie pulled away the moment Carmen entered the room.

"I thought I sent you to bed, Steph," Carmen said.

Stephanie stood and headed for her room, saying, "I'm going, Mom, I'm going."

Carmen sat down beside Stephen. "Okay. I want you to tell me exactly what happened down there."

She listened carefully as he told her exactly the same thing Michael had told her. When she questioned him—"What did they look like? What were they wearing?"—his answers were identical to Michael's, right down to what the man said: "He said, 'Toys, mere toys.'"

When he was finished, Carmen realized she was frowning. If the boys were lying, then they had to have made up the story in great detail before breaking the robot and telling her, otherwise their stories would not have been identical in every detail.

A chill fell over her like a blanket as she seriously considered, for the first time, the possibility that there *had* been three men in the boys' room.

Why would they come in just to whisper to one another right in front of Stephen and Michael, break a toy robot, then leave?

That was what she found so frightening about it: It was completely senseless.

Should I call the police? she wondered. *But what if they come and it turns out the boys are lying?*

She decided that if three men had indeed broken into the house, there would have to be some sign of entry somewhere, and it would have to be down in the basement.

"Okay," she said decisively as she stood. "That's all I wanted to know." She left the room and, as she started down the stairs, she heard Stephen call, "What're you gonna do?" But she didn't respond.

Downstairs, she was asked the same question by Michael.

"Just stay here," she said as she opened the French doors and went into the next room, reaching out to flick on the light. She looked around the room that was supposed to be Stephen's, saw that the two windows were still locked and went into the wide hallway beyond, turning on another light.

She checked the tool room at the end of the hall; the window there was untouched, too.

She walked up the ramp at the opposite end of the hall and checked the door. Locked.

In the next room, she tried not to look at the plank covering the blood tank—tried to avoid even thinking about it—and devoted all her attention to the two windows there.

Nothing had been broken or pried open.

She turned to the doorway that led to the morgue. Although she hadn't admitted it to Al or anyone else, she didn't like to go in there. She didn't think it was evil, or anything like that; it just made her . . . uncomfortable. But there were three windows in there and, although she was pretty sure the boys had been pulling her chain, she supposed she should check those, too.

With a sigh, she walked into the dingy room and turned on the light. It was much more tolerable since Al had painted it, but still . . .

She checked the window across from the door, then the two on the back wall.

There were footsteps behind her.

"Michael?" she said. "There's no way anyone could have—" She turned and her voice caught in her throat and she froze in place, mouth open, as the air around her became icy cold, as if she were standing in front of an open freezer, and just as she turned, she felt someone brush by her, rubbing against her only slightly, and felt the shift in the cold air as someone passed.

There was no one there.

Stephen went downstairs to find Michael sitting on the edge of his bed, frowning as he stared intensely through the open French doors. The light was on in the next room.

"Where's Mom?" Stephen asked.

Michael nodded toward the doors. "She went back there. I think she's—"

Suddenly, they heard a rush of movement in another part of the basement: footsteps, a rapid series of clicks as the lights were turned off, doors slamming, and Carmen walked quickly through the next door, flicked off the light as she came out and closed the French doors hard.

For a moment, Stephen thought she might scream. There was an odd look on her face, one he'd never seen before, one he thought, at first, was abject terror. Then she stood before them, set her jaw, and put her fists on her hips.

"There was no one in here tonight, you understand?" she said, her voice low but unsteady. "No windows or locks were broken. Everything's closed up. *No one* was in here. Now, if you thought that was funny, you're wrong, and if you do anything like that again, you're both gonna be in *big* trouble."

She spun away from them and stomped up the stairs.

Stephen and Michael exchanged a silent glance, then Stephen called, "Mom? There really was—"

"I don't wanna hear it, Stephen!" she snapped, turning back and pointing a finger at him. "I told you a long time ago to keep your stories to yourself, but you had to go and tell Michael and you got him all worked up and now you're both upset, which is exactly what I said would happen, remember? Well, *remember?*"

Slowly, Stephen nodded.

Carmen started up the stairs again.

Stephen turned to Michael, released a long sigh, then started slowly up the stairs behind his mom.

"Where do you think you're going?" she asked over her shoulder.

"I . . . um, I was just gonna come up and watch a little—"

"You're going to bed, is what you're gonna do! Both of you. And I don't want to hear a word from either one of you, got it?"

"Can I at least come get a glass of water?" Stephen asked quietly.

"Yeah, yeah, go ahead."

He waited on the step until she was gone, then turned to Michael again.

"Boy," Michael whispered, "she's pissed."

"Or something," Stephen said before going upstairs.

Carmen went into the living room and flopped into the recliner. The picture on the television screen disappeared in a blur of colors as tears stung her eyes. She sucked in a deep breath, wiped her eyes quickly and grabbed her pack of Marlboros from the end table. Her hands trembled as she lit her cigarette and she shook the match harder than usual, as if to shake the tremors out of her bones.

She leaned her head back, closed her eyes, and savored her anger. She was angry because, with their vivid story and their wide, frightened eyes, the boys had managed to convince her that strangers had been in the house. Three of them! She'd allowed her imagination to get caught up with her sons'.

"Yeah," she breathed, thinking, *That's all it was. Just my imagination and that stupid story of theirs. Right?*

But the tiny little voice of her conscience that usually spoke from deep within her mind remained silent.

8

School's In

"C'mon you guys, outta bed!" Carmen shouted down the staircase, clapping her hands sharply three times.

Stephen held his pillow over his head, but he heard a muffled groan from the direction of Michael's bed, then a groggy, "Errr, summer's over."

There were sounds of yawning and sighing as they stirred, sat up, and looked around with puffy eyes.

"You wanna shower first?" Michael mumbled.

"Uh-uh. G'head."

"C'mon, you're gonna be late!" Carmen called.

"H'come?" Michael replied as he trudged up the stairs.

" 'Cause my alarm clock didn't go off, that's how come. Breakfast is ready!"

Stephen flopped onto his back, rubbed his eyes, then stared at the ceiling.

He would not be going to school right away like Michael and Stephanie. Instead, he would have to go to the hospital for his treatment. Last week, Mom had met with the principal of the high school Stephen would be attending, as well as one of the counselors. She'd explained the learning problems he had faced while going to school in Hurleyville and told them of his illness and that he would be late for school every day the first week so he could get his treatments. She'd said they were very understanding and had assured her that they would do everything possible to see that he was comfortable and that his problems were dealt with properly.

Stephen had no way of knowing, of course, if they were sincere or not, but he hoped for the best. School was hard enough by itself, but going to a new school with total strangers made it even harder; he certainly didn't need any *more* trouble.

When it came right down to it, he didn't need anything other than those treatments. They were enough trouble all by themselves, thank you very much. He despised them even more than the doctors and nurses he had to deal with every day. There was nothing particularly wrong with them—except that they administered the treatments.

Each day he was put under a sinister-looking contraption that resembled an X-ray machine, only it was bigger and uglier and more threatening. The worst part was being abandoned by everyone while he was exposed to radiation. If they were all afraid of it, why were they leaving him in there?

He'd had a nightmare—several times, in fact—in which everyone left him in that sterile white room beneath that ominous machine . . . and they never came back.

Oh well, just a few more days, and then . . . well, as Dr. Berry said, "And then we'll see."

Stephen couldn't wait for the treatments to be over, and hoped he'd never have to have them again. He could think of nothing worse.

"Stephen?"

Nothing except that voice.

He sat up on the bed and listened.

"Stephen? Are you ready?"

He turned toward the French doors, but saw nothing through the glass panes.

"Are you ready, Stephen?"

It was the same male, voice, but now it was coming from another part of the basement.

"I'm waiting, Stephen."

Each time it spoke, it sounded closer.

Staring through the panes, Stephen thought he saw something . . . just a faint sign of movement . . . a shadow, perhaps . . . a shadow falling through the open door across the next room.

He shot from the bed and scrambled around the room, grabbing pants, a shirt, shoes, then—

"Time is wasting, Stephen."

He raced up the stairs, the sound of his breath loud in his ears, rounded the banister and hurried down the hall, his clothes clutched to his chest.

Carmen stepped out of the kitchen in front of him and they collided.

"Stephen!" She snapped, more frustrated than angry. "What're you doing?"

He started to speak, then snapped his mouth shut and just stared at her, trying not to tremble.

She held up a rigid index finger and said, "I don't wanna hear it, Stephen. Not now, not ever, but especially not now. This morning's been bad enough already. Go eat your breakfast, it's on the table."

She hurried past him and went into her bedroom.

Stephen stood in the hallway and listened, but all he heard was the shower. Relieved, but still tense, he headed for the dining room.

Carmen could not understand what had gone wrong with the morning. She *knew* she'd set her alarm for seven o'clock, but when she'd finally dragged herself out of a sound sleep, she found that the alarm button on top of the clock was still in the ALARM ON position, but the clock had been set for twelve and she was forty minutes late.

After waking everyone urgently, she'd tossed a quick breakfast together, thrown on some clothes—she always felt more awake when she was dressed—set her purse and keys on the kitchen counter so she'd be ready to take Stephen to the hospital, and somehow managed to get Stephanie and Michael fed and dressed in time to meet their bus, but not before asking them, "Did any of you fool around with my alarm clock?"

They'd all looked at her with puzzled expressions and said no.

"Okay. Just wondered."

Once Stephanie and Michael had gone, she was left with Stephen, who was even more quiet than usual, and Peter, who couldn't stop talking about the day when he would be able to ride to school in a big yellow bus, too.

Carmen sat across the dining-room table from Stephen and said, "Well, how about we go to the hospital and get this over with so you can get to school?"

His hair, wet from his shower, was combed straight back and clung to his head, making his thin face look almost skull-like. "Do I have to go straight to school afterwards?"

"Course not. You can come back here, if you want. Relax. Recover. Then I'll take you to school. In fact, if you don't feel like going at all, that's fine, too. It's only for this week, and they know all about it at school. It's up to you."

He nodded slowly, stared at the tabletop for a long moment, then looked at her, lips parted slightly, as if he were about to say something. Then he seemed to think better of it, closed his mouth and muttered. "Okay, let's go."

When everyone was ready, Carmen went into the kitchen to get her purse and keys.

They were gone.

She stared at the empty space on the counter where she had set them as Peter tugged on her hand and said, "Mommy, I'm pretending you taking *me* to schoo'!"

"All right, where's my purse," she said. Then, louder, "Stephen, have you seen my purse?"

"No," he called from the living room.

"Well, it was right here on the counter with my keys and now they're gone, so look for them, okay?"

"Where'd you put 'em?"

"Right *here*," she snapped.

"Okay, okay, I'll look."

They looked. They searched the entire first floor of the house, but the purse and keys were nowhere to be found. Carmen was near tears when she met Stephen in the dining room.

"Think they might be downstairs?" Stephen asked.

"I haven't been downstairs this morning."

"Okay. Just asked."

But that question made Carmen pause. She frowned as she thought about it. Then, against her better judgment, knowing her things couldn't possibly be down there because *she* hadn't been down there, she went downstairs and, a few steps from the bottom, she froze.

Her purse and car keys were on Stephen's bed.

She stared at her fists for a long time before clenching them at her sides and calling, "Stephen! Stephen, get down here right now!"

Carmen did not turn when she heard him coming down the stairs, she just continued to stare at her purse and keys on the bed. When his footsteps stopped, she pointed at the bed and said, "Did you put them there?"

"Nuh-n-*no*!"

"Then how did they *get* there?"

"I—I—I d-don't know!"

Finally, she turned to him, glowering. "Stephen, this has got to stop," she said, her voice almost a whisper, quivering with anger. "I mean it. I don't know what you're trying to do, but whatever it is, I'm sick of it!"

He stared at her, slack-jawed and horrified. "B-but I didn't—"

"Shut up!" she growled through clenched teeth. "I don't want to talk about it. Just see to it that this crap stops *now*, Stephen! I'm serious. If you're still pulling this stuff when your dad moves home, you're gonna be sorry, because he won't put up with it. And neither will *I*!"

She crossed the room, swept the purse and keys off the bed, then started up the stairs, calling back, "C'mon, let's go."

They didn't speak for a while; Peter was the only one who did any talking, babbling on about how he was pretending Mommy was taking him to school. Once they'd been on the road for a while, Carmen felt herself begin to relax. Other thoughts began to crowd her mind, making it easy for her to forget about her purse and keys being moved downstairs. Along with those thoughts came guilt.

"I'm sorry for shouting at you like that, Stephen," she said quietly. "But you made me very angry."

He turned to her suddenly and said, "But I didn't—" then stopped just as suddenly and faced front. He said nothing more.

Carmen was relieved by his silence. She was glad he'd thought better of denying it once again. She really did not want to hear it.

Because the quiet voice in the back of her mind kept whispering insistently that Stephen's denial might very well be the truth.

9

Sleepless Thoughts

Carmen could not sleep, so she sat at the dining-room table—her favorite spot in the house—and smoked as she thumbed absently through a back issue of *Vanity Fair* and half-listened to the radio call-in talk show that played softly.

Once Stephen's treatments had come to an end—for the time being, at least—Carmen expected him to change. For the better, of course. He'd been so quiet and brooding since they'd moved into the apartment, so unlike himself. She told herself it was due to his illness and, perhaps even more so, because of the grueling daily treatments for it. But the only change she noticed in him during the weeks following his final treatment was that his mood seemed to grow quietly and gradually darker.

At least Stephen had Cody to cheer him up. Cody's parents both worked and he was alone a lot, so he'd started spending most of his time at their house. Carmen didn't mind. She didn't like the thought of the boy's being alone so much, so she tried to make him feel at home.

Although she was glad that Stephen had a friend, Carmen was disturbed to see that the only time Stephen seemed truly happy was when Cody was around; otherwise, he was silent, depressive, and, if she asked him what was wrong, he made no more than a vague, monosyllabic reply.

She worried about him, but told herself that he'd been through a lot and might not be through all of it yet; as long as he had a friend who made him happy and was doing well in school, she was satisfied.

The only problem was Cody. There was nothing wrong with him that she could put her finger on—he was a nice enough boy, friendly and polite when spoken to but otherwise pretty quiet—he just seemed . . . different, like the kind of boy who might find it difficult to make friends. And yet he and Stephen had hit it off famously. Oh well. So they were friends. As long as they weren't knocking over liquor stores or burning down buildings for kicks, what was the harm?

You're just being a mother, she told herself. *Too* much *of a mother.*

She wasn't so hard on herself when it came to Stephen's idea that there was something evil about the house. Since Michael had picked up on it, Carmen often found the boys and Stephanie whispering among themselves, only to fall silent when they found they weren't alone. That had been going on for some time between Stephen and Stephanie, of course, but since Michael had come home, it seemed to happen more often. It got on her nerves, but she kept her feelings to herself.

On the weekends, Al didn't seem to notice the children whispering secretively. His mind was on other things. One hundred and six miles of driving every weekend was taking a toll on him, as was the stress of knowing he would be taking a step down and making less money once his transfer went through, making their financial bind even tighter than it was already.

When he was home, they didn't talk about anything

important or too serious. He'd go fishing (although Stephen didn't seem interested in going with him anymore) or spend time watching television. When they made love, he acted distant, preoccupied. And he didn't seem to be sleeping well at night, either. The last time he'd been home, Carmen had awakened very early on Saturday morning to find herself alone in bed; a couple minutes later, he'd come into the bedroom and gotten back into bed looking worried, his face twisted in a frown of creases made to look even deeper by the faint glow of moonlight outside the window.

"Whasmatter?" Carmen had asked.

Her voice startled him and he looked at her for a moment, that frown clinging to his face, then said, "Uh, nothing, nothing, go back to sleep."

So Carmen had more than her share of things to worry about: Stephen, his illness, and—no matter how hard she tried not to—his friendship with Cody as well; and money and Al. But, for the first time she could remember, she was actually relieved to have those worries. Those worries gave her a welcome excuse for some of the odd things she'd been doing . . . things she *thought* she'd been doing, anyway.

There was, of course, the voice she'd heard that day while she was alone in the house. She'd chalked that up to missing Al.

Then the plates and silverware had appeared to take themselves back into the kitchen the day Michael came home, and her purse had disappeared and her car keys had gone from the kitchen counter to Stephen's bed downstairs.

Last week, she'd found the bathroom faucet running and steam billowing up from the scalding water.

Yesterday she thought she'd bought two six-packs of soda, even remembered putting them in the refrigerator. That evening, they were gone; none of the kids had drunk them, hadn't even seen them. She tried to find the receipt, *knowing* she'd bought them and wanting to prove it to herself, but she couldn't.

She'd blamed it all on her preoccupation, told herself she'd just made a few absent-minded mistakes. But somehow, that just didn't work. So she buried it all by worrying about everything else.

As Carmen lit another cigarette, a female caller on the radio said, "Well, my problem is, like, I'm not sure of myself, you know? I'm not sure who I am. Like, am I a wife? Am I a mother? Am I a daughter? And no one seems to understand the crisis I'm having, or the space that I need to work it all out."

Carmen glanced at the radio and blew smoke as she chuckled coldly, "Get a life, lady." Then she went back to her magazine.

At roughly the same time, Al could not sleep either. He sat up in his motel room drinking a beer and smoking a cigarette. The room was dark except for the flickering light from the television, which was playing silently. Al was watching the images on the screen without really seeing them. Instead, he was, like Carmen, lost in his thoughts . . . thoughts about his last visit home. He could not get it out of his mind. He'd been thinking about it on the job as well as off. Even going to the occasional movie in the evening failed to stop the constant replay of the memory.

Oh, he had plenty of other things to worry about, there was no doubt about that. Stephen's illness, the gradual change in his personality, and Al wasn't sure he liked Stephen's friendship with that odd kid Cody, although he hadn't said as much to Carmen and was unaware that she sometimes felt the same way. And of course there was the matter of money; he would be getting less pay soon and they had to struggle enough as it was to make his current salary cover everything. But, in spite of all that, it was last weekend that weighed the heaviest on him.

The first thing had happened on Friday night. . . .

He'd been awakened quite suddenly by the sound of movement and voices in the house. He lay in bed for a while, listening. The voices were muffled, the sounds of movement made up of bumps and scuffles. And there was music, terribly soft, almost inaudible, tinny and . . . old, like music from a bygone era playing on a gramophone, its scratchy warblings coming from a yawning horn above a cranked-up turntable. It didn't sound like something any of the kids would listen to, but still . . .

He got out of bed, careful not to wake Carmen, and went down the hall in his undershorts. The sounds grew closer. He stopped and listened and realized they were coming from downstairs.

Quiet voices, soft, mournful music—obviously there was a gathering of some sort taking place down there. Al suspected Cody was involved somehow; in fact, it was probably his idea to sneak a bunch of kids into the house from the beginning.

But why were they listening to *that* music?

Stepping carefully in the dark, he started down the stairs, but stopped halfway down.

There was no light coming from down there, no light at all. It was as dark as the rest of the house. Al frowned, listened some more.

He could still hear the voices and the music, still heard the sounds of feet moving over the floor. He took the remaining steps cautiously, although he wasn't quite sure why.

In the bedroom below, he heard the boys' steady, sleepy breathing, and suddenly—

Nothing else. There was only the breathing. And the darkness.

The voices and music had stopped.

Al opened one of the French doors and leaned into the next room.

The empty darkness was silent, but cold. Al stepped all the way into the next room, squinting in disbelief. It was so cold in that room that he was pretty sure that if it weren't so dark, he'd be able to see his breath; it was like a meat locker. Concerned that a window might have been left open, he took a few more steps into the room, then stopped, realizing that, even if a window was open, it wasn't *that* cold outside.

Then he suddenly realized that the cold was gone. The room had returned to a normal temperature, but Al's skin crawled with goose bumps anyway.

He thought about it a moment, wondering how it could have happened, then decided he didn't *want* to know and backed out of the room.

He listened again to the boys' breathing. Yes, they were asleep, there was no doubt about that; Stephen was even snoring quietly, but a genuine snore, not a silly one that a kid might fake at the last minute to keep from being caught awake by a parent.

When he got back to bed, Al found Carmen awake. She asked him what was the matter and he told her to go back to sleep.

Al, however, did not sleep. Instead, he lay in bed listening for the voices and music again. But he did not hear them.

The following night, he was awakened again, this time by movement. His eyes snapped open wide and stared into the darkness as the bed vibrated.

It didn't shake, it didn't jerk, it *vibrated*.

Slowly, his eyes closed as he decided it was probably nothing more than the refrigerator coming on in the upstairs apartment. Carmen had mentioned to him that a family would be moving in upstairs. But his eyes snapped open again when he realized that they wouldn't be moving in for another week.

The upstairs apartment was empty. There was no refrigerator up there.

He stared at the ceiling as the bed continued to vibrate, its movement humming through him, oozing through his muscles and coiling around his bones.

Al got up and went to the living room, turning on lights as he walked, his hands trembling. He watched television for a while, smoked, had a couple of beers, and then, warily, returned to the bedroom. He sat on the edge of the bed.

The vibrating had stopped.

Although he was exhausted from the sleepless night before, he was unable to doze off for a while. He lay there waiting for the vibrating to continue. It did not. Finally, Al slipped away and slept late into Sunday morning.

Now he lay awake once again, staring at talking heads with no voices on the television, drinking a beer and filling the dark room with smoke.

There was a good chance that he would not have given either incident much thought if it weren't for Stephen . . . if it weren't for the things Stephen had said he'd seen and heard . . . the things he'd said about the house . . .

There was something else, too, something Al hadn't thought about in years. In fact, he thought he'd forgotten about it entirely, which would have been fine with him. It had happened years ago, when he was in the service. He'd seen something back then that had given him nightmares for the longest time. In fact, he still had one now and then. Until he'd seen . . . that thing . . . he'd laughed at the supernatural, and his laughter had been genuine. Since then, he'd continued laughing, but nervously and without as much conviction as before.

He'd told no one of what he'd seen back then, not even Carmen. He wasn't sure he ever would.

But what had happened at home last weekend had brought it to mind, and had reminded him that he was no longer closed to the notion of things that go bump in the night.

His transfer would go through soon and he would be able to move to Connecticut to stay with his family. He missed Carmen and the kids and was looking forward to being with them for more than just weekend visits.

But Al wasn't at all sure he was looking forward to moving into that house.

10

Making a Deal

Stephen knew his parents would not approve of the music he and Cody were listening to in Stephen's bedroom, but he realized that he didn't care. That had not always been the case. There was a time—very recently, in fact, although it seemed like ages ago—when their approval had meant something to him, and the mere knowledge of their disapproval would have been enough to make him think twice about lying there on his bed listening to Ozzy Osbourne's shrieking voice.

But now Stephen found himself feeling a certain amount of resentment toward Carmen and Al, enough to make him careless of what they might think.

Al's transfer had gone through and he'd been home for the better part of a week now, so there were two people around all the time who didn't believe him, who didn't even seem to trust him. He resented them for that disbelief, as well as for their eagerness to blame him for every little thing that went wrong in the house; they blamed him when the other kids got scared, and they blamed him whenever something in the house disappeared or was misplaced. He wondered what he'd be blamed for next.

But he didn't care. If they didn't care about what he thought, he would no longer care about what *they* thought.

"So, who would you rather sleep with," Cody said, "Madonna or Joan Jett?" He was lying on Michael's bed in the same position in which Stephen was lying on his own: face up, ankles crossed, hands locked behind his head with elbows jutting out at each side.

The day was coming to an end outside and the fading light of early evening shone through the windows. In spite of that, every light in the room was on. Stephen did that everywhere he went in the house now; he didn't like to be in any room that was not well lit.

"I don't know," Stephen said thoughtfully. "Which one's worth the most money?"

"What difference does *that* make? They're both hot."

"Yeah, but after I've had 'em, they'll be so grateful, they'll wanna shower me with expensive gifts and lotsa cash, so I want the one that's got the most." Concealed laughter was hidden in Stephen's voice.

Cody tossed his head back and laughed, then said, "You're so fulla shit, your ears stink!" Then he laughed some more before adding, "Madonna's got bigger boobs."

"Think so?"

"Oh yeah, yeah, I *know* so. Show you." He sat up and leaned down to get a brown paper bag on the floor beside the bed. It was full of rock magazines he'd brought over with him that he and Stephen hadn't looked through yet. He dumped the bag on the bed and began searching through the stack for the one he wanted.

Stephen liked Cody for a number of reasons, among them the fact that, unlike the only people he'd been able to hang around with back in Hurleyville, he was cool. Back home, being in all those damned special-education classes had kept him from being accepted by the popular kids at school; he'd ended up spending his time with the other boneheads in those classes while the kids he *really* wanted to be with had spent their time picking on him, laughing at him, and calling him names.

Well, maybe Cody wasn't what *they* would consider cool, but he was a good friend to Stephen and he had lots of cool things, like all those rock magazines he bought every month, a great collection of tapes, a boom box to play them on and—or so he claimed—a bunch of pornography (although Stephen had seen very little of it because, understandably, Cody had to be careful about flashing it around). He liked some of the same music Stephen liked—pop music, mostly—but had introduced him to a lot of stuff Stephen hadn't listened to in the past . . . because he knew how much his parents disliked it.

But what Stephen liked most was that Cody believed him when he talked about the things that had been happening. Not only did he believe Stephen, he accepted the stories to be true as nonchalantly as one might accept a newspaper headline to be true. He hadn't shown a flicker of doubt.

"Yeah, yeah, here it is," Cody said, holding one of the magazines open—it was a back issue of *Rock Scene*—as he got up and went to Stephen's bed.

Stephen sat up and looked at the picture Cody indicated: a shot of Joan Jett onstage at a concert wearing a very tiny black bikini.

"See?" Cody said. "Great bod, but flat as a board."

"Yeah, but how much money does she have?" Stephen said, and they both laughed, until—

Cody's laughter stopped as if he'd choked on it.

Stephen looked up to see Cody's eyes opening wider than seemed possible as they stared to Cody's right. His mouth opened and closed several times, but he made no sound, just dropped the magazine onto Stephen's lap as his face lost some of its color.

Following the direction of Cody's eyes, Stephen's gaze

fell on the French doors and on the old man who stood beyond them.

Stephen kicked his legs and tumbled clumsily off the bed until he was on his feet, then spun around toward the French doors.

Both boys stood frozen in place for a long moment, staring.

The man's skin was white. It wasn't clown-white or sheet-white or even merely pale; it was the white of skin that had been drained of blood, of life, a sick, milky, splotchy white. The skin was wrinkled beyond the effects of old age, unnaturally wrinkled and flabby, as if nothing lay between it and the bones beneath. What was left of his white hair was stringy and hung in thin patches to varying lengths. He wore a dark suit that appeared old in both style and condition; it looked ragged and tattered, even dirty. The white hands that dangled from the sleeves were gnarled, and long thick nails curved downward over the fingertips.

The old man did not move, just faced the boys. He would have been staring at them had there been anything besides empty, glassy white orbs in his eyesockets.

Cody ran first, but Stephen wasn't far behind him. They quickened their pace as they rushed past the French doors, then thumped loudly up the stairs, leaving the music playing in the room behind them.

They were halfway down the hall when Carmen stepped out of the dining room and snapped, "Why do you always have to *run* up those damned stairs! How many times have I told you—" She stopped when she got a good look at their faces and saw that they were gasping from fear rather than exertion.

Stephen pointed back down the hall and said, "There was a-a . . . w-we saw a-a-a *man* . . ."

"Oh God, Stephen, not again." For a moment, she sounded very weary, as if Stephen had told her she was going to have to take another in an exhausting series of long, uphill runs. Then she sounded angry. "Dammit, Stephen, this is getting really old, and I'm—"

"No, we *did*!" Cody insisted. "There was an old man down there, just st-standing there and staring at us!"

She just looked at them, from Stephen to Cody and back again, silent and stern. Then she said, "It's a good thing Al's not here, Stephen."

"Where is he?"

"At the grocery store. He's really getting sick of this business of you seeing people in your room. And so am I. You're liable to get your butt grounded if you keep—"

"But it's not just *me*!" Stephen insisted, frustrated.

"No, Mrs. Snedeker, it's not," Cody added. "I saw the guy, too. I saw the guy *first*!"

Carmen's shoulders sagged as she let out a long sigh. "Okay, let's go." She led the way down the stairs.

As the boys followed, Stephen muttered, "Here we go again. Nothing there . . . makin' it up . . . stop lying . . ." Then he looked at Cody and rolled his eyes.

Carmen faced the boys at the foot of the stairs, unable to keep herself from wincing at the sounds coming from Cody's boom box on the nightstand between the beds. "Okay, where were you? What were you doing?"

"We were on the beds," Stephen said.

"And this, um . . . *music* was playing?"

They nodded. "We were lookin' at rock magazines," Cody said.

Carmen glanced distastefully at the magazine on the bed, open to a mostly naked, angry-looking woman. She pushed the magazine aside, and sat on Stephen's bed.

"Okay," she said, "go upstairs. Go outside if you want, I don't care. Just go."

Stephen asked, "What're you gonna—"

"Just *go*." She sounded irritable enough for them to know better than to stick around asking questions.

When they were gone, Carmen stared at the French doors.

"Okay, Carm," she breathed, the words barely audible, "what the hell're you doin'?"

Although it was difficult to think with the rancid sounds pounding out of the speakers behind her, she decided she was calling Stephen's bluff. She'd sit on that bed and watch and wait and see what she could see. The conditions were exactly the same as those under which the boys claimed to have seen this old man. She was giving herself a chance to see him, too, that was all.

Her inner voice spoke up then, shattering her sense of self-satisfaction, of self-security.

Giving yourself a chance to see him? it whispered. *Don't you mean you're giving it a chance to finally show itself? Don't you mean you're looking for whatever it is that's been moving things . . . taking things . . . talking to you in a familiar voice from an empty room? Of course that's what you're doing . . . whether you admit it or not . . .*

Carmen shook her head sharply, as if to rid it of the gnawing voice.

She leaned forward, elbows on her knees, chin on her knuckles, and continued to stare at the French doors, waiting.

The music was truly awful and, as she listened to the lyrics, she decided she'd have to have a word with Stephen about what music did and did not get played under this roof.

As she waited, Carmen thought. No matter how she tried to hold her wandering thoughts in check, they went back to her inner voice, to the things that had been happening to her in the house . . . and for a moment, she thought she heard the sound of cautious movement from some other part of the basement.

She sat up straight, her hands clutching together between her knees as she listened.

Silence, except for the awful music.

Then the song—if it could be called that—ended and, a moment later, another began.

Was that more movement Carmen had heard in the brief silence? Was it moving closer? Or was it just—

Your imagination? her inner voice muttered.

She suddenly felt as if her skin were shriveling around her bones.

The hair at the base of her skull bristled.

Although Carmen tried to listen for the sounds she'd *thought* she'd heard deeper in the basement—she tried to listen hard—she could not bring herself to stay there a moment longer and bolted from the bed.

Halfway up the stairs, she tried to slow her hurried pace and calm her rapid breathing. Once she was in the hall, she had returned to what she hoped was her normal appearance; although inside, she still felt icy, unsteady and afraid . . . but afraid of *what?*

"Where've you been?" Al asked from the kitchen.

His voice startled her. She hadn't heard him come in. She wasn't even sure how long she'd been down there and, as a result, had a silly, almost girlish feeling of guilt, as if she'd been caught doing something she shouldn't.

"Downstairs." She went in the kitchen and found him loading the refrigerator with the groceries he'd gone to get.

"What's the matter with Stephen and Cody? I found them sitting on the front steps looking . . . I don't know, like they got into trouble, or something."

"Oh really? Well, they came running up the stairs earlier saying they'd seen a ghost. Another ghost, I should say."

"Oh shit." Al opened a bottle, closed the refrigerator and took a couple gulps. When he looked at Carmen, his face was dark; he was wearing his half-angry-half-fed-up expression. "Well, that's it," he said, leaving the kitchen.

"That's the last of it." He went out the front door and said firmly, "Okay, Cody, I think it's time for you to go home for tonight."

The boys' heads snapped up to look at him.

Stephen said, "But his parents are—"

"I'm sorry, but Cody's gonna have to go home."

"Can I get my stuff out of Stephen's room?"

"Sure."

Carmen stood at the top of the stairs while Al went down with the boys and waited as Cody got his things together, said good-bye and left. Then Al pointed a finger at Stephen and said, "No more ghosts. You understand me? We've had enough. No more voices, no more people in your room, that's it, it's *finished*. One more word about any of that stuff and you're gonna be sorry. And we'll start with you staying down here for the rest of the night. No TV, no music—and no more of that crap I heard playing down here a little while ago, you got it? I don't want that trash in this house. You can go from here to the bathroom and back. That's it. I don't wanna hear another word out of you till tomorrow. And turn off some of these damned lights! Every light in the room is on! You start running up the bill and you can *pay* for it."

Al started up the stairs and Carmen expected Stephen to say something, to protest, to call up to him. The room downstairs was silent, though. Al took another swallow of beer as he walked by her.

"Don't you think that was a little too much, Al?"

"Why too much? You mean you're not getting sick of it? What else're we gonna do, *encourage* him? Next time, he gets something worse. He gets grounded, or he can't watch the television or use the phone or . . . or something. I've had all I can take of this *Twilight Zone* shit."

Then Al went into the living room and turned on the television.

Stephanie was in the back yard with Peter and Michael was down the street playing with a friend; it was time to call them in. But first, she wanted to have a word with Stephen. She felt somewhat responsible for the tongue-lashing he'd gotten because she'd told Al about what he and Cody had "seen."

Of course, she hadn't—and wouldn't—tell Al about her little experiment afterward, about how she sat in the room waiting to see what *she* could see.

Downstairs, she found Stephen lying on his bed, staring at the ceiling with his hands locked behind his head. She sat on the edge of his bed and said, "Sorry about the outburst, but I think—"

"I don't give a shit what you think!" Stephen said through clenched teeth without looking at her.

Carmen gasped and stood up. "Don't you *ever* talk to me that way again or I'll slap your mouth halfway around your head, young man!"

Very quietly, jaw still locked, he said. "You don't care what I think; I don't care what you think. You don't wanna hear what I have to say; I don't wanna hear what you have to say."

Carmen's voice trembled when she spoke again. "Whatever's wrong with you had better be gone by morning, Stephen. I mean it, that kind of behavior just doesn't cut it around here, so you'd better get over feeling sorry for yourself, or whatever the hell you're doing, right now. You might be a teenager, but you're still not too old to get your ass whipped!"

She spun around and stomped upstairs to bring the other kids inside.

When she was gone, Stephen undressed for bed. He still hadn't turned the lights off in his room. The darkness outside the window was now complete; no sunlight remained. Turning those lights off would let some of that darkness inside, and Stephen did not want to do that.

Instead, he got into bed with the room fully lit; even the bedside lamps were on.

He turned onto his side and tried to relax, although he knew he would be unable to sleep for a while. He was too upset, so upset, in fact, that he was experiencing feelings he'd never known before. He wanted to . . . break something, to pick something up and just smash it against the wall with all his might. His frustration was a viscous congestion in his chest that seemed to seep between his ribs and press against muscle and flesh.

He closed his eyes tightly, blocking out the light, and pressed his head into the pillow.

"Stephen?"

His eyes snapped open.

He was alone in the room.

"Stephen? Are you ready?" the voice asked, ever so quietly.

He didn't move for a long while, just waited for it to continue. When it didn't, he opened his mouth, took a moment to ask himself if he was sure he wanted to do this, then said, "Yes."

"That's my boy."

"If . . . only if you'll leave me alone. I'll, um . . ." He sat up a little. ". . . I'll do whatever you want if you'll just leave me alone. Deal?"

That familiar chuckle, like ice cubes clattering over glass. "Very good. *Very* good. It's a deal, my boy."

"It's a deal? So . . . you'll leave me alone?"

"You will have to hold up your end of the bargain first. You will have to do whatever I want, just as you said. Then . . . we'll see."

Stephen realized someone was coming down the stairs and quickly dropped back onto the mattress.

"You talkin' to somebody?" Michael asked.

"Uh-uh." Stephen covered half his face with the sheet, afraid the lie would show.

"I thought I heard you talkin' down here."

"I said *no*."

"Okay, okay. Mom and Dad say I'm supposed to make sure the lights are off down here. Most of 'em, anyway."

Stephen thought about that a moment, pictured the room dimmer, even completely dark. For the first time since the move, the idea of darkness was not as frightening, even a little comforting.

"Yeah," he said. "Go ahead. Leave one of 'em on, though."

"You okay, Stephen?"

He suddenly found Michael annoying. He wanted to think, to go over what had just happened, but his brother wouldn't shut up. As he turned over on his belly and pulled the sheet up further, he growled, "Yes, I'm okay, dammit, what's the matter with *you*?"

When Michael spoke again, he sounded hurt. "N-nothing. Just asked." His footsteps started up the stairs. "I'll be back in a little while."

But Stephen did not respond. He lay in bed, wide awake, thinking about what he had done, wondering what kind of deal he had just made . . . and with whom.

11

Changes

The changes that took place in the Snedeker family over the following months were very subtle, but not so subtle as to go unnoticed by Al and Carmen; they were —with the exception of the changes in Stephen's behavior—simply not discussed.

Their lives went on as they always had, with the usual problems and the usual highlights. They went to church every Sunday, attended church functions and school functions on weeknights, occasionally rented a video to watch. If there appeared to be anything different about them on the outside, it was only that they seemed to settle into their new home and were finally feeling comfortable.

The changes were not, however, exterior. They could not be seen by unfamiliar eyes; they were hardly visible to familiar ones. They were taking place under the skin, growing slowly, spreading like the cancer that had afflicted Stephen, but doing so without attention, without treatment of any kind.

Without knowing the other was doing the same, Al and Carmen individually fought to cling to that stable exterior while trying to ignore little things that continued to happen all around them, silly things that, taken one at a time, would be insignificant at best. But together . . . together, these incidents formed a pattern that Al and Carmen did not want to know about or even be aware of; so they fought to ignore it, and held even tighter to that normal, clean exterior they had built for themselves.

And all the while, Stephen's behavior and personality changed. Later, Al and Carmen would say it had been instantaneous, but that was only because the initial changes were so gradual, so subtle, that when the transformation was complete, it caught them completely off guard.

There were many things that, during the next several months, would catch them off guard.

"Things seem to be going well for you guys," Fran said to Carmen one day while changing a messy diaper. Carmen was on the sofa drinking a diet cola and enjoying the sound of the baby's coos and burbles.

"What do you mean?"

"Oh, well, you said Stephen's better and—"

"No, no. I said his cancer seems to have gone into remission. That doesn't mean it won't come back, it just means he's okay for now. We're thankful for that, though, and we've put it in God's hands."

"Yeah, but that's better than before, right? So, Stephen's better for now; you seem . . . oh, I don't know, you seem more at ease, I guess. Like you're not so tense and anxious as you were before. 'Course, I suppose you had a lot to be anxious about, what with the move and Stephen's cancer. You just seem . . . happier, I guess. That make sense?"

"Yeah, I suppose so," Carmen said, although she was frowning. That was, of course, the effect she'd been trying for, she just hadn't realized she'd succeeded.

"Be right back," Fran said, taking the baby in her arms. "I'm gonna go put her down for a while."

Carmen nodded absently, then returned to her thoughts.

She certainly hadn't *felt* happy or at ease. In fact, there were days when, if she allowed herself, she questioned her sanity, wondered if maybe the stress of Stephen's illness and the sudden move had caused some sort of delayed reaction, a nervous breakdown, perhaps.

Sometimes, when she was alone in the house, walking from one room to another, she spotted movement in the corner of her eye, a flash of gray that darted from one piece of furniture to another. At first, she thought it was Willy; they usually kept him locked downstairs, but occasionally he weaseled his way up to the living room and wiggled around, playing hide-and-seek with them. But he was always locked up when she saw this blurred movement to her right or left; when she investigated it, there was never anything there.

Twice, she'd stood in the kitchen with her back to the refrigerator—washing dishes one time, chopping vegetables another—when she'd felt a wave of ice-cold air hit her back, as if the refrigerator door had swung open. But when she turned around, it was closed. The cold faded quickly, until it seemed as if the drop in temperature had never occurred—if, indeed, it had.

Also, twice she'd awakened to find the bed vibrating, almost as if it were one of those tacky motel beds and someone had dropped a quarter in the slot . . . but without a sound. Beside her, Al had slept soundly. She'd gotten up both times, had a cigarette, gone to the bathroom, and when she'd returned, the vibrating had stopped.

Each time something happened—movements, vibrations, the kitchen floor bleeding, or a voice or two she'd thought she'd heard when she knew no one else was in the house—she thought of Stephen. She thought, of course, of the things he'd said about the house, the things he'd supposedly seen, but she also thought of what had become of him since they'd moved into the house.

First, there had been his fear of going downstairs; that had been very unlike Stephen, who, in spite of the treatment he'd received from his peers at school, had managed to remain an outgoing, even aggressive boy who had shown fear only when fear was sensible, not when there was nothing of which to be afraid.

But lately, something else seemed to be happening. It was nothing physical, not like the result of his cobalt treatments; instead, this was a change in his personality. Her first exposure to it was when he'd snapped at her while lying in his bed that night.

I don't give a shit what you think, he'd said, and his words had cut into her like rusty blades. He'd never said such a thing to her before and it had hurt. The hurt had come out as anger, although she'd wanted to hunker down beside his bed in tears and ask, *Why would you talk like that to me, honey? Why?*

But that had only been the beginning. He'd become very quiet after that. He seemed anxious to separate himself from the family altogether. He spoke only when words were dragged out of him, and even then he sounded as if he were talking to people he held in the utmost contempt. There had been three occasions on which he'd said rude, horrible things to Carmen that made her hurt just recalling them. And when he said them, he even *looked* different; his face tightened, became almost reptilian.

She'd often wondered if perhaps this change in Stephen would have taken place had they not ignored what he'd said about the house—or if they had not moved into the house in the first place.

"—dinner tonight, Carmen?"

She jerked upright, eyes wide, and turned to see Fran standing before her, hands on her hips.

"What?" Carmen said. "I mean, um, I'm sorry?"

"I said, what're you planning for dinner tonight?"

"Um, well, um . . . I'm not sure, really." She was nervous, fidgety, as if Fran had been watching her thoughts unnoticed. "How about you?"

"Oh, probably a frozen dinner. Marcus won't be home from work until late tonight."

Carmen suggested that, instead of eating alone, Fran and the baby should come over for dinner, providing they didn't mind something simple. Fran agreed happily.

"You know," she said, "in all this time, I think I've only been in your house once, and then for just a few minutes."

Carmen thought about it; she was right. She wondered how she'd gone so long without having Fran over. After all, she spent a lot of time in Fran's house.

Ashamed of your house, maybe? her inner voice asked. *Afraid of what she might see or hear?*

Carmen looked away from Fran, blinked her eyes rapidly and quickly dismissed the thought.

Carmen had already started dinner when the doorbell rang. Fran held the baby in her arms as she entered, smiling.

But her smile faltered a bit and she frowned as she looked around her.

"Something smells good," she said, her smile quickly recovering.

Carmen noticed it, though she chose not to ask for an explanation. "Pot roast, potatoes, and vegetables. Like I said, something simple. You want something to drink?"

Fran had a beer, Carmen a diet soda, and the two of them sat at the dining-room table, Fran holding the baby —who was cooing contentedly, looking around with wide eyes—in her lap.

"Where're the kids?" Fran asked.

"Outside. Except for Stephen. He's downstairs."

"I thought he didn't like it downstairs."

"Not anymore. He's been spending a lot of time down there. He even mentioned something about moving back into his own room. I don't know, he seems . . ." She shrugged, but didn't go on.

Fran was frowning again, looking off to her left, as if she'd seen someone or something.

"What's wrong?"

Fran blinked at her. "Um . . . nothing. I just thought I, uh . . . I don't know."

"Maybe Al drove up. He should be here any time now."

Looking to the left again, Fran murmured, "No, I don't think . . . oh, well." She grinned at Carmen and said with forced cheerfulness, "Can I help with dinner?"

"No, just relax."

They talked. As the conversation progressed, Fran appeared more and more ill at ease, as if the chair she sat in were uncomfortable. Nervous tics came alive in her face and her eyes darted around warily as she held the baby closer to her.

"Is something wrong, Fran?" Carmen asked quietly.

"What? Um, no. I mean, um . . ." Her eyes darted around again, then she smiled nervously. "I'm sorry." She looked down, sipped her beer, and kissed the baby's head.

"Sorry for what?"

Fran didn't look up for a long moment, then: "Would you mind terribly if we didn't stay for dinner, Carmen?"

Carmen flinched. "Well, I thought—"

"I'm really not that hungry, and I usually put her down pretty early and, um . . ." She stood. "Could I have a raincheck? Or how about if you and Al come over next weekend for a barbecue?"

Carmen stood, too. "Wait a minute, Fran, hold it." She followed Fran into the hall. The skin at the back of her neck felt prickly and she sensed that something was very wrong here. "There's something wrong. What is it?"

Fran would not meet Carmen's eyes as she reached for the doorknob. "Um, Carmen, I'm, uh . . ." She laughed again, a breathy, staccato sound that rattled up from her throat. She opened the door a few inches, turned to Carmen timidly and asked, "Promise you won't laugh at me?"

"Well, of course not, Fran. What's the matter?"

"It's just that I'm—I'm uncomfortable here."

"What? What do you mean, you're un—"

"It's this house. It's . . . there's something, um . . ." She shook her head and started out the door again. Carmen clutched her elbow, a little harder than she intended, and held on tight. Her heart was in a frenzy in her chest, even throbbing in her throat, and she was afraid to ask the question she needed to ask. "What about this house, Fran?"

Fran replied after a long pause, whispering half her words. "I'm not sure. But there's something, um, something wrong here. It's not just the house, it's . . . the *air*. I feel it no matter what I do. It's like I'm trapped in a tiny room that just keeps getting smaller and smaller, you know? A claustrophobic feeling."

"But you've been here before and you never noticed any—"

"Only for a few minutes, never this long. I don't think I had time to see anything. And I didn't—"

"*See* anything? What did you see?" Carmen's mouth was dry and chalky and her palms were sweaty. She released Fran's elbow and rubbed her hands over her hips to dry them. "You didn't say anything about *seeing* anything."

Another edgy laugh. "It's nothing, Carmen, just—"

"What did you *see*?"

"I'm not sure. I kept seeing . . . well, it looked like something was moving around in the hall. Moving fast. Something small. I'm sure it was just me. It is, really, it's just me"—another laugh—"and I'm not gonna be very good company, is all. Tell you what, I'll see you later, okay?" She opened the door. "Call me tonight, we'll make plans for this weekend, okay?" She stepped out onto the porch. "A barbecue. Our place. See you later."

Then she was hurrying across the lawn toward her own house.

Carmen stood in the doorway for some time after Fran left, then she closed the door hard and leaned back against it, eyes closed.

Thoughts raced through her mind and she tried to slow them down. *Maybe it was just all the things I'd told her about Stephen, about what he'd said, about what the kids claimed to have seen and heard*, she thought.

She smelled dinner, remembered she had a roast in the oven and hurried into the kitchen to prepare the rest of the meal, trying to ignore the trembling of her hands.

Al had been trying to ignore a lot of things, too.

Like the music and voices coming from downstairs, for example. He'd heard them a number of times. Enough times, in fact, so that he didn't even get out of bed anymore, just lay awake staring into the darkness, listening.

Sometimes the bed vibrated, too, the way it had that first night. Of course, the family had moved in upstairs —Ben and Alice Farraday and their son and daughter, nice folks, friendly—so Al was able to use his upstairs-refrigerator theory to dismiss the vibrating; it took some pushing, but he managed to convince himself, and a few extra beers before bed helped him to get to sleep in spite of the disturbing thoughts he tried to bury.

Even when he slept as well as usual, however, Al found himself feeling as though he hadn't been, as if he'd been spending his nights tossing and turning between sweat-soaked sheets. He got through work with the help of a lot of coffee, and he started getting ready for bed as soon as he got home by opening his first bottle of beer.

He lay in bed one night, awake, but with his eyes closed. He wondered if he was drinking too much beer, if maybe it could be behind the things he'd been hearing and feeling and thinking; maybe, just *maybe*, Stephen had been right about the house. But then he told himself he'd been drinking more *because* of all those things, and he couldn't imagine himself not drinking, not without going crazy, not without blurting it all out to Carmen and, at the very least, *looking* crazy.

After a while, with the steady and soothing sound of the alarm clock ticking on the nightstand, Al slept. . . .

He awoke suddenly and harshly to find himself shaking and his first thought was, *Oh God, oh my God, it's shaking now, not vibrating*, shaking!

It was Carmen. She was clutching his shoulder, shaking him hard and hissing, "Al. Al! Wake up, Al, it's the bed! The bed!"

"Wh-what?" He sat up, squinting in spite of the darkness and blinking furiously, as if his eyes had something in them.

"The bed, Al, the *bed*!"

Once he'd emerged from the thick fog of sleep, he realized that it was happening again. The bed was vibrating. Its silent thrum moved through Al's body, wrapping around his bones like twine.

He thought fast and came to a decision: If it worked for him, it would work for Carmen, too.

"Whassamatter with it?" he asked, trying not to look

like he was in a hurry as he tossed back the covers and got out of bed. He stood there rubbing his eyes and running his fingers roughly through his hair.

"You can't feel that?" Carmen said, speaking louder now. She stood on the other side of the bed in her long nightshirt with a picture of Opus the penguin on the front. "It's *vibrating* is what's the matter with it. Feel it."

"What?"

"Just feel it!"

Al tried not to flinch as he put his hand on the bed and felt the familiar, somehow malignant sensation ooze up the middle of his arm. After a moment, he pulled his hand away, nodded at Carmen and said, "Yeah, well?"

"Well? *Well*? The bed is vibrating, Al, what is it? Why is it doing that?"

"It's from upstairs," he said quietly, calmly, his voice even and thick with the indifference of sleepiness.

"From what?"

"From the refrigerator upstairs. That's all. It comes on and vibrates, then comes down here and we feel it in the bed, is all. Go back to sleep. It'll stop after a while."

She stared at him, lips parted, as he turned and headed for the bathroom.

Once in the bathroom, Al turned on the light and locked the door. He didn't need to use it, but it was the only place he could think of to go in the middle of the night without having to give Carmen some sort of explanation.

He put the toilet lid down and sat on it, elbows on his knees, his face in his palms, and exhaled slowly. He hoped the vibrating had stopped and Carmen had gone back to sleep. He even prayed for it silently. After a while, he crossed himself, stood and then stopped when he heard a loud noise from somewhere outside the house. The noise repeated again and again, stopped for a moment, then continued.

Al frowned as he left the bathroom, muttering, *"Now what?"*

It was a dog barking. He almost ignored it and went back into the bedroom, but it was so close, he thought he'd check it out.

He went to the front window in the dining room, which seemed closest to the barking, and separated the blinds with two fingers.

A bright moon cast a dull light over the ground like a luminescent bruise. A large dog stood at the edge of the front yard—in the poor light, it was difficult to tell what kind of dog—barking at the corner of the house. It was barking at the house the way a dog might bark to warn its master of an intruder, or the way a dog might bark at its own attacker: vicious and rapid barks punctuated by snarls and growls.

He had never seen the dog before and couldn't tell if it was wearing a collar or not. He didn't move for a while, just watched the dog as it barked persistently. He kept expecting it to stop and leave, but it didn't. If anything, its barks only became angrier and more threatening, more desperately fierce.

Al felt a bead of sweat trickling down over his temple and he moved the back of his free hand across his forehead. He was perspiring. His heart was pounding.

This house, he thought. *It's barking at the house because . . . because the house scares it.*

Pulling his hand away from the blinds, Al stepped back and just stood there, staring at the closed blinds awhile as the dog barked . . . and barked . . . and barked . . .

Secrets grew like tumors in the Snedeker household.

Carmen did not tell Al when she heard someone laughing in the kitchen although she was alone in the house.

Al did not tell Carmen when he heard footsteps following him around the house one weekend, although no one was there.

And Stephen only talked to them when he had to. When he was not at school, he spent most of his time in his room, often with Cody, who brought along tapes for them to listen to, the newest from the heaviest of metal bands, with lyrics that spoke only of sex and death, violence and suicide, torture and necrophilia. He didn't spend much time with Michael anymore, mostly because Michael wanted to do things, was interested in things that held no appeal for Stephen. As a result, Stephen was considering moving into the room that had originally been his.

The idea of having a room of his own was, once again, appealing.

There would be nothing to interrupt the voices then. . . .

Late one night, Stephen lay awake in his bed listening to the sound of a dog barking outside. He'd heard it before, but had given it no thought until his dad complained about it one morning over breakfast before going to work. Al had said they needed to find out whose dog it was and call them; it had been sitting outside their house barking for several nights in a row.

Curious, Stephen got out of bed and went upstairs, moving comfortably through the dark. He went to the window in the dining room and saw the dog outside in the moonlight, barking and snarling at the corner of the house. Nothing else—not a squirrel, not a cat—just the house.

Although he didn't realize it, one corner of Stephen's mouth curled up.

So he wasn't entirely alone. The dog somehow knew

the house held something unusual. The dog somehow knew it was occupied by something other than a mother and a father and four children.

The dog knew. . . .

12

Ghosts of Christmas Present

By Christmastime, Stephen had obtained a battered old leather jacket on the back of which he put a skull and crossbones and the logo of some heavy-metal group that combined an upside-down cross with a bloody dagger.

He was wearing it one day when he came home from school. It was the last day of school before the beginning of Christmas vacation; outside, everything was blanketed in snow, and Stephen brushed flakes off his scarf and jacket before coming through the front door. As he walked through the house, Carmen stopped him.

"Stephen? Could you come here a second?" she called from the dining-room table.

She wasn't looking forward to the talk she was about to have with him—about to *try* to have—because she had a pretty good idea how it was going to end up.

Carmen and Al had talked with Stephen a lot lately—together and individually—about things ranging from the foul language he'd been using around the house to his personal hygiene, which, for reasons they could not understand, had gone steeply downhill over the past weeks.

There were a lot of things they didn't understand about Stephen lately.

Now there was the jacket. It was something he never would have considered wearing before their move. He'd always been a clean boy, a natty dresser, so polite and well-spoken.

Not anymore.

"Sit down, Stephen," Carmen said quietly, smiling.

With an annoyed sigh, he pulled out a chair and flopped into it, thumping his elbows onto the table, resting his chin on his fists.

In spite of the fact that his cancer had gone into remission, Stephen still looked pale and thin and, although not as distinct, yellowish-gray half-circles still darkened the slightly puffy flesh beneath his eyes.

"Where did you get that jacket?" Carmen asked.

"Somebody gave it to me."

"Leather jackets aren't cheap."

He shrugged. "It's old. He didn't want it anymore. He gave it to me."

"Well . . . it's not a bad jacket, really. So why did you put that stuff on the back?"

Another shrug, a long, slow blink, then: " 'Cause I like it."

She leaned closer to him. "Stephen, you know we don't want you wearing things like that."

"Like what?"

"That's the *cross* you've got on your back, and it's upside-down."

"So?"

"Oh, don't play dumb with me, Stephen, you know what I'm talking about." She was getting frustrated and angry already and her voice was showing it. "It's sacrilegious and . . . well, if you ask me . . . *you* were the one talking about evil a few months ago and, well, as far as I'm concerned, that's evil, what you've got on your back. We've given in with the music, so you pretty much get to listen to whatever crap you want to as long as you keep it to yourself, but *that* is too much!"

"Well, what's the difference? I don't understand. It's part of the music, it's what the music stands for, it's—"

"I know, that's why your dad and I don't like the music. That cross you're wearing on your back is a very important symbol. Christ died on that cross so we could—"

Stephen rolled his eyes. "Yeah, yeah, I know. I learned all about it in Sunday school."

"So how can you wear such a thing!"

"You're so worried about evil, so scared of it, but you've got it all around you and you don't see it, just ignore it. I'm tellin' you, this house is evil!"

"That again. I just . . . Stephen, I don't understand you. I don't understand what's wrong with you."

Then Stephen did something that made Carmen drop her mouth open and gasp, shocked and hurt.

He laughed, shook his head and said, "You don't understand much of anything, do you?" He stood from the table and went to his room, leaving Carmen staring at the place where he'd sat, her mouth still open, her wide eyes full of pain.

Finally, she lit a cigarette and exhaled wearily. Her next step, of course, would be to talk to Al about it, but she wasn't too eager to do that, either.

Al seemed very short-tempered lately, especially where Stephen was concerned. He had no tolerance for the changes that had taken place in the boy; Carmen had to admit she felt much the same way, but at least tried to be fair and civil about it, tried her best to see Stephen's side (something that was getting more difficult all the time, since he seemed so unwilling to share his side). She was afraid that, sooner or later, she would tell Al about something Stephen had done or was doing, and Al would lose whatever restraint he'd been showing and come down on the boy hard, *really* hard, with something besides the usual grounding or suspension of telephone privileges— like harsh physical punishment, for example. Although she understood the desire to do that—Stephen had pushed her tolerance to the edge, too, especially with his response to her complaint about the jacket—the thought of it made her cringe.

But the back of Stephen's jacket made her cringe, as well.

She would talk to Al. If he did no good, she would have to take stronger measures. . . .

Although she waited until after dinner that night, hoping he would be relaxed, Al was furious. He went downstairs and, from the living room, Carmen could hear him shouting at Stephen. She even heard what sounded like something being thrown against the wall.

Peter was dozing on the sofa beside her; Stephanie and Michael were on the floor watching television, their backs stiff, their eyes fixed on the screen as they fought to ignore the sounds.

Then, after a brief silence, she heard Al's footsteps thumping up the stairs and his voice barking angrily, "That's it, I give up! You wanna go around looking like some kinda satanic punk, that's fine, just don't tell any-body you live here! Spoiled little shit is what you are! Don't know where it comes from, but it doesn't come from us!"

As he came down the hall, his tirade continuing, Car-men could hear the faint sound of Stephen's laughter from downstairs. She hurried into the hall to meet Al.

"I don't know what the hell to do with him," he growled, going into the kitchen and getting a beer from the refrigerator. "He wants to keep his fucking jacket—"

"Al," she chided, wincing.

"—he can keep it, I don't give a damn. Wants to go

around looking like a thug, like a damned criminal or some kinda—I don't know, some kinda cult member—then fine." He leaned back against the edge of the counter and tilted his head back as he drank.

"Well, there's *something* wrong, I just don't know what."

"He's a goddamned spoiled brat, is what's wrong."

"Oh, what, it's my fault, is that what you're saying? It's *my* fault he's behaving this way?"

"Hey"—he spread his arms and raised his eyebrows—"*you* said that, not me."

Carmen spun around, stretched out her arm and leaned against the refrigerator with her elbow locked. She closed her eyes a moment, lips pressed together tightly. She knew this could turn into an ugly argument if she pursued that thinly veiled accusation any further. She decided against it, took a deep breath and turned around.

"I think I should take him to see Father Hartwell."

Al took another slug of beer and sighed. "You think it'd do any good?"

"Couldn't hurt, could it?"

He thought about it a moment, frowned, became rather distant. Then he said quietly, as if to himself, "It's just been since we moved here . . . into this house . . ."

Carmen was surprised by his words—could he possibly be entertaining some of the same thoughts that had haunted her?—but hid her surprise quickly.

"You think that has something to do with it?" she asked.

"Hm? Oh, no. Course not. Just . . . an observation, is all. He's changed a lot in a little time."

"That's why I think he should talk to Father Hartwell."

"Yeah. Yeah, it couldn't hurt."

* * *

She called Father Hartwell the next day and explained the problem, and he agreed to see Stephen. Against his protests, Carmen took Stephen to the church and dropped him off while she went to the grocery store. When she was finished shopping, she returned, picked him up and headed home, resisting the urge to go inside and ask Father Hartwell how it went and what was wrong with her son. Instead, she tried to start a conversation with Stephen.

"So, what did you and the father talk about?" she asked.

Looking out the side window, he shrugged. "I dunno. Not much. Just . . . talked, I guess."

And that was the most she could get out of him. She could only hope and pray that Father Hartwell would be able to do some good.

But that was not enough for her. When she got home, she called Father Hartwell on the bedroom telephone.

"How did it go, Father?" she asked.

"Well, Carmen, if you don't mind, I'd rather not talk about it in any detail. I will say this much, though: You did the right thing in bringing him to see me. I'd like to see him again. Tomorrow, in fact. If that's okay?"

"Of course it's okay. I'm so glad. I mean, I was worried that . . . well, Al and I were both worried that . . ." She didn't finish, afraid that her voice would break and tears would start.

"Listen, Carmen," Father Hartwell said softly, "I'm here for you, too. I think Stephen needs these talks right now and I suspect we might make some progress. But if you need someone to talk to, don't hesitate."

"Thank you, Father," she whispered.

"Same time tomorrow?"

"Same time."

But Carmen was not able to drive Stephen to see Father Hartwell the next day.

That evening, Carmen received a call from her brother Cal in Alabama. The instant she heard his voice at the other end of the line, she became tense; he only called her when he needed something—or when something was wrong. Like their father, he was an alcoholic who had no intention of treating his problem; Carmen's heart went out to him and he was always in her prayers, but she'd finally realized a number of years ago that there was only so much she could do for him and, if he was ever going to be saved, he was going to have to take the first step himself.

"C-Carmen? You're, um, you're gonna have to come home. Right away." His voice was wet and quavery.

"What's wrong, Cal?"

"Dad. He's, um, he's dead, Carmen. Somebody killed him. He's been murdered. You gotta come."

Carmen was stunned into cold silence for a while. When she could speak again, she told Cal it was snowing in Connecticut, but she would catch the next available plane and be there as soon as possible.

After she'd hung up, she plopped onto the sofa and stared at nothing as she thought about her father. Her parents had divorced when she was twelve and she'd never been close to her father, had hardly known him, really, unlike her brother, who had remained in constant touch with him. In spite of that fact, Cal had always held their father's lifestyle in contempt—his constant drinking, his lack of care for himself, his hand-to-mouth life on the edge—but not enough, apparently, to keep himself from following the same pattern. The presence of that pattern in her family kept Carmen from touching alcohol, and was responsible for the gnawing concern she had about Al's attachment to beer, something she had not yet found the courage to mention to him.

She called the airport. Carmen was able to find a plane leaving that evening. Al had to scramble to make arrangements at work so he would be able to take care of the kids while Carmen was gone. He cringed at the thought of doing such a thing so soon after starting at the quarry, but it was one of those unpredictable and unavoidable crises that happened to everyone from time to time, and his boss would just have to work it out.

After driving Carmen to the airport, Al and Stephanie and Peter picked up a pizza on their way home; Al had never been able to cook and had no intention of trying now, so, until Carmen returned, they'd live on take-out and frozen dinners.

That night, once the pizza was gone, Stephen retreated, as usual, to his room. He'd spent most of the evening there, anyway, taking his dinner downstairs with him. Tension was growing between Al and Stephen; the room was quieter when they were together, the air somehow thicker. They spoke to one another only when necessary, which was slowly becoming less often as time passed. That was fine with Al; he didn't care to have much to do with the boy until he cleaned up his act. Maybe that was harsh, but it was the best he knew how to do. There was no reason for Stephen's recent behavior, and to act as if nothing was wrong seemed no different to Al than telling him it was okay.

Al and Michael watched a football game on television while Stephanie and Peter did some pasting and coloring at the dining-room table. There was no school tomorrow, so Al wasn't concerned with how late they stayed up. But they had grown used to going to bed early and it wasn't long before they were all sleepy enough to retire to their rooms.

Al was left alone after the game, watching sitcom reruns. And thinking.

He didn't look forward to going to bed. Not alone.

Alone, he might just lie awake . . . waiting . . . for the music . . . the voices . . . the vibrating . . .

Three hours later, his eyes were heavy and his head kept drooping forward as he watched television. Finally, he gave in, turned off the television and the lights and went to bed.

Once beneath the covers, his weariness vanished and, just as he'd suspected he would do, he lay awake, twisting and turning to find a comfortable spot, a soothing position.

He did, eventually. His eyes closed on their own, he felt the heaviness of sleep wash over him, was aware of his breathing becoming slow, felt himself slipping away, until . . .

He heard music and his eyes snapped open. He sat up. It was the same music he always heard: old and tinny, conjuring black-and-white images of rooms full of cobwebs, old photographs in ornate frames, and antique furniture.

Al lay back down, pressing the heels of his palms into his eyes and groaning.

Faint voices laughed. The music continued. And there was something else.

Barking. The dog was barking outside once again.

I'm going to ignore it, he thought. *All of it. I may not sleep, but I'm not getting out of bed.*

The music went on. The voices continued to talk and laugh festively. The dog's barking became more intense.

Al rolled over and pressed his head into the mattress, pulling the pillow down over his ear.

But he could still hear it. The phantom party, the persistent barking . . .

And then he felt the familiar vibration ooze through his body, through his bones. It curled its long and bony fingers around his elbows and knees, over his shoulders and over the top of his skull, increasing its pressure, vibrating deeper and deeper.

Al rolled onto his back and began to kick frantically at the blankets, his breath hissing through clenched teeth as he rolled off the bed and thunked to the floor, then crawled a few feet away from the bed before clambering to his feet. Moving backward, he bumped into the dresser, stood there and stared at the bed.

He could see nothing. There were no visible signs that the bed was filled with some kind of sinister movement. He reached behind him and flicked on the small lamp on the dresser, but still there was nothing to be seen.

There was, however, plenty to be heard.

Music played from somewhere deep in the house, and muffled voices and soft laughter mingled with it.

Outside, the dog barked as if it were ready to attack and kill.

Al turned the overhead light on, slipped on his pants and went into the short hallway outside the bedroom, turning on lights as he passed the switches, his movements rapid and jerky.

The music continued.

The voices murmured on.

Once again there was only darkness downstairs.

Al was halfway down when the sounds stopped.

Silence.

He felt a sharp pain in his hand and realized it was because he was gripping the bannister so hard.

Outside, the dog continued to bark so hard that it was becoming hoarse.

Al turned, went back up the stairs, into the living room—he switched on two lamps there—across the hall and into the dining room, where he froze.

Someone was standing at the front window, looking out into the night; the blinds were raised and the figure was silhouetted in the dim moonlight that ˙reflected off the snow.

Al held perfectly still in the doorway, except for his hand, which crawled over the wall, searching for the light switch as the figure turned and faced him.

˙ Al flicked the switch, filling the dining room with light as he sighed with relief, "Stephen."

"Somebody's dog is"—he chuckled—"kinda carried away out there."   .

"Were you playing music just now?"

Stephen rubbed the back of his neck and started to walk slowly out of the dining room. "Music? No, *I* wasn't playing any music."

Al gently held his arm as he passed through the doorway. "You didn't have anybody in here? You didn't sneak some friends into the house?"

"Why? It's crowded enough in here as it is."

Al let go and the boy went down the hall . . . down the stairs . . .

Later, Al would wonder about Stephen's words and how he had spoken them; they would bother him, even give him a chill when he recalled them. But for the moment, he took them only at face value. When Stephen was gone, Al went to the window and looked out at the dog.

It looked like a Lab and was closer to the house now, but seemed tense, ready to run if necessary. Much closer and it would actually be biting the corner of the house.

After lowering the blinds, Al went back to the bedroom, dressed, and went outside. He ran along the front of the house toward the dog, waving his arms and calling, "Get out of here! Git! Go! Beat it!" He threw, even kicked, snow at the dog, but it was surprisingly difficult to tear the animal's attention away from the house. When he finally did, the dog hurried off, stopped and

urned, whined a little, gave Al a few insistent woofs,
hen went away.

Back inside, Al undressed, then stared at the bed a
moment, wondering if it was safe to lie down again. He
realized it didn't matter because he was wide awake. In
his robe, he went to the kitchen and opened the refrigerator.

"Damn, that's right," he whispered. "No beer."

He was still staring into the refrigerator's glaring light
when the barking started again.

Al slammed the refrigerator door. Glass clinked and
cans rattled inside. He clutched his fists at his sides as the
barking got closer, louder, more vicious. Eyes closed,
breathing harshly though his nose, Al thought, *Boy, oh,
boy . . . sure could use a beer.*

In the living room, Al settled into his recliner. His
thumb trembled as he used the remote to turn on the
television.

"Gonna have to talk to somebody about that damned
dog," he breathed as he flipped through the channels.

Its barking was relentless.

He settled on an old western and put the remote on
the end table, where he spotted a rosary. Carmen kept
them all over the house. He picked it up idly in his trembling hand, silently telling himself it wasn't necessary,
that he wasn't upset, wasn't frightened, just restless, that
was all.

The dog went on barking and barking . . .

Al whispered, "Hail Mary, full of grace . . ."

. . . barking . . . barking . . .

In the back of his mind, Al thought—but he wasn't
quite sure because it was faint, so faint—he heard the
tinny sound of music. . . .

Carmen returned three days later.

Her father had been found in his small, rundown

trailer. No bullet holes and a minimum of blood were found in the trailer, so it was presumed he was murdered elsewhere with his own .22-caliber pistol and brought back to his trailer. Although they didn't say as much, of course, the police seemed to think that finding the murderer was of little importance; after all, the victim had been an old drunk who barely subsisted, and who associated with the shadiest of characters, the kind of people most likely to do such a thing casually.

Carmen and her brother made the burial arrangements and, because she wanted to get back home as soon as possible, she left Cal as the executor of their father's estate—what there was of it.

She was glad to be home, and Al was glad to have her back. Everything had gone smoothly in her absence, he told her, but she had been missed.

Everyone seemed fine, Al included. But somehow, Carmen felt something was wrong. She couldn't put her finger on it . . . it was nothing visible . . . nothing anyone said . . .

Just my imagination, she told herself. *After the last few days, everything looks pretty dark.*

They began the usual Christmas activities. Al brought home a tree and Carmen and the kids—except for Stephen—decorated it.

Al had taken Stephen to see Father Hartwell every day while Carmen was gone, and she kept it up after returning. She resisted the temptation to ask Stephen about his visits with the father, telling herself that the results would begin to show soon. But they didn't. Stephen was still rude and profane when he spoke, quiet and brooding when he didn't.

If the talks with Father Hartwell didn't work, she hoped her prayers would. She wanted her son back.

Carmen put a wreath on the door, some holly and garland here and there in the house, and brought out the records and tapes of Christmas music they'd collected over the years. She played the music often, kept egg nog in the refrigerator.

Michael, Stephanie, and Peter made a snowman in the front yard and Carmen gave them a broom and an old scarf and hat to put on him.

They watched *A Christmas Carol* and *It's a Wonderful Life* again, as they did each year.

They did all the things they did every Christmas, all the things that made them feel good, put them in the holiday spirit, and made that time of year different from any other. But this year, as Christmas neared, then passed, none of those things quite worked. It wasn't the same. Something was missing, something other than Stephen's usual willing and cheerful participation.

Carmen didn't know how the others felt, but no matter how hard she tried to work at it, it just didn't feel like Christmas. She didn't feel the way Christmas always made her feel.

No matter how silly it sounded, Carmen simply did not feel safe.

Not even in her own house.

Perhaps especially in her own house.

13

The New Year Begins

Christmas decorations disappeared from store windows and were soon replaced with Valentine hearts and candy boxes. Strands of colored bulbs and sparkling garlands were boxed up and returned to storage. Christmas records and tapes were returned to their shelves where they would stay until the following December. Trees were removed and dry pine needles were vacuumed from the carpet.

All over town, naked toppled Christmas trees lay waiting for garbage men to carry them away; strands of tinsel and bits of garland still dangled from their brittle branches, sometimes blowing in the wind over the snow and ice.

The sky remained a dark steel gray and the air a blade sharp enough to slice flesh. The stripped branches of the trees reached skyward like arthritic claws. The snow-flakes eventually turned to raindrops and the snow on the ground became a thick, icy mud. . . .

"We've been meeting for some time, now, yet I don't feel as though I've really learned much about you. Why is 'hat?"

"I dunno. Maybe because I haven't said much about me, you think?"

"Yes, I suppose. Why is that?"

"Mm. Don't like talking about myself, I guess."

"I see. Well, would it be easier if I asked questions?"

"All you've been doing is asking questions."

"Yes, you're right. Well, then . . . I guess I'm at a loss. You see, your mother asked me to speak with you, oh, a few months ago, I guess, because she was noticing what she thought were some unpleasant changes in you. So I agreed. For a while, it was five days a week, then twice a week, down to once a week. All that time, I kept thinking that if I gave you a chance, you would tell me what was bothering you, what was wrong. Now I'm beginning to think that perhaps I was mistaken. Perhaps your mother was mistaken as well. So, tell me, Stephen. Were we? Mistaken?"

Stephen sat where he always sat in Father Hartwell's study, the way he always sat there: on the brown leather sofa, right foot dangling over his left knee, hands locked behind his head, elbows pointing upward on each side of his head like small wings.

Father Hartwell sat in a straight-back chair on the other side of the coffee table in front of the sofa, facing Stephen. He was leaning forward, elbows on his knees, thin hands joined loosely. He was in his forties, bald on top with a wreath of brown-and-gray hair around his head. He had glasses with brown tortoiseshell frames and thick lenses; he had a habit of removing them to pinch the bridge of his nose between thumb and forefinger.

Stephen asked, "Were you mistaken about what?"

Father Hartwell did it again—removed the glasses, pinched the bridge of his nose—as he released a soft sigh. "Oh, I'm not sure really. Were we mistaken about, um . . . about there being something wrong with you? Tell me, Stephen, has something upset you lately?"

"How lately?"

"Well . . . anything at all?"

"Yeah. Cancer. That upset me." His voice was not sarcastic; it remained low, level and without expression.

"Of course it did. That's perfectly understandable. But our prayers have been answered. Your cancer is in remission and you seem to be doing very well. Physically, I mean. I'm talking about something that might have hurt your feelings, something that might be making you angry, or . . . or even scared. Is there anything like that?"

Stephen's lower lip slowly moved inward until he held it between his teeth, nibbled on it slightly as his eyes moved gradually around the room, finally stopping, once again, on Father Hartwell.

"No," he said. "No, nothing like that. I'm fine."

"You don't believe you've been behaving differently?"

He shrugged. "I don't know. Different than what?"

"Different than . . . usual?"

"Uh-uh. Not that I know of."

"What about the way you dress? Your clothes?"

"What about 'em?" The slightest hint of defensiveness showed itself in his voice.

"Well, they're not the kind of clothes you usually wear. Are they? I mean, the jacket, for example. The T-shirts you wear around the house."

"T-shirts? What, you been talking to my mother?"

"Of course. She says you wear T-shirts with rock-and-roll groups and slogans on the front that are . . . well, offensive. Even blasphemous. Like your leather jacket."

"So? What's wrong with that? Lots of kids wear them."

"But your mother says you never *used* to wear such things, or listen to such music."

He shrugged. "I do now."

"Yes, but your mother seems to think the sudden

change was brought on by . . . well, by something. Is that true? Did something happen that—"

"No. My friend Cody played his tapes for me one day. I liked the music. He gave me a couple old shirts, this old jacket. They just don't like it, is all. The music, the clothes. So they're making like there's something *wrong* with me because of it."

"Well, I must admit, Stephen, the jacket *is* blasphemous. The cross on your back is—"

"But there's nothing wrong with *me*. If that's why I've been coming here, then"—another shrug—"I've been wasting your time. I'm sorry."

Father Hartwell looked at Stephen a long while, studied his face through narrow, thoughtful eyes. Then: "Would you like me to tell that to your mother?"

"I dunno. What do you think you should tell her? You're the priest."

"Well, I suppose if you think these visits are a waste of time . . . then they are. If they stop, would you promise me something, Stephen?"

A shrug.

"If ever you need to talk to someone about something that . . . well, that you might not want to discuss with your parents or a school friend . . . will you come to me? I'd be happy to sit down with you anytime."

"Yeah. Sure." Stephen smiled.

"I have to admit, Carmen, your boy is going through the throes of adolescence."

"What do you mean? Exactly?"

"Well, he's rebellious. He enjoys doing things that shock you, offend you. That's why rock-and-roll stars are able to make so much money without being talented." He chuckled. "Because the kids know their parents don't like them."

"But it's more than that, Father." Carmen clutched

the receiver tightly, pressed it hard against her ear. "He's
. . . changed. His personality, his behavior . . . it's like
he wants nothing to do with us anymore. He stays down
in his room almost all the time. Only comes up to go to
the bathroom or eat. He sits down there in the corner
and mumbles to himself while he listens to that horrible
music on headphones. He wears those shirts, that jacket,
rings with little skulls on them, all that heavy-metal par-
aphernalia. I don't even know where he gets it, although
I suspect it's got something to do with the boy he's been
hanging around lately. Stephen is just not the same boy,
Father."

"Yes, it seems they all reach an age where they are no
longer the same child. But some change more drastically.
It sounds like that's the case here."

"Yes, it is." She closed her eyes and smiled slightly,
relieved that he was finally beginning to understand.

"Unfortunately, I didn't see any of that during my
visits with Stephen. Oh, he was cranky now and then, a
little impatient. But he was well behaved. And yes, I
noticed the jacket and the rings. I think your suspicions
about Stephen's friends are correct. He mentioned a boy
named Cody who got him into the music. He sounds like
a bad influence to me."

"Tell me, Father. Did he talk about . . . our house at
all? The house we live in here?"

"No. No, I don't remember him mentioning it at all.
Why do you ask?"

"Oh, no reason. So, you don't think . . . I mean,
there's nothing more you can do."

He laughed. "Carmen, dear, I'm only a priest. But, if
you'd like, I can recommend a therapist."

"Therapist?"

"Yes. A good Catholic therapist who specializes in this
very situation. He works well with teens."

Carmen frowned. "A therapist?"

"Is that so bad? I think it would be a wise move."

"Do you think Stephen is . . . well, you know, mentally ill?"

"Of course not, dear. I just think he's troubled. In fact, I suspect that a boy that age who *isn't* troubled is likely mentally ill. Growing up is a difficult project, and Stephen is going through some of the toughest times right now. In fact, he's had the added burden of his illness, something most teens don't have to deal with. No, Carmen, mental hospitals are for the mentally ill. Therapists are for people who've had a little too much dropped in their lap at one time. They're for people who are having trouble with the problems life hands all of us at one time or another. Therapists are for *everyone*. No, my suggestion of therapy does not mean I think your son is mentally ill. Not at all."

Carmen could think of nothing to say. She did not agree with Father Hartwell, and that bothered her even more than her situation. So, she just sighed quietly into the telephone.

"Do you have a pen, Carmen? Let me give you his name and telephone number. You call, explain the problem, and make an appointment for Stephen. If you'd like, you can make an appointment for the whole family. It's up to you."

Father Hartwell recited the name and number. Carmen did not write them down.

Stephen decided to move into the room that had originally been his, but told no one except Michael. First, he moved all of his things into the room, then, with Michael's help, moved the bed.

"You sure you want to move over here?" Michael asked.

"Yeah. Why?"

"I thought you didn't like this room."

"Oh, it's not so bad."

Michael frowned. "You didn't even like *our* room at first."

"Yeah, well, I guess that was stupid."

Michael's frown did not go away. Hands on his hips, eyes narrowed, he stared at his brother with concern. "It wasn't so stupid a while ago. Why the sudden change?"

"I just want a room of my own. Is that so bad?"

"You sure you're all right, Stephen?"

Stephen laughed. "Why?"

" 'Cause you've been . . . well, kinda weird lately."

Another laugh. "You're startin' to sound like them." He jerked a thumb upward, toward their parents upstairs.

"Yeah, but . . . I hardly ever see you anymore. You're always spending time with Cody. And you're always wearing them weird shirts and rings, listening to that music and—"

"Oh, you're just too young yet. You'll be listening to that music, too. You'll wear these shirts 'cause you like the groups. You'll see."

Michael's frown faded slowly. His mouth curled into a half-smile. "You think so?" he asked.

"Sure."

"Oh, well." Michael shrugged.

"Look at it this way. You've got your own room again."

"Yeah, but . . . I kind of liked it when it was *our* room."

"You'll get over it," Stephen chuckled.

The month's bills were spread before Carmen on the dining room table, but her attention was directed toward one in particular. Carmen noticed that Al—he was seated at the end of the table to her left—was looking at the power bill, which she'd already seen; she watched his mouth become a tight, straight line, his eyes become wider and wider, his shoulders sag from shock, until he finally exploded.

"Holy shit, have you *seen* this?"

Carmen could only nod.

"This is . . . I mean, son of a *bitch*, this is ridiculous, what've we been doing, lighting up the whole neighborhood?"

He looked at her, mouth open, holding the bill out before him, waiting for an answer.

"Um, I think," she said hesitantly, "it might be because of the lights being left on all night downstairs."

"Are they still doing that?" he asked, his voice so low she almost couldn't hear them.

"I think so."

He stood and slammed his fist onto the table hard. Carmen could hear his teeth grinding. He turned and left the dining room, turned right in the hall and started downstairs.

Carmen got up and followed him, moving quickly, hoping her presence would keep him from getting too carried away.

"Stephen?" he called on his way down the stairs. "Stephen, where—what the hell is going on down here?"

Carmen reached the basement in time to hear Stephen explain that Michael was helping him move into his original room.

"So, if you're not afraid to move into a room by yourself, why in the hell have you still been leaving the lights on all night down here?" Al bellowed.

Stephen and Michael stared at him silently.

Al held out the bill. "Look at this. The power bill. You wanna count all the numbers in that little box at the bottom? You know why they're there? 'Cause you've been leaving these goddamned lights on all night, that's why!"

The boys said nothing.

Al jerked the bill back, slapping it against his thigh. "So, you know what I'm gonna do? I'll *show* you what I'm gonna do!"

Moving as if he were in a terrible rush, Al first made his way through Michael's room, then Stephen's, removing every single lightbulb from every socket. He put them in an empty cardboard box he found in the corner of Stephen's room.

"Please don't do this," Michael said quietly.

"Nope, too late for that. You should've thought of that when you were leaving the lights on all night, running the power bill through the roof. Should've thought of it *then*."

"But how're we gonna do our homework?" Michael asked.

"Do it upstairs. Come down here when you're ready to go to bed." Holding the box under one arm, Al stood at the foot of the stairs and faced the boys. "No spending money or allowances for a while. They'll be going toward this goddamned bill." Then he stomped up the stairs.

"Well, boys," Carmen said, folding her arms over her chest, "I don't know what to tell you. I think the law has just been laid down."

Michael sighed and bowed his head.

Stephen just stared at her. He hadn't said anything so far, just stared without expression, his face giving away nothing.

Carmen shrugged and said quietly, "You should've listened to your dad in the first place."

"He's not our dad," Stephen said. His voice was low and flat; his lips had hardly moved as he spoke.

Carmen jerked her head toward him, shocked. Stephen had never said such a thing before. He'd always called Al "Dad," always introduced Al to his friends as "my dad."

"You don't say much," Carmen breathed, "but when you do, you sure know how to say something rotten, don't you?"

"Well," Stephen shrugged, "he isn't."

"I think that's about enough out of you," she said. She turned to go back up the stairs, but stopped and turned to Stephen again. "If he's not your father, I'd like to know who is. Who's done everything for you that needed to be done over the years? Who's always taken you fishing? Who wanted to drop *everything* so he could be at your bedside while you were sick? And who was—"

"That doesn't make him my father," Stephen said.

His voice was a whisper, but he could not have hit her more forcefully with his hand. She'd thought, for a moment, that perhaps she was getting through to him, that maybe she was finally saying something that would work, that would stick, make him think.

She realized, as she looked at his dull, expressionless face, that she'd been wrong.

Carmen spun around and hurried up the stairs, hoping the boys had not noticed that she was crying.

"You didn't have to say that," Michael said angrily after their mother had gone. He stood at the foot of the stairs watching Stephen, who stood in his own room.

"What?"

"About Dad. It was a shitty thing to say."

"But it's true, isn't it? I mean, even if we *call* him Dad, that doesn't *make* him our dad, does it?"

Michael cocked his head to one side and narrowed his eyes as he stared at his brother; one corner of his mouth turned up in a look of disgust and he shook his head slowly. "What's wrong with you, Stephen? What's the matter with you?"

Stephen's head tilted back slightly as he laughed. "I dunno. What's the matter with *you?*"

Still laughing, Stephen reached out and closed the French doors.

Michael heard his brother's muffled laughter continue as he stared through the glass and watched Stephen flop down on his bed.

Al was deep in a calm, dreamless sleep—a rarity lately— when he was jerked awake suddenly. At first, he thought it was the bed again, but he was wrong.

He sat up to find Michael standing beside the bed in the dark.

"I'm sorry," Michael whispered.

"Whatssamatter?"

"My light's on. In the bedroom. It woke me up."

"Well, jeez, Mike, turn it off." Al started to lie down again, started to roll over, get comfortable and go back to sleep.

"But, Dad, you took out all the bulbs."

Al froze. He became alert suddenly when he realized that he had, indeed, taken out all the lightbulbs downstairs earlier that night.

Facing Michael again, Al whispered, "Whatta you mean, the light's on?"

"It's . . . on. It's shining."

"Did you put a bulb in?"

"No."

"Then Stephen must've—"

"Uh-uh. There's no bulb."

Al turned to Carmen when she stirred and made a breathy noise in her sleep. When he was sure she wasn't going to wake up, he tossed the covers aside, got out of bed and put on his robe. He followed Michael out of the room and into the hall.

He was certain Michael had been dreaming. He was sure it was nothing more than that. He told himself it was nothing more than that over and over as he followed the boy.

As Al started down the stairs, he realized there *was* light down there.

"Okay, c'mon Michael, what'd you do, take one of the bulbs from the drawer in the kitchen?"

"No!" Michael hissed. "There's no *bulb*!"

Al stopped halfway down the stairs. The back of his neck tingled and he felt his stomach tighten, felt his testicles shrink upward into his body.

Michael continued down the stairs until he realized Al was not following him. He stopped and looked back.

"Are you coming?"

Al's voice was dry and hoarse when he finally spoke: "Yeah, yeah, I'm . . . I'm coming."

He continued down the stairs, but much more slowly now, his hand clutching the bannister as he went. Once at the foot of the stairs, he stood for a long moment in a pool of light shining from his left before turning to follow Michael into the bedroom.

"See?" Michael said, his voice groggy. "See what I mean?"

Al turned.

His breath caught in his throat as if it were a rock.

An empty light socket was glowing with a strong, off-white light that made Al squint. It was not a normal light, though. There was something very odd about it, something deeply unnatural.

Al stared at the light, mouth open and working slightly, as if he were to speak, but he said nothing, just stared at the glaring malignancy of the grayish-white light.

The light disappeared and left them in darkness.

Al pressed his lips together and took in a long deep breath, then let it out slowly.

"See what I mean?" Michael whispered.

Al didn't speak for a while. He knew his voice would give him away. He hoped Michael had not looked at his face when he'd first come into the room.

"See what?" he barked.

"The light. It was just—"

"It's pitch black in here, dammit, what light?"

The soft moonlight from the window glistened in Michael's wide, disbelieving eyes. He said nothing.

"What the hell is the matter with you? You wake me up in the middle of the night to . . . juh-just-just go to bed, goddammit, go to bed right *now*."

Al spun away from Michael and hurried back up the stairs, clenching his fists so his hands would not tremble.

In the bedroom, he removed his robe and sat on the edge of the bed and then shot back to his feet immediately, turning to look down at the bed.

It was vibrating.

Without realizing it, Al began to make small noises in his throat. He looked at Carmen and hoped, prayed, that she would not wake up as he backed away from the bed, leaned down for his robe and hurried out of the room.

In the kitchen, he turned on the light and opened a beer. He was halfway through it before he realized there were tears on his cheeks and he was sobbing quietly.

"You were right, you know," the voice whispered.

Stephen lay in the dark, alone in his room, wide awake.

"He is *not* your father. Is he?"

Stephen shook his head slowly on his pillow.

"He believes nothing you say. He has no faith in you. No respect for you. Does he, Stephen?"

He shook his head once again.

"Does he?"

"No," Stephen breathed.

"He will never do you any good. Will he?"

"No."

"He will only prevent you from growing. Isn't that right?"

"Yes."

"He will only prevent you from becoming what I have promised you can become. Correct?"

"Yes."

"You do not want that, do you?"

"No."

"And why is that?"

"Because . . . you've said so."

"And who am I, Stephen? Who am I that I should say so?"

"My father. You are my father."

"Who am I, Stephen?"

"You . . . are God."

"That is right, Stephen, my son. That is right. . . ."

14

Winter into Spring

As the temperature outside the Snedeker house gradually rose and the gray of winter gave way reluctantly to spots of green here and there, the temperature inside dropped steadily and the mood grew slacker.

It was becoming more and more common for most of the conversation that took place in the house to be coming from the television, which was on constantly. None of them talked much anymore. They only ate around the dining-room table on the weekends, and sometimes not even then; instead, they put their plates on their laps or on TV trays.

It wasn't as if they were angry with one another; that wasn't the case at all. Instead, it seemed as if they were preoccupied with their own private, silent thoughts, as if they were too busy going over and over things that disturbed them, examining them in their minds, gnawing on them.

Stephanie and Peter were the only two people in the house who remained their usual playful selves, but even they seemed to notice the change and seemed a bit troubled by it. They also seemed to realize it would be best not to ask anyone what was wrong and, instead, spent much of their time together, playing and talking.

Michael spent as much time as he could away from the house with friends. He used to hang around the house a lot with Stephen, but they were seldom together anymore.

Stephen was his own company. He stayed downstairs when he was home, the electric squeals of his heavy-metal music muffled by the closed and latched French doors. Sometimes he could be heard, alone in his room, laughing. . . .

How did it happen? Carmen wondered one day. *When did it start? When did we become like this?*

She sat at the desk in the sun-room smoking a cigarette, trying to identify the point at which her family had changed. It was a subtle change, yes, but a definite change nonetheless. A chill had fallen over her home, over her family, and she was powerless to do anything about it. It made her feel almost as helpless as she'd felt when she'd learned that Stephen had cancer.

Stephen . . .

Sometimes she actually found herself *missing* him, as if he were away on a trip, or something. It seemed as if he had gone away and been replaced by a stranger who roamed around the house ignoring everyone, smiling for no reason, sometimes mumbling to himself, sometimes laughing, wearing those horrible T-shirts with skulls and demons and desecrated religious symbols on them. He even *looked* like a stranger; his hair was growing longer and he seemed unconcerned about his appearance and, although she couldn't pinpoint the specific change that had occurred in them, even his eyes no longer looked familiar.

"Al, don't you think we should do something about

Stephen?" she'd asked a few nights ago as they were
getting into bed.

"Do *what*? I mean, what're we gonna do? He's old
enough to know how he's behaving, he knows what he's
doing so what're we gonna do?"

Al had changed, too; he'd become more quiet than
usual lately, but when he did speak, he sounded as if he
were on the very edge of anger, running his words together in a rush as if he were trying to get them out
before they exploded inside him. He was drinking more,
too, and his breath had smelled strongly of beer that
night.

"Well, what I mean is," she'd said, "maybe he *doesn't*
know what he's doing."

"He's gotten weird, but he hasn't gotten stupid."

"No, I mean . . . well, Father Hartwell suggested
that maybe, um . . . maybe Stephen should get some
therapy."

He barked out a couple of sharp, cold laughs. "Therapy? You know what that costs? An *hour*?"

"But if there's something wrong, it might be worth
it."

"If there's anything wrong, it's that damned kid he
hangs around with, but *you* think he should be able to
have his friends, *you* think that'll help him. No. I don't
believe in hiring somebody to do what a family should be
able to do on its own."

"Well, so far, we haven't been about to do it on our
own."

"Oh, okay, so I suppose you think that's my fault, or
something?"

"I didn't say that. I'm just worried about him. There's
something wrong with him, and I keep thinking there's
something we should be doing. Mom says he's going
through a stage, but she hasn't spent any time with him
lately like we have. And how can this be a stage, he's just

acting too weird, he's not even the same person anymore, and I don't think—"

"Well, I hope it is a stage," Al said, rolling over and turning his back to her. "And if it is, he'd better get through it fast, or I'm gonna kick his butt through it."

Carmen had lain awake for a long while that night, worrying about Stephen.

And now she was worrying about him once again.

But Stephen was not her only worry. . . .

There were the voices.

They were never quite loud enough for her to be certain she'd actually heard, rather than imagined, them. They were never quite identifiable, either, though they always sounded familiar.

Sometimes they whispered her name. Sometimes they laughed at her. At other times, she thought she could hear a small child calling her from somewhere in the house when she knew she was alone. Still other times, their murmurings sounded angry, threatening. She still thought she saw things now and then, too, things that flitted around her quickly but were gone the moment she turned to them; once, she'd hurried into her bedroom to get something from her dresser and, for just an instant, she could have sworn she'd seen a figure—it appeared to be a man, but it was impossible to tell—sitting at the foot of her bed, but it was gone when she stopped and turned toward it.

Then again, it could have been Willy skittering around the house, or a squirrel chattering in the backyard, or children playing in the neighborhood, or even her own troubled imagination, which was working overtime on the possibility that Stephen *did* need therapy, that perhaps he *was* mentally ill, that maybe his relationship with Al would never heal, that Al would just go on drinking until it became a real problem and he was just as much a stranger to her as Stephen had become.

And in the middle of all her worrying, she kept re-membering Stephen's words on their first day in the house:

Mom, we have to leave this house. There's something evil here . . . something   evil . . . something   evil . . . evil . . .

Carmen needed someone to talk to. She'd tried talking to Al, but that hadn't worked. She used to be able to talk to Stephen about almost anything, but, those days seemed to be over. Of course, there was always Fran—*if* Carmen could get her to hold still long enough to have a conversation.

Ever since leaving the house in such a hurry that one evening a few months ago, Fran had kept herself busy enough so she wouldn't be able to talk at length with Carmen. For a while, Carmen had been hurt. Then she began to get angry, wondering why she was suddenly getting such chilly treatment from her friend. It was partially her fault, though, for not pinning Fran down and talking with her. But she hadn't done that because she was afraid to talk with Fran. Just before leaving, Fran had said something about seeing things in the house, about the house making her uncomfortable. Carmen missed the time they used to spend together, the talks they used to have . . . but she didn't want to hear Fran's explanation for what she'd said.

She stood from the desk and went into the living room. Peter was in his bedroom napping, the others were still at school. She stood in the living room a moment, staring through the window at Fran's house.

How bad could it be? she wondered. *What could she say that would be so awful?*

After checking on Peter to make sure he was still sound asleep, she went over to Fran's.

As soon as Fran opened the door, Carmen said, "Okay, let's sit down and talk."

"Oh, hi, Carm. Gee, you caught me at a bad time. I was just going to—"

"Really, Fran. We need to talk. *I* need to talk. Please?"

Fran stood in the doorway chewing on a thumbnail. "Something wrong?"

"That's what I'd like to know. One day you run out of my house like it's on fire and we've hardly talked to each other since. So . . . what's wrong? What happened?"

Fran sighed and gave Carmen a sad smile. "Yeah, I suppose we do need to talk. C'mon in."

They sat at the small kitchen table and Fran poured them coffee. The baby was sleeping in the living room and a talk show was playing low on a small AM radio on the table.

For a few minutes, they made nervous small talk, then Carmen asked her exactly what had happened that day she'd left the house so suddenly.

"I haven't said anything because . . . well, I knew how stupid I would sound," Fran said hesitantly.

"Said anything about what? If it'll explain why you hurried away that day without any explanation, I don't care *how* stupid it sounds, I want to hear it."

"Well, your house . . . I was very uncomfortable in there. I didn't want to say anything because . . . well, because of what the kids had been telling you for so long, I knew how much that had bothered you, and . . ."

"You said you kept seeing things."

"Yeah. In the corner of my eye, like someone, or something, was hurrying through another part of the room, or the house. But there was no one there. And I felt . . . I just didn't feel right."

"So, you think the house really is—"

"Absolutely not, and that's exactly why I didn't want to say anything. I knew that you'd think that I thought

that the house was haunted, and I don't, okay? I think
. . . well, I just think that . . ."

When Fran didn't go on for a moment, Carmen
asked, "What *do* you think, Fran?"

She laughed nervously. "Well, I'm not sure. It was
probably just, you know, what you'd told me about what
the kids had said, and the history of the house . . .
knowing what it used to be . . . that's all, I'm *sure*
that's all."

Carmen thought about that a while, sipped her coffee,
lit a cigarette. "If that's all it is," she said, "then why
don't you ever come over? Why have you been avoiding
me?"

"Well, like I said, I was embarrassed. And I don't
want to impose on you with the baby and—"

"You know it's no imposition."

"The house just makes me uncomfortable, Carmen,"
she sighed. "That's all. It's stupid. It's childish. But I
know what it used to be and I think about what used to
go on there . . . and it makes me uncomfortable."

"You're afraid of my house."

Fran's sudden laughter sounded rather forced as she
took her coffee mug to the sink and rinsed it.

"You are," Carmen said, following her. "You're afraid
of it."

"Carmen, please stop it."

"Well, what if I told you I feel the same way sometimes? What if I told you that I see things sometimes?
That I hear voices sometimes? Or that I—"

Fran turned around suddenly and interrupted:
"You're joking, aren't you?"

"Not at all. Sometimes I think I'm going nuts over
there. And Stephen . . . well, you say he's going
through a stage, but it's a stage that didn't start until
right after we moved into that house."

Fran's eyes narrowed and she whispered, "You really hear voices?"

Carmen nodded.

"So, do *you* think the house is . . . y'know, haunted?"

"I haven't let myself use that word yet and I'm not sure I want to hear myself use it. But I'd be lying if I said it hadn't crossed my mind."

"What about Al?"

Carmen shrugged. "We haven't talked about it. I don't know what he thinks—or if he has an opinion about it at all. I'm afraid he'd think I was nuts. And we've already talked about getting a therapist for Stephen, so . . . one in the family's enough, thanks."

Fran leaned against the bar that separated the kitchen from the dining room. "So, what are you gonna do?"

"What *can* I do? I can't talk to Al, and the last thing the kids need is for their mother to tell them the house is haunted. They've heard that enough from Stephen. But I had to tell somebody. That's why I came over. It feels good to . . . well, spill my guts."

"Makes me feel a little better, too," Fran chuckled. "At least I wasn't imagining things."

Carmen lit another cigarette. "I don't know. Maybe it *is* just imagination. Things haven't been going well over there for any of us, that's for sure. I think everyone's kind of tense. I know I am. And, like you said, the house does have a pretty strange background. That alone is creepy."

They were silent for a while. Voices droned through the ghostly static on the radio.

Suddenly, Fran drummed her fingers on the tabletop decisively. "You ever listen to this show?" she asked, nodding toward the radio.

Carmen shook her head. "I don't think so."

"I like it better than most talk shows because they get

some really interesting guests most of the time. Reall *bizarre* guests, you know? And just the other day, the had a couple on who might be able to help you."

"What?" Carmen laughed. "Why would they be abl to help me?"

"They're this married couple, see, the Warrens. An they're, well, ghostbusters, I guess. Only for real, none o that Bill Murray stuff," she laughed.

"You're kidding, right?"

"No, no, really. That's not the first time I've heard o them, either. I read an article that—" She snapped he fingers and stood. "In fact . . ."

She left the kitchen and Carmen heard her shuffling around in the living room. When she returned, Fran wa paging quickly through a magazine. Once she wa seated, she found what she wanted, folded the magazin open and slapped it down on the table.

"There they are," she said, pointing to a photograph

Carmen picked up the magazine and studied the ma and woman on the page, half her mouth curling up i amused disbelief.

"These people? You mean, these people are"—sh laughed—"ghostbusters? But they look normal."

"They *are* normal. You should hear them. They'r perfectly normal. Pleasant, intelligent, very *un*-nuts."

The man and woman in the picture wore broac smiles. Both in their sixties, the man, stocky and barrel chested, had graying hair and wore metal-rimmec glasses, and the woman had sparkling eyes and dark hai that was drawn back in a bun. They looked pleasant warm, like someone's favorite set of grandparents. Th caption read, "Demonologists Ed and Lorraine Warre reside in Connecticut, but travel extensively to lectur and continue their research."

"You can take it, if you want," Fran said. "It's a rea interesting article. They talk about all the signs of a haunting, you know, like sudden changes in temperature, things moving around the house by themselves or disappearing, flashing lights—'ghostlights' they call 'em —and all kinds of stuff. They say that children and animals are usually the first to notice 'cause they're really sensitive to things like that, y'know. They tell stories about some of the cases they've worked on, too, and they—"

"Children and animals?" Carmen asked quickly.

"Huh? Oh, yeah. They sense those things a lot better than adults."

Carmen frowned and stared at her hand on the table. "Children and animals." She thought of Stephen insisting from the very beginning that there was something wrong with the house, and of—

"That dog," she whispered to herself.

"Huh? What dog?"

"Oh, um, just . . . remember that dog that was barking outside almost every night for a while?"

"Oh, you heard him, too, huh? Yeah, I thought I'd go crazy. Why?"

"Al finally wandered around the neighborhood one day a few weeks back until he found out who owned it and told them to keep it locked up at night. But it barked outside our house. Every night. It stood at the front corner on this side and barked like it was about to attack the wall."

Fran cocked her head and frowned. "Really?"

"Yeah. It only woke me a couple times—I can sleep through just about anything most of the time—so I only saw it twice. But Al—it woke him up every time, I guess. Said it always stood right there, barking . . . at the house."

Fran wore a troubled expression as she stared thoughtfully at Carmen for a while. Then she tapped a finger on the picture of the Warrens and said, "I think you should call them."

"Call them? Why? I mean, what would I say? I was just"—she laughed—"just making an observation, is all."

"What could it hurt? They just live over in Monroe. They have a museum there at the house, they hold lectures and teach classes there on demonology, and—well, it's all in the article. Take it, read it. You could at least ask them what they think of your situation."

Another laugh. "You know what Al would do if I he knew I called a couple of ghostbusters to tell them our house might be haunted? He'd pitch a fit."

"He doesn't have to know, does he?"

She scanned one column of the article, thinking. "No, I don't think so. I'm sure this just . . . well, I've been stressed out lately and . . . it's just me, Fran, just us. Things are pretty tense with us these days, that's all."

"Is anything wrong?"

"Oh, nothing serious. I don't think, anyway."

"Well, at least take the magazine with you and read the article."

"Yeah, sure. Sounds interesting."

Carmen did take the magazine home with her, but, instead of reading it, she dropped it on top of a stack of other magazines beneath an end table in the living room.

But she did not forget about it. Not quite . . .

Carmen was not the only one who had been giving a lot of thought to what Stephen had said that first day in the house.

Al had been haunted by the boy's words, haunted the way the ghost of a murder victim might haunt its killer: with cruel and dogged persistence.

So he drank more. He was aware of it, and he didn't like it, but he didn't know what else to do. Sleep did not come easily at night, and neither did waking up in the morning. It was difficult keeping his mind on his work during the day and when he got home in the evening, he was almost too wound up and rundown just to hold the simplest conversation. So, some beers seemed to be the best solution.

All because of some phantom music at night, a damned barking dog (until a couple weeks ago, anyway), vibrations in the bed, and Stephen's claim that the house was evil—combined with what the house used to be.

And, of course, there were the disturbing changes in Stephen. Al didn't even like to look into the boy's eyes anymore; they were the cold eyes of a threatening stranger and they made Al's neck hairs bristle.

It wasn't just his eyes, though. The sound of his laughter coming up the stairs when he was alone in his room was unnerving, and his quiet mumblings as he walked along the hall. He didn't even spend as much time with Cody as he used to, and they had been inseparable. Cody still came over, they still went downstairs together and listened to that music. Sometimes Al caught them exchanging glances or whispering to one another in a way that made him think they shared some unhealthy secret.

One evening, the whole family had been watching television in the living room when Stephen had surprised them by coming in and joining them. He sat on the floor in the corner behind them and folded his knees up against his chest.

No one said anything to him; they just exchanged quick, surprised glances, then turned their attention back to the television.

Then he'd started mumbling to himself.

They'd ignored it at first—although Al had found that very difficult—but it continued.

His words were indistinguishable, his voice a low,

throaty drone punctuated occasionally by a soft chuckle. All the while, his distant eyes remained locked on the television screen.

Al's right hand began to squeeze the bottle of beer tighter and tighter until—

"Will you stop that goddamned mumbling!" Al shouted. "What the hell is *wrong* with you? You're acting like a crazy person, a sick person! Now, will you shut the hell up or go to your goddamned room!"

Everyone else in the room had stiffened at Al's shouting. Stephen just sat there a few moments longer, stared at the television, and continued to mumble to himself. Then, he stood and said quietly, "Okay." He left the room without looking at anyone, his lips twitching into an icy smirk as he passed Al.

They heard his footsteps as he went down the stairs . . . his footsteps and his quiet laughter.

Al hated it—Stephen's mumbling, his own shouting— but he didn't know what to do about it and had no idea where it had come from. It was so foreign. Their family had been so quiet and content before.

He kept hoping that it would pass, that it would just go away and things would be as they had always been.

Until then, he would do his best to ignore it.

The day Carmen had talked with Fran about the house, Al came home from work feeling the way he usually felt —wrung out. He was looking forward to a good dinner and a few relaxing beers.

That was not what awaited him.

When he walked through the front door, he heard Carmen crying. He stepped into the dining room to find her seated in one of the chairs from the dining-room set; it had been turned to face the doorway to the kitchen. She was leaning forward, elbows on her thighs, chin resting in her palms with her hands over her cheeks as she stared into the kitchen and sobbed.

"Carm?"

She jerked upright and cried out in shock.

"What's the matter?" he asked, unable to hide his annoyance.

Trying to catch her breath, she wiped her eyes, then pointed into the kitchen. She tried to speak, but only sobbed again.

Al walked over to the doorway and looked into the kitchen. White chunks of crockery were scattered over the floor amid a pool of dried, sticky-looking maroon-colored juice and thick chunks of some unidentifiable substance that appeared to have crawled over the linoleum.

"What happened?" Al asked.

"Willy. He was out and I—I didn't know it. He g-got up on the counter and knocked over the pitcher of juice, and my casserole."

Al sighed and put his arm around her. "Well, why are you so upset? That's no big deal, is it? I mean, it's just . . . well, it's just a mess, right? It can be cleaned up."

She looked up at him slowly. Her mouth was curled downward, lips pressed hard together.

"Okay, then *you* clean it up!" she shouted. "*You* mop that fucking floor! See what it does to *you*!"

Al took a step back, his mouth hanging open. "W-what?"

"That floor! You just go ahead and see what—no, no! I'll show you myself!" She stood. "You just watch, just watch!" She shot from the chair and left the dining room.

Al stood beside the chair looking confused. Was Stephen's craziness catching? What was *happening* to his family?

In a few minutes, Carmen returned with the mop and

a bucket full of water. She kicked off her shoes and bent down to roll up her pants.

"Now, you just watch," she said.

Still looking as though he'd been slapped in the face for no reason, Al watched as Carmen began to mop the kitchen's red-brick floor.

Michael, who had heard his mother's shouting, joined him.

So did Stephanie and Peter.

They watched as Carmen mopped. They watched as the mop turned a dark color. They watched as her bare feet began to slop through a reddish-brown liquid that formed quickly on the linoleum.

And they smelled the coppery odor.

Carmen was still crying, stopping now and then to wipe away her tears with the heel of her hand. After a while, she stopped and turned to Al, ignoring the children.

"You see this?" she shouted. "This right here, *this* is what I deal with every time I mop this damned floor! *This* is why I'm upset! You explain this to me! What the hell *is* this?"

Al gawked at the reddish mess for a moment, then stepped forward and put a hand on Carmen's shoulder.

"I'll tear this linoleum up," he said. "We'll replace it. The landlord'll pay for it. It's just old, is all. It runs when it gets wet. We'll replace it and it won't happen anymore."

He squeezed her shoulder and forced a smile.

Carmen looked at him as if she were surprised.

"Really?" she asked.

"Yeah, sure, no problem. We'll just get rid of the damned lino. It's old, that's all. I mean, think about it. How old is this house?"

He gave her another smile, and he almost believed that one.

"We'll call Campbell and tell him, then I'll do it this weekend," he said. "That's all it is, honey. Really."

She stared at him. "You mean it?"

"Yeah, sure."

Her shoulder sagged with relief. She leaned toward him and he embraced her.

"What's wrong with the floor, Mommy?" Stephanie asked.

Al answered. "It's just old, honey. So, when it's mopped, the color comes out of it in the water. Looks almost—"

"Looks like blood," Michael said, with dread in his voice.

"Yeah," Al laughed. "Looks almost like blood."

"But what's that smell?" Carmen asked.

Al shrugged. "Just the linoleum, is all." He turned to Carmen. "You want me to clean this up, hon? I will."

"Would you?"

"Sure. Just let me go to the bathroom first." He kissed the top of her head and left the dining room, went down the hall, holding his breath all the way, and into the bathroom, where he closed the door, locked it, and put a trembling hand to his forehead. His head was suddenly aching, *throbbing*, and his heart was beating in his throat.

His calm was gone. The reassurance he'd shown Carmen was not only gone with it, but had not really existed in the first place.

He'd groped desperately for the explanation he'd given Carmen for the floor and, to his surprise, it had worked. The only problem was that he did not believe it himself.

"Dear God," he breathed tremulously as he slid down the door to a sitting position on the floor, "what's happening?"

15

House Guests

It was on a Sunday afternoon in June, a couple weeks after the end of the school year, that Carmen got the call from her sister Della in Alabama.

Michael and Stephanie were playing outside and Peter was in the backyard with Al, who was trying to get the barbecue started to make hamburgers.

Stephen, of course, was downstairs in his room.

Della had diabetes and had been very ill lately. On top of that, she and her husband were going through a very difficult separation, complete with screaming fights and threats and the digging up of old offenses which were best spoken of privately in hushed tones—not in front of their two daughters. She was calling to ask if Carmen would mind taking in the girls, Trish and Kelly, until the situation improved.

"Well, I, um, sure, it wouldn't be . . . can I call you back in a few minutes? I really should talk to Al first, and I promise to call you right back, okay?"

As Carmen hung up, the front door opened and Michael came in looking sweaty and out of breath. He tossed her a wave as he passed the doorway on his way downstairs.

Carmen went out to the backyard and told Al about her conversation with Della.

"Yeah?" Al said when she was finished. "Well, if she needs help with them, sure. It's fine with me. How long, does she think?"

"She didn't say."

"Well"—he shrugged—"that's all right. Yeah, go ahead and tell her to send 'em."

"Thanks, hon." Carmen went back into the house, picked up the telephone and was starting to dial her sister's number when she heard—

"*Mawwm!*"

Michael's scream was so piercing that Carmen dropped the receiver.

"C'mere Mom, c'mere *now!*"

She hurried down the hall to the stairs. "What?" she called as she started down the stairs. "What is it?"

Michael stood at the foot of the stairs, pointing into his room, mouth gaping as he hopped lightly up and down; his other arms waving, beckoning Carmen to come quickly.

"Hurry, *hurry!*" he shouted.

Once at the bottom, she stood beside Michael and looked into the room and saw—

Nothing.

She stared, waiting for something, anything that might explain Michael's behavior. Nothing happened.

"Michael, what's *wrong* with you?" she scolded.

"But he was there a second ago! He ran all the way around the room on the shelf!"

"Who was there? *Who* ran around the room?"

"He-he was—there was a-a—" As Michael stammered, he pointed into the bedroom, his hand jittering anxiously.

"Okay, Michael, calm down, what is it?" Carmen's

voice broke. She realized Michael's behavior was making her very uneasy.

"It was a boy, Mom! A little boy! He was, he—he was black and—and he was wearing pajamas, Superman pajamas, red and blue, and he ran all the way around the room from that end of the shelf to *that* end, and then he . . . he disappeared."

"Disappeared where?"

His body relaxed then, as if his excitement were suddenly being drained out of him. He turned to her slowly and bowed his head, suddenly ashamed.

"In . . . into the wall," he muttered.

Carmen looked around the room silently for a moment. She didn't know what to say or do. How would she explain this sort of thing to Trish and Kelly? What would she tell them? Worse yet, what would they tell their mother when they went back home?

She was jarred from her thoughts by the sound of muffled laughter behind them. She turned to see Stephen standing on the other side of the French doors, which were open a crack. He wore only a pair of undershorts that looked in need of a wash, and a pair of headphones with a cord that stretched to the small stereo by his bed. Apparently, he'd drawn something on his chest: a star of some sort with a circle around it.

He was laughing at them.

"Did you do something to scare your brother, Stephen?" Carmen asked angrily.

He laughed again. "*I* didn't do anything."

"Did you see it?" Michael asked hopefully.

Stephen held up his hands, palms out, and took a couple of steps backward, chuckling, "Hey, no way, I'm not breakin' the rule. We're not supposed to talk about it, remember? No ghosts, no voices. Otherwise, we get yelled at."

"Well, if you saw something, I *want* you to talk about it, Stephen," Carmen insisted.

Another laugh as he shook his head. "No fuckin' way." He reached out and closed the doors, then turned and walked to his bed.

Carmen spun away from the door, running a hand through her hair as she hissed, "*Damn!*" To Michael: "I'm sorry, hon, I just don't have time for this right now, I've gotta call your aunt Della." She headed up the stairs, trying to ignore Michael's sad and heavy sigh.

Her thoughts returned quickly to her nieces. The girls would think they were all crazy. Should she warn them first? If they knew about what the kids kept insisting they were seeing, if they knew about the history of the house, would they come . . . or would they decide to go stay with someone else for a while?

That's not what you're worried about and you know it, her inner voice murmured. *You're not worried that they'll think you're crazy or about what they'll tell their mother, are you? No, of course not. So what are you worried about, Carmen? What?*

As she picked up the telephone, she knew exactly what was worrying her.

She was worried that the girls would not be safe in the house.

Michael went into Stephen's room and stood by the bed, where Stephen lay listening to his music, eyes closed, head resting in the cradle of his interlocked fingers. The muffled music coming from the headphones sounded like a swarm of tiny insects to Michael.

He reached down and shook Stephen's foot.

Stephen opened his eyes and stared at Michael, but did not remove the headphones at first.

"You saw it, didn't you?" Michael asked.

Annoyed, Stephen slid the headphones back off his ears. "What?"

"I said, you saw it, didn't you? The ghost. That little black boy in the Superman pajamas."

"How do you know it was a ghost?" Stephen asked with a sly smile.

"You don't think it was?" Michael studied his brother's face, the taunting, knowing expression he wore. "You *know* what it was, don't you? You know all about it. *Don't* you?"

Stephen laughed and put the headphones back on, closed his eyes and began to jerk his foot to the beat of the music.

Michael backed away from the bed slowly and left Stephen's room, closing the French doors behind him. He didn't feel very good all of a sudden and went up the stairs slowly, trying not to think about his brother, about whatever it was that Stephen wasn't telling them, whatever it was that Stephen knew. . . .

Trish and Kelly arrived three days later. Al went to the airport, picked them up and brought them home to one of Carmen's festive meals.

Trish was twelve years old, a quiet girl with golden blond hair and a sweet, fair face. She was seven the last time Carmen had seen her, and she hardly recognized the girl.

Even more startling changes, however, had taken place in seventeen-year-old Kelly. She had grown into a tall and beautiful young woman with a svelte and shapely figure and full dark-blond hair that fell to her shoulders.

The girls put their bags in Stephanie's room. For the duration of their stay, Stephanie would sleep in Peter's room and Peter would share Michael's room.

They talked as they ate the big lunch that Carmen had

prepared. While Trish was quiet and shy, Kelly seldom stopped talking. She was animated and boisterous and the house rang with her laughter.

That laughter would not last.

While everyone else was eating and talking upstairs, Stephen was sitting on his bed, legs crossed Indian-style, in a pair of cutoffs with a large sketchpad open on his lap. Heavy-metal music played over his headphones as he drew on the pad with a black felt-tip pen.

The music was terribly loud, even too loud for Stephen, but that was the way he liked it . . . the way he needed it. He kept it that loud for a reason.

The voice had been speaking to him with more and more frequency over the months. It used to frighten him; now, at the most, it merely unsettled him. Sometimes, as the voice spoke, images appeared in Stephen's mind: ugly, violent images that haunted him, gnawed at him until he put them on paper, made crude sketches of the faint images that passed back and forth behind his eyes. The pictures were just as ugly as the things the voice said to him . . . bad, evil things.

He'd been playing the music on the headphones at deafening levels hoping that it might drown out the voice—although now, he didn't really care anymore. Only occasionally did he feel a chill as he listened to it, to the things it wanted him to do.

After all, what was there to be afraid of? As it had told him at the beginning, and many times since, Stephen was hearing the very voice of God . . .

As his pen scratched over the pad, the music made him deaf to the laughing voices upstairs, until—

"Stephen."

It was so sudden and unexpected, so clear through the raucous music, that Stephen's hand jerked, pulling the pen over the paper in a jagged line as he lifted his head.

"Stephen, they're here," the voice said.

Who? he asked silently, in his mind. He'd learned that it was unnecessary to speak out loud to the voice. It could hear his thoughts.

"Your cousins. Your lovely cousins. You haven't seen them in a while, so you don't know how lovely they are, but . . . they are, Stephen. So young and smooth-skinned. They would feel sooo good . . . taste sooo good. . . ."

As the singer screamed out of the headphones, backed up by shrieking guitars and thunderous drums, Stephen heard the voice laugh gently, that cold, icy laugh that sounded like wet rocks clacking together.

"I think you should go see your cousins, Stephen," the voice said.

Okay.

Stephen set aside the pad and pen, slipped the headphones off and stood up quickly. He didn't hesitate anymore when the voice told him to do something.

"No, no. Not now, Stephen."

He sat down on the bed again, slowly. Waiting.

The pinched music coming out of the headphones beside him sounded like a recording of a massacre.

"Later," the voice said. "I'll tell you when. Maybe some time during the night. If not tonight, some other night."

"Stephen?"

His mother's voice startled him; he hadn't even heard her coming down the stairs or opening the French doors. He jerked his head toward her.

"What're you doing?"

"Just . . . drawing."

"The girls are here. We're having lunch. Just wondered if you wanted to come up and see them and eat with us." She sounded cautious. She sounded cautious around him a lot these days.

"Oh. No. Uh-uh." He lay back on the bed, locked his hands behind his head and stared at her.

"You're not hungry?"

"Uh-uh."

Frowning, she approached his bed and got down on one knee.

"Stephen, listen to me," she said softly. Hesitantly, almost as if she were afraid to, she reached out and placed her hand lightly on his. "I'm not sure what's . . . wrong with you. You're not yourself anymore, and I think you know that as well as I do. I keep hoping that . . . well, that if something's bothering you, you'll come to me and talk about it. But I'm worried that . . . well, I keep thinking that maybe, um . . . maybe your illness . . ."

"Has come back?" he prompted her, starting to smile.

She nodded.

Stephen laughed. "Don't worry about that. It's not gonna happen." Then he laughed again.

"What do you mean?"

"My friends aren't going to let it happen."

Her eyes widened slightly as her eyebrows huddled above them.

"What friends? Who?"

"My friends here in the house. Oh, that's right"—he put a hand over his mouth and snickered into his palm —"you don't want me to talk about them. You don't believe in them. But that's okay, Mom. They believe in me. And they won't let me get sick again."

She rose to her feet slowly, her jaws flexing as she clenched and unclenched her teeth. She stared at Stephen as if, before her very eyes, he had been replaced by someone she'd never seen before. For a moment, she looked as if she were about to speak, but then her eyes fell on the open sketchpad, on the picture Stephen had been drawing.

Stephen's eyes followed hers to the figure on the page.

It was a man with a mustache and dark hair, wearing a plaid shirt, a man not unlike Stephen's stepfather, Al. Gouts of black blood gushed from the giant fishhook that pierced the man's neck.

Stephen grinned at his mother as she turned to him slowly, a cold look of shock on her face.

Finally, she turned and left the room.

Stephen laughed as he listened to her climb the stairs, and he heard the voice laugh with him.

16

Kelly

Carmen had been wondering when it would happen. It seemed to happen with everyone, so why not the girls? She just didn't think it would be quite so soon.

It was the morning after their arrival. Al had gone to work a few hours ago, everyone had eaten breakfast and Kelly had helped Carmen with the morning dishes. Trish had settled down in front of the television—she was watching a soap opera that she never missed—and the kids were outside. Carmen and Kelly seated themselves at the dining room table with tall glasses of iced tea.

They had made small talk as they worked in the kitchen, but Kelly had been unusually quiet. Yesterday, Carmen had thought it impossible for the girl to so much as calm down. But she *was* calm, even frowning a little, as if something was troubling her.

"So, how'd you sleep?" Carmen asked.

"Oh . . ." Kelly shrugged.

"I know it's hard to sleep in a strange place sometimes. Takes a while to get used to a different bed than your own."

Kelly nodded.

After a moment: "You didn't sleep well, did you?"

Kelly's features tightened as she thought a moment. "Aunt Carmen, something's . . ." She took a deep breath, sighed.

"What?"

"I don't like this house."

It was Carmen's turn to sigh. Less than twenty-four hours had passed and already . . .

"What don't you like about it?"

"Well, Mom told me it used to be a—"

"I wish she hadn't done that."

"Oh, that doesn't bother me, really. It's something else. The way I felt last night in bed like, um . . . well, like I wasn't alone in the room."

"Trish was with you."

"No, that's not what I mean. I felt like there was somebody else there in the room. Somebody . . . moving around, maybe. In the dark."

"And?"

"Well, there wasn't, of course. But it *felt* like there was."

Carmen thought before she spoke. She could tell Kelly the same thing she'd told Fran, but why open that can of worms? Even *she* didn't quite believe that.

"Honey, I'm afraid you've walked into a very weird household," Carmen said. "At least it's weird at the moment. You know about Stephen's illness, but . . . well, things have been tense here ever since then." She told Kelly briefly about the changes that had taken place in Stephen since his illness and their theories as to the cause —his illness, the treatments and medication, the move, and perhaps, in part, his association with Cody—and the stress his change had put on the entire family. She told Kelly of Stephen's feelings about the house—that it was evil, haunted, possessed by someone or something—and how that had affected the other children and frustrated Carmen and Al to the point of anger.

She did not, however, tell Kelly of her own experiences in the house. Mostly because she was trying to forget about them herself.

"I suspect what you're picking up on," Carmen said, "is the tension in the house. That's all."

"So Stephen thinks the house is haunted, too, huh?"

Carmen could not hold back a small flinch. "Then . . . that's what *you* think?"

Kelly shrugged. "Well, I'm not sure. But I know I felt something weird last night. And it *wasn't* tension, Aunt Carmen. It was . . . well, it felt bad. Dark. It's hard to explain. But, to be honest, I don't feel comfortable in here right now."

Carmen closed her eyes a moment and considered her response. A sudden wave of dread passed through her. Having another person in the house who insisted it was haunted would only make things worse.

"I hope, Kelly, that you'll keep your feelings about the house to yourself. Please? Don't say anything to the kids. And *especially* don't say anything to Al. He's sick to death of this. He'd go through the roof."

Kelly agreed to say nothing.

"But it still makes me kind of nervous . . . being here, I mean."

"Just new surroundings, that's all. You'll get settled."

Carmen forced a smile that did not feel—or look— very convincing.

17

Summer into Fall II

After a while, the girls began to behave as if they were living at home. By the second week of their stay, they were comfortable enough to lounge around in sloppy clothes, or go to the refrigerator and get something whenever they wanted. They became regular members of the family so easily that everyone else quickly forgot that they were really guests.

But as comfortable as they became, Kelly was never quite able to relax. She always felt as if something deep down inside was bothering her, making her tense and anxious, nervous and sometimes even a little nauseated. But it *wasn't* anything deep down inside. Kelly knew exactly what was making her feel that way.

The house.

The worst thing about it was that she couldn't put her finger on precisely what it was that bothered her. It was just a feeling.

Sometimes it was a cold feeling, a bone-deep chill that passed over her, *through* her, then disappeared in a moment's time as she walked down the hall or passed through a doorway. Other times, it was the feeling she was being watched as she undressed or showered; there had been a couple of instances, in fact, when she'd cut her shower short because of the overwhelming, almost smothering feeling that someone was in the bathroom with her and was about to rip the shower curtain aside and laugh at her—though all she had to do was look around to see that she was alone.

Sometimes she felt that she was being followed through the house or—and this was the worst—she felt someone brush by her in a doorway or in the hall. But there was never any evidence that her feelings had merit. There was never anyone nearby to make her feel that and, no matter how hard she looked, she never saw—or even heard—anything to explain her feelings. At least, not yet. . . .

As the days and weeks passed, Kelly started hearing some strange sounds. Al had brought a small fold-out cot into Stephanie's room and the girls had flipped a coin to see who got the bed; Kelly had won. Sometimes late at night, while Trish was sound asleep, Kelly thought she heard footsteps walking slowly around her bed in the dark. They were soft, cautious footsteps that barely tapped against the wood floor as they moved along one side of the bed, around the foot, and up the other side, then back again.

The second night it happened, Kelly woke her sister.

"Trish. Trish! Wake up Trish!"

In a moment: "Huh? Hummuh? Whum? Whassamatter?"

"Listen!" Kelly hissed.

"What?"

"Just *listen!*"

Silence.

"Listen t'what?" Trish asked groggily.

"You don't hear anything?"

"No."

"You don't hear, y'know, footsteps?"

"Aw, c'mon, get real Kelly, I was asleep." She rolled over again and ignored her sister.

Other times, she thought she heard someone walking around outside. Even though it didn't make sense—she *knew* it was impossible—Kelly thought she could hear someone walking all the way around the house again and again all night long.

Sometimes, when she was sitting in a room alone—on the living-room sofa reading, for example—she thought she heard a voice whispering to her unintelligibly from a shadowy corner of the room.

After Aunt Carmen's reaction to her first remarks about the house, she was afraid to say anything more to her. And after what Aunt Carmen had said about Uncle Al, she was certainly afraid to mention it to him.

So she kept it to herself. She continued to tell herself that it was just her imagination . . . even though deep down inside, she knew it was not.

It wouldn't be long before she realized that she was, indeed, right.

Very late one night, when Stephen was deep in a rare restful sleep, the voice said to him sharply, "Stephen! It's time to get up! Now!"

Stephen's eyes snapped wide open and he sat bolt upright in bed, his back stiff, fists clenched. In spite of the depth of his sleep, in spite of the fact that it had been a while since he'd slept so well, he was awake instantly.

"Get up, Stephen," the voice said. "It's time to go visiting."

Stephen knew immediately what that meant. He swept the covers aside and got out of bed, left his room, and crossed Michael's, being very careful to wake neither Michael nor Peter. Once upstairs, he passed through the living room, went down the hall and very, very carefully opened the door to Stephanie's room. Once he was able to stick his head in, he waited for signs that he'd disturbed Kelly and Trish from their sleep. When he heard nothing, he entered the room and closed the door silently behind him.

Pale, dim moonlight illuminated the room through the window at the far end and Stephen used it to maneuver himself between the bed and cot.

For a long time, he watched them sleep. He turned from one to the other slowly, his eyes caressing their defenseless faces, watching them as they dreamed.

An urge built up in him slowly as he looked at them, an urge he could not long ignore. Finally, as he stood there in the moonlit darkness, he gave in.

Staring at Kelly, who lay on her back leaning to the other side of the bed, he reached down and very carefully placed his hand on her shoulder to see how she would react.

Nothing.

He lowered his hand to her upper arm.

Still nothing. Her slow, rhythmic breathing continued.

He moved his hand over to her breast.

"Feels nice, doesn't it?" the voice asked quietly.

Wonderful, Stephen thought dreamily. *It feels wonderful.*

"You'd like to feel more, wouldn't you? You'd like to *do* more?"

Yes, I would.

"But she's too big. She'd defend herself. She'd only get you into trouble. You need someone smaller. Someone younger."

You're right. I don't need that kind of trouble.

"Turn around." The voice laughed.

Stephen turned around, as was told. He looked down at Trish.

Smaller. Younger. Definitely unable to defend herself.

Stephen smiled, lowering his hand first on the girl's shoulder. Then on her arm.

"That's better," the voice whispered. . . .

It was two days later when Carmen drove home with a backseat full of groceries to find Kelly and Trish on the front porch. Her attention was drawn to Trish in particular; she was sobbing uncontrollably.

Carmen pulled into the driveway, killed the engine, and hurried to the porch.

"What's wrong, what's the matter?" she asked; she hadn't seen the girls this way since they'd come to Connecticut, and her voice sounded frantic.

Kelly put an arm around Trish. "Aunt Carm, something terrible's happened. You may not believe it, and if you don't, I don't know what I'm gonna do with myself."

Carmen sat down beside Kelly and said, "Just tell me, please, I'll believe you."

It took a while for Kelly to get it out, but finally, she said, "Stephen, um . . . he molested Trish."

Carmen could only stare at them in numb shock. She knew in her gut, the moment that Kelly said it, that it was true. It was even unsurprising. It seemed a natural direction for his behavior over the months to finally take.

"When?" she asked.

Kelly said, "This afternoon. While you were gone. He didn't, um . . . get very far, if you know what I mean. I caught him first."

"Okay," Carmen breathed, realizing that she was suddenly, for some reason, out of breath. "Okay, okay, I'll, uh, take care of it. Right now. Where is he?"

"In his room," Kelly said.

Of course, Carmen thought as she got up and went into the house. She went downstairs to find Stephen, as usual, sitting on the side of his bed wearing headphones and drawing in his sketchpad.

Carmen reached out and plucked the headphones off.

"What the hell did you think you were doing?" she asked angrily.

"Doing when?"

"Today. With Trish. You *know* what I'm talking about!"

He said nothing. His mouth curled upward into a smile and he laughed.

"Okay, that's it, I mean that is really it. We've tried so hard, God knows we've tried, but nothing seems to make any difference. You don't change. You just get worse. And this is the *last* of it, Stephen." She spun around and left the room, went upstairs and straight to the telephone.

Carmen called the police.

Stephen was taken away by the police that afternoon. He was questioned, at which time he confessed that he'd been fondling the girls while they slept at night, and that he'd attempted unsuccessfully to have sex with his twelve-year-old cousin. Then he was delivered to the juvenile detention center, where he was later interviewed by a psychiatrist.

In the meantime, Carmen was at home riddled with guilt. Al would be home soon and she worried that he would be furious; at the same time, she suspected he would be very happy, and that would make her feel even worse. But she had done what she had thought best.

They had dealt with the unpleasant changes in Stephen long enough. Obviously, those changes had gone way too far, and something had to be done. This might, at least, get him some help.

When Al got home, he wasn't furious, but he wasn't

happy, either; he simply thought Carmen had done the right thing. He told her that maybe it would turn out for the best, that maybe it was the kick in the pants Stephen needed.

As it turned out, Stephen needed more than that. The psychiatrist who had talked with Stephen called Al and Carmen and told them it was his opinion that Stephen was schizophrenic—in other words, drastically out of touch with reality—and was in need of at least a sixty-day observation period in an appropriate mental hospital. He suggested Spring Haven. He recommended, however, that he spend the night in the juvenile detention center. He didn't think the family would be safe with Stephen in the house overnight.

They were devastated. Their son was, indeed, just as they had suspected, mentally ill. What had they done wrong? Every parent makes mistakes in raising their children, but what mistakes had they made that would bring their son to this?

They wondered how they could have been so callous. All that time he'd spent telling them he was hearing voices and seeing things, they had only gotten angry at him—when his real problem was a serious mental illness that he could neither help nor understand.

Their guilt and sadness were weighing heavily on them when, the next day, they picked Stephen up, took him to Spring Haven Psychiatric Hospital and admitted him.

It was an attractive building with lots of green grass around it shaded by a number of enormous oak trees. A tall solid fence stretched all the way around the sprawling grounds and patients and attendants strolled the grass calmly.

Stephen said nothing to them the entire time. He ignored their apologies, their offers of help, their pleas for him to talk to them. He remained silent until the moment they left him at the hospital. Then he looked at them, smiled darkly with expressionless eyes and said quietly, "Now that it doesn't have me to talk to it's going to come after you. All of you."

Al and Carmen left, saddened by his remark, thinking it was nothing more than another of the many symptoms of his illness.

Unfortunately for them, their children and Carmen's two nieces, they were wrong.

18

The Ghost Hunters

At a small, modest house in Litchfield, Connecticut, around the time Al and Carmen Snedeker were leaving their oldest son at Spring Haven Psychiatric Hospital, a forty-eight-year-old woman named Delores Cavanaugh was floating several inches above the chair in which she'd been firmly positioned just a few moments before. Her body, still in a sitting position, was tense and her face pale with horror as she stared at the others around her.

Those people included her fifty-five-year-old husband, Ross, and their twenty-one-year-old daughter, Caroline. With them were a tall, rather regal-looking woman standing beside a burly, barrel-chested man, both in their early sixties: Lorraine and Ed Warren.

For a moment, all four of them watched in shock and horror, then Ed stepped forward, waved to Ross, and said, "Get her away from there." As Ross stepped toward his wife to pull her away from the chair, Ed raised his right hand and, in a booming voice that echoed off the walls of the house like the strike of a hammer, he barked, "In the name of Jesus Christ, I command you to leave these people and go back to the place from which you've come!"

A framed picture on the wall dropped to the floor.

Two rows of porcelain bric-a-brac on a small shelf were swept through the air by an invisible hand and thrown against the next wall, the pieces shattering over the floor and a small dining table.

Ross Cavanaugh embraced his wife and held her close as he led her across the room.

An oak hutch with a glass front and shelves of china inside shook as if the earth were moving beneath it.

The four chairs around the dining table abruptly slid away from it simultaneously as the pane of a nearby window rattled wildly.

Ed turned, watching each event as it happened. Lorraine held a small cassette recorder in her right hand; it was recording the sounds of everything that happened around them.

As the chaos continued, Ed raised his right hand once again and repeated in the same booming voice, but even louder and more firmly this time, "In the name of Jesus Christ, I command you to leave these people and go back to the place from which you've come!"

The rattling and shaking continued for a few seconds, then—

The house fell silent.

Everyone remained frozen in place for a moment, then Ed turned, gave the Cavanaughs a cautious but comforting smile, and said, "I think it's stopped."

"It's only stopped for now," Mr. Cavanaugh said wearily, his arm still firmly encircling his wife's shoulders. "Uh, Mr. and Mrs. Warren, when we talked to you on the phone, this is exactly what we were talking about. It's been happening all the time."

Ed turned to Lorraine and asked, "Did you pick up anything?"

She placed a hand on her chest and sighed heavily. "This is definitely an evil spirit, Ed. It's not a poltergeist, like we first thought when we heard their story. It's an evil spirit and its intentions are malignant and strong."

He nodded toward the recorder. "You getting this?"

She nodded. "It's still on."

Ed moved toward the Cavanaughs, smiling at their daughter, who was so horrified by what she'd seen that she still stood—beside her parents now and away from the area of activity—with her back stiff and both hands pressed over her mouth, eyes wide.

"I'd like to ask you a few questions," he said quietly. "Why don't we go into the living room, sit down and try to relax?"

Lorraine followed them as they went into the next room and everyone took a seat. She sat beside Ed on the sofa and placed the recorder on the coffee table.

"I think the first thing we need to know is this," Ed said, clasping his big hands together. "Does most of the activity surround you, Mrs. Cavanaugh?"

She opened her mouth, but couldn't speak. She simply nodded her head.

Her husband said, "Yes, definitely. Always, in fact. It always involves her, somehow. She's never been hurt." They were sitting together in a loveseat and he placed a hand on her knee gently, looked at her, and asked, "Have you? I mean, not that I've ever known."

She shook her head and finally spoke in a hoarse voice. "No. Never. Just . . . terrified. It terrifies me."

"Of course it does," Ed said. "It *should*. But if it hasn't hurt you, we're ahead of the game. I just wanted to know if it pays more attention to you than anyone else. Um . . . tell me, does anyone in your family dabble in the occult? Any ouija boards, tarot cards, demonology, that sort of thing?"

Mrs. Cavanaugh shook her head firmly. "Never. Not in all our years."

Caroline was shaking her head too and Ed turned to

her questioningly. "No. I don't live here anymore but, I mean, I'm an only child, so I should know. I've never played with any of that stuff and, as far as I know, neither have my parents. I mean, why would they? We've always been a Christian family and we just don't believe in getting involved in that sort of thing."

"Okay," Ed said, nodding, "that's good. Here's another question, and please don't think it insulting. It's just something we *have* to ask in our work, only as a precaution, and I hope you'll answer honestly. Do any of you take drugs or drink heavily?"

"Oh, no, definitely not," Ross said.

Caroline added, "Even when I was younger, I never did any of that."

Ed nodded thoughtfully, then looked at Ross and Delores again. "You've been the only ones living in the house for . . . how long?"

"Almost three years."

Another nod. He turned to Lorraine and asked, "You wanna look around?"

"Well, I can, but it's a very small house. I don't know if I need to. We've already seen quite a lot."

"Yeah, we have, that's for sure. Mr. and Mrs. Cavanaugh, we're going to get some researchers in here right away to spend some time with you. If it's not an inconvenience, they'll be spending day and night in the house recording everything that happens. We'll be back within the next couple of days with a video camera to record an extensive interview with you and get all the facts from the very beginning. I mean, we'll get what you've told us already and more. We want everything, and I mean *everything*, on the record."

"It wouldn't be any inconvenience at all," Ross said.

"Good. The next step would be to bring in a member of the clergy. Are you religious people?"

"Well, we've always been Catholic, but . . . we haven't been practicing Catholics for many years."

"But you wouldn't object if we brought in a priest?"

"Not at all."

"Because I suspect we're going to need an exorcism."

"Can you tell me something?" Ross asked. "Can you tell me why it's after my wife? She seems to be the center of it. It always surrounds her. This isn't the first time she's floated like that. We don't understand it."

"I honestly don't know. But I suspect that after we've asked you a few more questions, we might have some idea as to why that's happening."

Ed was being diplomatic. He knew from experience that when something like this took place it was usually for a reason. He suspected that, in spite of what they'd said, they'd been involved in some sort of occult activity. Perhaps Mrs. Cavanaugh, on her own and without the knowledge of her husband, had been consulting a ouija board or a psychic, or had been attending séances to contact some dead relative or friend. But he didn't want to say that now because it had been his experience that such accusations tended to anger people, even if they were true—sometimes *especially* if they were true.

They left the Cavanaughs with smiles and handshakes (although Mrs. Cavanaugh was still so shaken that she remained on the loveseat in the living room, cold and silent) and went to a nearby coffee shop to discuss what they'd learned.

It was a busy coffee shop with lots of noise around them and they had to speak louder than usual to be heard.

"I think Mike would be best," Lorraine said. "I think we should send him. He's had experience with situations like this before and I think he could handle it."

"Yeah, that's probably a good idea." He sipped his coffee. "So, you think it's an evil spirit, huh?"

"Positive. And I think it's probably there for a reason."

"You mean they brought it on?"

She nodded. "Somehow. Since it's focusing on the wife, I suspect it's probably something she's doing. But that's the way it usually is, right? Even though they don't realize it."

Ed nodded, releasing a heavy, weary sigh. They'd both put in a long day—a long week—and they were tired.

"You want something to eat?" Ed asked.

"Sure, I'm hungry. But remember. No red meat. You're gonna cut back, right?"

"Yeah, yeah, yeah. And you're gonna kill me, is what you're gonna do," he murmured.

They picked up the menus and browsed through them in the comfortable silence of a couple who have been married for years.

When Ed was five years old, his family moved into the top floor of a two-family house on Jane Street in Bridgeport, Connecticut. It was directly across the street from St. John's Church, the church Ed's grandparents attended and that his family began attending from then on.

That house on Jane Street was to start what would be a lifelong interest for Ed Warren, a passionate interest that would lead him into some very strange places and show him some frightening things. At a very young age, that house was to change Ed forever.

That house was haunted.

On numerous occasions, every member of the family —Ed, his twin sister, his brother, and his parents—saw the apparition of an old woman who always looked less than friendly.

Ed's father was a police officer and a stern but sensible man. Not wanting his children to be frightened, he tried

to tell them that there had to be a logical explanation for
what they had been seeing. But they all knew better.

Every Sunday, Ed's grandparents joined them for
breakfast and the sound of Grandpa coming up the stairs
became very familiar: his labored steps, the thump of his
cane, his heavy, wheezing breaths.

When Grandpa finally died a number of years later,
Grandma was understandably devastated and Mom frequently checked up on her to make sure she was okay.
One day, Mom was gone later than usual and it wasn't
until very late in the evening, when the children were
ready for bed, that they heard the door open downstairs.
Thinking that Mom had come home, Ed left his bedroom and turned on the light so she wouldn't fall on the
stairs. As he started back to his room, he realized it
wasn't Mom coming up the stairs at all. He heard shuffling steps, a thumping cane, wheezing breaths. . . .

It was Grandpa coming up those steps, Grandpa who
had been gone for some time. Ed heard him go into the
kitchen and walk in circles for a while.

At about that same time, Lorraine was attending a
Catholic school and trying to hide from the nuns an ability that she had only recently, at the age of nine, discov-
ered she possessed.

Lorraine could see colored lights around people. The
colors followed the outlines of their bodies. They were
very pretty, but Lorraine didn't know what they meant
—if anything.

The sisters constantly discouraged her from even
bringing the colors up in conversation. She was told she
had a vivid imagination, that was all. She learned
quickly to keep the colors to herself. But that did not
keep her from seeing them.

There was no one in Lorraine's world to answer her
questions about them. It wasn't until much later that
Lorraine realized she was seeing the human aura, and

that, being clairvoyant, she was able to see and feel many other things that most people couldn't.

They met when they were sixteen. They were drawn together. Lorraine proudly told friends, "Ed is the only man I've ever dated."

After they were married, Ed graduated from art school and, in a 1933 Chevy he had bought for fifteen dollars, they took to the road selling his paintings here and there. But whenever they heard of a haunted house in the paper or by word of mouth, they would travel there and Ed would paint the house. Then Lorraine would go to the door with the painting and say, "My husband has sort of made a habit of painting haunted houses, and he's painted yours. We'd like you to have the picture." That almost always got them in the door so they could question the people who lived there, ask about the haunting and get the story directly from them.

Over the years, based on their research—which became more and more extensive as the years passed—Ed and Lorraine began to develop theories about how hauntings worked, about why they took place, about what brought them on. They read countless books on the subject but, as Lorraine said in the midst of their research, "It sounds like all these guys are reading the same books *we're* reading!" So they did not depend on the regurgitated and incestuous work they read to develop what was to become the New England Society for Psychic Research; they depended only on their own experiences, on the things they had witnessed.

As the years passed, books were written about them. Later, movies were made about them. They began to teach classes on what they had learned, turning students into researchers. They traveled the country and lectured at colleges about their experiences and what they had learned from them.

Ed had turned an experience in a haunted house as a

child into a life's work, and Lorraine had joined him to use a talent that, as a child, had been taken seriously by no one.

And now they were in a loud and busy coffee shop in Litchfield, Connecticut, waiting for their orders.

Somewhere in the coffee shop, a telephone sent out its electronic chirp.

Lorraine scooted away from the table and stood.

Ed laughed and said, "Hey, hey, what're you doing?"

Lorraine stopped, her mouth dropped open and she pressed a hand to her chest. "Oh my goodness. I was getting up to answer the phone." She put a hand over her mouth and returned to the table.

Ed laughed a deep, resonant laugh, his whole body shaking as he shook his head. "Oh boy, Lorraine, that's rich, that's good."

She laughed, too, and said, "Well, the phone at home is ringing constantly, and it seems every time I turn around, I'm getting up to answer it."

"Yeah, yeah," he laughed, "but a *coffee* shop. You know what that tells me, Lorraine, you know what that says to me? We need a vacation. We need a vacation really bad, 'cause we've been workin' too hard."

"Well, we've just taken on another case."

"I have a feeling it won't last too long. I mean, it probably won't take much to get the church to sanction an exorcism for this one. What's going on there is pretty obvious. But as soon as this one's over, we take a little vacation. We need a break."

Months would pass before that case came to its close and a grueling, church-sanctioned exorcism was held, thus relieving the Cavanaughs of the demons that plagued them in their home.

But, of course Ed and Lorraine were unaware of the

Snedekers and the things that had been taking place in their home.

The vacation Ed had said they needed so much would not come for some time.

19

The Darkness Closes In

Al and Carmen Snedeker were saddened by what Stephen had done to his cousin and by his hospitalization, but they assumed that, because he was gone, the atmosphere in the house would improve. It had been so tense and charged with hostility for so long that they were hoping for a relief, a return to some sort of normalcy. They assumed the younger children would be more relaxed without Stephen's stories of ghosts and apparitions, and Kelly and Trish would sense that and, as a result, feel more relaxed also.

They were wrong.

During the following weeks, the small, strange things that had been occurring now and then in the house—the noises, the fleeting glimpses of something darting here and there around a room, the sudden changes in temperature and the inexplicable feelings of being watched, or of simple, heart-clutching dread—would begin to escalate, would grow in severity and frequency, until those strange things were no longer small at all.

In fact, before Stephen left the house, their troubles had hardly even begun.

Whatever presence lurked in the Snedekers' house

wasted no time now in making itself known to the rest of the family.

The evening after Stephen left, Al was watching television and having a beer while Peter and Stephanie sat on the floor taking turns on Etch-A-Sketch. Michael was in his room doing homework and the girls, Kelly and Trish, were in the kitchen cleaning up with Carmen.

Since the incident with Stephen, Carmen had been making an effort to pay special attention to Trish; she'd made sure Trish wasn't physically hurt, had apologized to the girl profusely and told her to speak up if she wanted to talk to someone about what had happened. Trish had told her, however, that she didn't want to stay there anymore. Carmen understood perfectly and called her other sister right there in Connecticut and asked if she'd mind keeping Trish for a while; she said it would be fine and she'd pick Trish up in the morning.

Everyone went on, doing whatever they were doing, the children giggling quietly on the living-room floor so they wouldn't disturb Dad as he watched an old black-and-white war movie, and Carmen and the girls laughed and talked in the kitchen as water ran in the sink and the dishes clacked together while being washed.

Al finished his beer a moment before the movie was interrupted with a set of commercials. He left his chair, went into the kitchen, tossed the empty bottle into the trash and opened the refrigerator to get another.

His hand stopped abruptly on its way to the refrigerator's second shelf as the entire house shook with a powerful, deafening *bang*!

Everyone fell silent and did not move, their bodies frozen in place.

It happened again. The windowpanes trembled. Bottles rattled and clanked inside the refrigerator.

It happened a third time and then . . . nothing.

Footsteps thumped rapidly up the stairs and Michael

shouted, "Dad! *Dad*!" In his socks, he skidded to a halt on the kitchen floor.

Stephanie followed him, holding Peter's hand, their eyes wide.

"What *was* that, Dad?" Michael asked, his voice hoarse.

"I don't know, but I'm sure as hell gonna find out. An earthquake maybe?" he asked, turning to Carmen.

"I don't think so. It sounded like an explosion of some kind."

"Yeah, okay. I'm gonna look around." He started out of the room and turned to Carmen again, pointing at the ceiling with his thumb. "Are the Farradays home?"

"No, they're out of town, remember? They were gonna be gone for three days. They'll be back tomorrow night."

"So there's nobody up there?"

"It didn't come from up there, Al. It sounded like it came from down here, right here in the house."

"Shit," he hissed as he left the room.

The others didn't move, they just stayed in place and exchanged fearful, nervous looks.

Al went through the entire house, including the basement. He looked out every window, he looked behind every door; he frantically searched each room for damage, even sniffed the air for the smell of smoke or gas or electricity. But he found nothing.

He returned to the kitchen, very puzzled, where everyone was still gathered, a bit more relaxed, but no less confused.

"Did you find anything?" Carmen asked nervously, quietly.

"No. No, I didn't find anything." Al actually felt ashamed to have to say that. The three pounding noises they'd heard were big, not sounds from the neighborhood but sounds from inside the house. The fact that he was unable to find anything meant it was out of his control and he knew that everyone was depending on him for an answer; he had none. Far too many things had been happening in the house lately over which he had no control.

"But it was right here," Michael said, "in the house."

The telephone rang.

"I'll get it," Carmen said. She went to the living room, dropped onto the sofa and answered the telephone. "Hello?"

"Carmen? It's Fran."

Carmen leaned forward and brightened. "Did you hear it?"

"Hear what?"

"The sounds. Three of them. Big pounding sounds, almost like explosions. Did you hear them? Is that why you're—"

"No, I didn't hear anything. I'm calling because . . . well, I know this is gonna sound weird, but I just happened to look out the window and, um . . . did you know that there's a very strange-looking woman walking around in the room above you?"

Carmen's mouth dropped open for a moment. "What?"

"Really, I'm not kidding, I saw her. There's a woman up there and she's green and she's glowing. I saw her walking back and forth in front of the window. She looks, um . . . upset. Angry, maybe."

Every single strange and frightening thing that had happened over the past year flashed through Carmen's mind and tears came to her eyes. "Please, Fran, please . . . tell me you're joking, tell me this is a joke."

"You think I would call to make a *joke* like this?" she asked, incredulous.

"No. No, you wouldn't. Hang on, please. Don't hang up." She put the receiver down and rushed into the kitchen. "Al, it's Fran on the phone. She says there's someone walking around upstairs by the window."

He frowned. "*What?*"

"Um, c'mere a second." She led him through the dining room into the hall and whispered, "She says it's a green glowing woman."

He rolled his eyes. "Carmen, would you please—"

"No, I'm serious. She's not joking. Al, *think* about it!" she hissed. "What's been happening in this house? We can't explain most of what goes on, can we?"

He thought about that a moment, then shook his head and said, "No. No, we can't, really." He reached out, squeezed her hand briefly, and said, "I'll go outside and look up there, see if I can see her. Because, you know, their door is locked and—"

"Yeah, I know. Go ahead. Get out there."

Al went outside and Carmen went back to the telephone.

"Fran? Al is going outside now to look."

"No, she's gone. I'm at the window right now and I've been watching. She's gone. I don't see her."

"You're kidding. She's gone? Really?"

"Yeah, I don't see her. She hasn't been by the window for a while now."

Carmen sighed. "Okay. I'm gonna go now, Fran. I'm gonna go out with Al and tell him."

"Wait a second, Carmen. Remember that magazine I showed you? You took it home. It had those people in it, the Warrens, Ed and Lorraine Warren? I really think you should call them. *Really.* You've got something really weird going on over there and I think you *need* them."

"Yeah, well . . . I might think about it. Thanks for calling."

Carmen hung up and hurried outside to join Al. He was standing away from the side of the house, near Fran's, looking up.

"Fran said she was gone," Carmen said as she approached him.

"*What?*"

"She said the woman was gone. She hadn't seen her in the last few minutes."

"Well then she was probably seeing things," he said angrily.

"Al, you know that's not true. Something really weird is going on in our house."

"Oh, shit, you listened to Stephen too much. He's cra—he's sick, Carmen. You know that now. He's very sick, and the things he said he saw and heard, those were just symptoms. That's all, nothing more."

"Oh, come on, Al, you mean you can explain all the things that have happened in our house? You mean nothing has happened in there that has scared the hell out of you? Because I don't mind saying I've had the hell scared out of me by quite a few things! I mean, what just *happened* in there? What was that noise? What shook the windows? What *was* that?"

Al's lips curled into an angry sneer and she heard him grind his teeth. "Look, I don't wanna hear this shit, okay? I don't wanna hear it! Anything that happens in this house can be explained, you understand me? Don't start sounding like your goddamned crazy son!"

Al spun around and left her standing there in the night, alone. She looked up at the window one more time, but saw nothing. Then she followed Al inside.

Within the next hour, everyone, one after another, still puzzled and more than a little nervous, decided to go to bed.

Carmen went downstairs with Michael and Peter where, earlier that day, Al had moved Stephen's bed back into Michael's bedroom. She could tell they'd been upset by the explosive sounds, even though they weren't saying anything, and she certainly hoped they hadn't overheard any talk of that green glowing woman in the window upstairs; that would really scare them. She was afraid they weren't going to want to sleep downstairs—she didn't want that to start again—so she wanted to make them feel as comfortable as possible.

Once they were in bed and quietly listening to music on the radio on the nightstand between them, Carmen gave them each a goodnight kiss, went back upstairs, and checked on Kelly and Trish.

Kelly was sitting up in bed wearing a gray T-shirt three sizes too big for her and reading her Bible by the light of the bedside lamp. Trish was curled on her side, a mere lump beneath the covers.

"Is she asleep?" Carmen whispered.

Kelly shook her head. "I don't think so. She just . . ." She looked over at her sister. "I don't think she wants to talk to anybody."

"Oh. Well, how are you?"

She shrugged, then hesitated a moment before speaking. "Aunt Carmen, remember what I said about this house? About . . . how it makes me feel?"

Here it comes, Carmen thought. "Yes, I remember. And you think those sounds tonight confirm your feelings."

She nodded. "And I heard what you said to Uncle Al about that woman upstairs. Aunt Carm, I think there's something really weird about this house. Even if . . . you don't believe me."

"Well, Kelly." She sat on the side of the bed and touched her niece's arm. "Even though I don't like to admit it, I'm beginning to think you just might be right." She nodded toward the open Bible on Kelly's lap. "But that'll help. That always helps."

"I know," Kelly said.

Before leaving the room, Carmen went to the cot where Trish was curled up, motionless and silent. She placed a hand gently on Trish's shoulder and said, "You asleep, honey?"

Trish shook her head against the pillow.

"Are you okay?"

She nodded against the pillow.

"You're sure?"

Trish rolled over and faced Carmen. "Are you mad at me 'cause I want to leave, Aunt Carmen?"

"Of course not! I understand perfectly. I'd probably want to leave, too, if I were you. Tell you what, you just get a good night's sleep and Aunt Vicki will be here to get you in the morning, okay?"

She nodded and rolled back over.

Carmen waved at Kelly as she left the room and went to Peter's room where Stephanie was sleeping. The lights were on and Stephanie was sitting up in bed.

"I don't feel sleepy, Mom," she said.

"Well, would you like to look at a book? Or color? You can listen to music, if you keep it low. You want the radio on?"

"Oh . . . I think I'll just color a little while."

"Okay, sweetheart. You do that."

When she left Stephanie, she felt better about going to bed, too. She was more worried about everyone else than she was about getting any sleep herself.

In the bedroom, she found Al already asleep. That made her feel better. She couldn't imagine any conversation that night being a good one, not after the incident with the green woman upstairs.

Carmen undressed, brushed her teeth and put on her nightgown, then quietly crawled into bed, careful not to disturb Al from his sleep.

Kelly was reading the Twenty-third Psalm—the most encouraging and comforting part of the Bible to her— when she thought she felt something moving over her bare legs beneath the covers. She frowned and kicked her legs, stopped . . . waited . . . and felt nothing. She went back to reading.

It happened again, something crept right up her left thigh and she began to kick.

It stopped.

Goose bumps crawled over her skin. It didn't feel like a twitching nerve or even an insect.

It felt like fingers.

When it happened again, it started at the very top of her thigh and moved upward rapidly.

She gasped loudly when she felt the sensation of fingers pressing between her legs with great determination.

Kelly sat up straighter and threw back the covers.

There was nothing there but her legs, which were spread and trembling.

Once again, she felt fingers between her thighs, probing and, a second later, entering her even as she watched and saw *nothing*.

Kelly shot out of bed and ripped off the blankets and sheet with her. She searched the bed carefully, went over every inch of the mattress, searched the folds of the sheet, the blankets, but there was nothing in the bed. There was no sign that anything had been there.

She considered waking Aunt Carmen, but what good would it do? She had no proof that something had touched her. If she told anyone, they would think she'd fallen asleep and had been dreaming, plus it would be embarrassing to bring up.

Instead, Kelly put her pillows on the floor, pulled the covers down with her and lay down beside the bed.

It was a long time before Kelly went to sleep, and even then, she had some very ugly nightmares.

* * *

Stephanie was coloring the pictures in her coloring book when she saw something move silently and uneventfully through her room.

She was first aware of it as a dark movement in the corner of her eye and looked up from her coloring book to see a shapeless blob that closely resembled a dark shadow . . . except for the fact that it was moving out of the wall and passing through the center of the room, a shadow cast by nothing, dark and yet transparent, its globular shape changing liquidly as it moved, until it passed through the bedroom door smoothly, without a sound, and was gone.

Stephanie showed no reaction, but she could feel her heart beating rapidly.

She considered waking someone, telling them . . . but why? Stephen tried to tell them for so long, and they wouldn't listen to him. Why would anyone listen to her?

She reached over and turned on the radio, cuddled down beneath her covers, heart still pounding in her throat, and continued to color the picture in her book.

Michael lay in bed listening to the slow, regular breathing of his brother, wishing he could fall asleep, too.

He'd left on a small night-light in the corner because he just didn't feel very comfortable about being in the dark tonight.

He was staring up at the shadowy ceiling when he first heard the whispers. He couldn't understand what the whispering voices were saying, he couldn't pinpoint the source of the whispering—but it was definitely there.

With wide eyes, he looked all around the room as he lay rigid in his bed.

The whispering sounded urgent; one voice spoke, then another, as if they were exchanging secrets of pressing importance.

He stared at nothing for a long time, listening.

Then it stopped.

He wondered if he should go upstairs and wake his parents, but then he remembered how Stephen's stories had been received and decided against it. Instead, he just lay there in bed, unable to sleep, waiting for the whispering to start again.

Then Peter began to scream as if he were dying, writhing in his bed as if in pain.

Carmen sat up in bed, startled from sleep by her son's screams.

She reached over and shook Al, trying hard to waken him.

"Al, wake up," she hissed, "c'mon, wake up!"

But he didn't budge.

"Al, get up!"

Nothing.

She stopped and listened. The screaming had stopped, but she heard faint, muffled voices. She got up and went downstairs to find Michael and Peter talking.

"What's wrong, sweetheart?" she asked, hurrying to Peter's bed.

He looked up at her, his eyes puffy, cheeks striped by tears, and said, "I was stung! Something stung me! Like bees! Like when I was stung by that bee!"

"Were you dreaming, honey?"

"No, no! I wasn't dreaming!"

She pulled back his covers and unbuttoned his pajama top to look him over. She saw nothing. No marks, no welts.

"I don't see anything, Peter," she said quietly.

"But something stung me!" he shouted. "Something stung me over and over!"

"I don't *see* anything, sweetheart. Maybe you were just dreaming."

His eyes squinted and his lips curled upward as he began to cry.

"I'm sorry, baby, but I don't see anything."

He just continued to cry silently, tears trickling down his cheeks.

"Would you like me to sit here with you until you fall asleep again?"

He nodded silently.

"Okay. I promise I won't go away until I know you've gone back to sleep. Okay?"

Another nod.

Carmen looked over at Michael, who was sitting on the side of his bed, watching with concern.

"I'll stay here awhile," she whispered.

"Good," Michael said with a nod, slowly getting back into bed. " 'Cause, Mom? Whether you think so or not, there's something really weird about this house . . . and I'll get to sleep a lot easier if I know you're here."

Carmen smiled and nodded and whispered, "Okay, honey." But deep inside, Michael's words made her feel as cold as ice.

Carmen awoke suddenly at a little before five in the morning and was unable to go back to sleep. The house was quiet; nothing had happened to disturb her sleep.

She got up, put on her robe, went to the kitchen and made some tea. She went through her stack of magazines in the living room until she found the one Fran had given her. She opened it to the article on Ed and Lorraine Warren and read it carefully and slowly as she sipped her tea at the dining room table.

Later, a while before she knew everyone would start to get up, Carmen started a big breakfast. As usual, it wasn't long before the aroma of eggs, bacon, and coffee had wafted through the entire house and, one by one, sleepy-eyed and yawning, everyone followed their noses to the dining-room table.

But no one spoke. There were no "Good mornings," not even any sleepy, mumbled greetings. Even Peter, who was usually the most boisterous member of the family so early in the morning, was silent.

An invisible dark cloud grew over the table as everyone ate in silence. Tension built as forks and knives clanked against plates and jaws chewed behind tight lips.

Finally, Carmen put down her fork, swallowed her food and locked her hands together beneath her chin, elbows on the table's edge. She spent a moment running her tongue back and forth between her upper lip and front teeth, trying to buy some time. And then:

"You know, since last night, I've been thinking—"

"Yeah, I know, and I don't wanna hear it," Al said quietly without looking up from his plate.

"No, please, just give me a second, here." She cleared her throat. "I've been thinking that maybe, um, maybe we were a little quick to, you know, punish Stephen the way we did . . . to dismiss what he was saying about the house . . . about there being something, you know, something weird here."

"Yeah, that was it," Al said, his voice more stern, "*that* was what I didn't want to hear. And I don't wanna hear any *more* of it, understand? That's just plain bullshit. Stephen was sick, he *is* sick, and now he's being treated. He just spooked us with all his stories, is all."

"Then how do you explain those sounds last night?" Carmen asked.

"I don't know, but I'm gonna look into it. There's gotta be some explanation."

With her hands in her lap, staring down at her plate, Kelly said in a near-whisper, "I kept . . . feeling something . . . touch me . . . my legs and . . . and . . ." She suddenly sucked in a breath and closed her eyes a moment, then lifted her head and looked at them. "It was a hand. Touching me. Like a man would touch me, only . . . rough and . . . and angry."

"I saw something move through my room last night," Stephanie said while chewing a piece of bacon, speaking in that casual, offhand tone that only a child can use when talking about something so bizarre. "It was like . . . a shadow. A big shadow-blob. Didn't make any noise, just moved in through the wall and out through the door."

Al dropped his fork angrily onto his plate and stopped chewing, his eyes darting from one to the other of them at the table.

"Look, I'm not in the mood for this, okay?" he whispered unsteadily. "I can't wake up this morning, I feel like I've been drugged, so just . . . lay off, okay?" He picked up his fork again and continued to eat.

"So, that's why you wouldn't wake up last night, huh?" Carmen asked.

"What?"

"Last night, when Peter started screaming. I tried to wake you, but you wouldn't budge. He said he was being stung."

"It hurt, Dad!" Peter piped up. "Like bees! It was like bees was stingin' me all over!"

"You were dreaming!" Al barked, making Peter flinch and fall silent.

"I heard whispers in the room," Michael said timidly. "Voices whispering somewhere in the room."

He threw the fork down this time, pushing away from the table and slapping his napkin down beside his plate.

"Goddammit!" he snapped. "I'm going to work."

He left the room, said good-bye to no one and, in a little while, they heard the front door slam.

Eventually, everyone continued eating and, as they

did, Carmen said, very quietly, "Don't worry, kids. I believe you. And sooner or later, your father will, too."

Nothing happened again until that evening, as if whatever presence had taken up residence in the house only
came out in the later part of the day, when the daylight
was replaced by long, dark shadows and the moon was
making its way into the sky.

Dinner was over and Carmen was clearing the table,
where Al was still sitting, drinking a beer and reading
the paper.

Stephanie and Peter were watching television in the
living room and Michael was, as usual, in his room doing
homework.

Trish had gone to her aunt Vicki's to stay.

And Kelly was in the bathroom. She'd hung her robe
on the back of the door and was standing before the
mirror in her bra and panties brushing her hair slowly.

She could hear the sound of the television set and the
children's voices in the living room.

She heard Aunt Carmen's muffled voice from the dining room.

Then, as she ran the brush through her hair again and
again, she felt something tug on her bra strap from behind, as if someone were trying to snap the strap against
her back. But when she looked in the mirror, of course,
she saw no one behind her. She spun around, but she
was alone in the bathroom.

She didn't move for a moment, frowning and suddenly feeling very cold. Then she continued to brush her
hair.

A coarse hand slid between her legs and clutched her
inner thigh.

Kelly gasped and shouted, "Hey!" She spun around
and jerked herself away from the hand—or what *felt* like
a hand—but it stayed with her, groping, thick fingers

pressing upward against the material of her panties, clutching at the elastic around her upper thighs.

Another hand moved up over her stomach to her breasts, squeezing them roughly, painfully, then curling its fingers beneath Kelly's bra and pulling.

"Help, please, God, help!" Kelly screamed, throwing herself at the bathroom door. She turned the knob and pulled. It opened a few inches but, almost as if someone were pulling it hard from the other side, the knob slipped from her hands and the door slammed shut loudly.

"Aunt Carmen!" Kelly shrieked as her panties tore away from her, as her bra snapped and was flung to the floor. "Somebody, Uncle Al, please, *help me*!"

Al let the newspaper slip to the dining room table and put down his beer while Carmen dropped a casserole dish into the sink and both of them dashed toward the bathroom.

"What is it! What's the matter?" Al cried, hurrying down the hall.

Peter and Stephanie hurried in from the living room and Michael pounded up the stairs as Al tried the door. It wouldn't open.

"Kelly, you all right?" he asked. "Get away from the door and I'll—"

"I'm not by the door!" she screamed in a ragged, sobbing voice. "Help me, help me, please God, please help me!"

Al took a few steps back, then bounded forward, slamming his shoulder against the bathroom door with a heavy grunt. It did no good. But before he could do it a second time, the explosive pounding started again, rattling the windows and jittering the pictures on the walls. There were no pauses between them this time; they came again and again and again, deafening, so loud and deep that they could feel the sounds in their bones.

All the lights in the house began to flash off and on simultaneously.

"Mommy!" Peter screamed, pressing himself against Carmen and hugging her legs.

Stephanie joined them on Carmen's other side and cried, "What's happening?"

Michael simply huddled against the wall, eyes wide, fists clenched.

"I don't know what's happening, sweetheart," Carmen shouted, putting her arms around Stephanie and Peter, "but you'll be all right, I promise!"

Al threw himself against the door again. And again. But suddenly he screamed in pain, doubled over clutching his stomach and fell to the floor. Carmen dropped to her knees beside him with a gasp.

"What, Al, what's the matter?"

"I've been stabbed!" he said through clenched teeth, his voice raspy. "My God, I've been *stabbed*!"

Carmen reached for his hands and gently pulled them away from his stomach, expecting blood; or some sign of injury.

She saw nothing.

The thunderous pounding continued and the lights went on flashing and flashing.

In the bathroom, Kelly was still screaming.

"You're okay, Al," Carmen said, leaning close to him. "You haven't been stabbed. There's nothing there."

She felt him relax against her for a moment, then, moving cautiously, he got up, reached for the doorknob again, and—

Everything stopped.

The pounding silenced.

The lights went out, plunging them into shadowy darkness.

And the bathroom door slowly swung open.

"Oh, my God," Carmen breathed, hurrying into the bathroom.

Kelly was stretched out on the counter, naked, legs spread, one arm dangling over the counter's edge.

"Oh, God, Kelly, what happened?"

Kelly's shoulders quaked as she cried silently. "Hands," she whispered. "Hands . . . all over me . . . ripped off my underwear . . . th-they felt me . . ."

"Whose hands?"

Kelly shook her head. "I could only . . . feel them."

"I'm calling the police," Al said from the hall.

Carmen spun around, stepped out of the bathroom and hissed angrily, "The police? What are the police gonna do? Arrest somebody? A ghost, maybe? You still think there's some damned explanation for all of this Al? Cause if you do, you're the one who's crazy. We don't need the police here. We need a priest. And we're gonna get one."

There was one more tremendous, thunderous pound and then, a voice that seemed to ooze from every inch of the darkness around them declared in a guttural, raspy tone:

"There is no one who can help you. You are mine."

20

A Skeptical Blessing

Carmen called Father Hartwell first thing in the morning. She'd slept little, and although nothing more had happened for the rest of the night after the lights came back on, Carmen was just as jittery as if it had all happened just a few minutes ago. So it was difficult for her to give Father Hartwell a coherent explanation of the problem. She stuttered and stammered as she tried to make him understand that something supernatural, something evil, had invaded their house and that their son Stephen, now in a mental hospital for hearing voices and behaving so strangely, had tried to tell them that all along. But Hartwell could make little sense of it all.

It was very obvious to him, however, that *something* was wrong, even though he wasn't quite sure what it was yet. He promised her he'd be over the moment he could tear himself away, probably in an hour, two at the most.

Al went to work reluctantly; he didn't want to leave Carmen and Kelly and Peter alone. Carmen would rather he stay, too, but they both knew he couldn't afford to miss work.

Stephanie and Michael went out to meet the bus, both quiet and tense, and, until it came to get them, they

tood by the road looking back at the house again and
gain.

As Carmen waited for Father Hartwell to arrive, she
kept Peter close to her at all times. Kelly stayed close as
well. She didn't *want* to be alone.

They were sitting on the sofa with Peter kneeling before them and playing with his Merlin game when Carmen said quietly, "You know, if you'd like, Kelly, you
can go over to your aunt Vicki's with Trish."

Kelly frowned and shook her head slowly. "No, I
don't think so. I just don't feel as comfortable with Aunt
Vicki as I do with you and Uncle Al. Besides, I want to
help."

Carmen was surprised. "Even with . . . all this?"

"Well . . ." Kelly shrugged.

"I just want you to know that, if you decide that's
what you want to do, it's fine with us. Really, we'll understand. So will you let us know?"

She nodded. "Yeah. I'll let you know."

When Father Hartwell arrived, Carmen had the front
door open before he'd even come up the walk. She
ushered him into the living room anxiously and seated
him in Al's recliner, all the while whispering to him,
"Oh, I'm so glad you came, Father, you don't know how
badly we need you here, I'm *so* glad you came."

Once they were settled, Father Hartwell asked, "So,
exactly what is the problem?"

Carmen told him. She told him everything. It spilled
from her in a flood because she'd been holding it back
for so long. But, as she spoke, she saw the expression on
his face change gradually, and she knew what that
change meant: disbelief.

When she was finished, she waited, hoping for a positive response, but not really expecting one.

Father Hartwell, who had been leaning forward in the
recliner as he listened to her, settled back with a sigh and

his frown relaxed. Half his mouth turned up in a reluc
tant smile and he said softly, "Carmen, I'm going to say
the first thing that comes to my mind. Your entire family
has been through a great deal. Stephen's serious illness
as you yourself told me, put a great deal of strain on all
of you." He added quickly, "Please don't misunderstand
me, I'm not saying this is all a figment of your imagina
tion or anything like that, I think it's perfectly under
standable. Stress can do the most . . . well, the most
incredible things to people, and I'm saying this from ex
perience, both my own and the experience of my parish
ioners who have come to me as you have."

After seeing the changes in his face, in his eyes, Car
men was not surprised by his response. She was even
ready for it.

"All right, Father," she said, "if this is because of the
stress and strain brought on by Stephen's illness—and
I'm not saying it isn't, I'm just, um . . . I'm just . . ."
She closed her eyes and thought a moment about what
she'd just said. "Yes, I *am* saying it isn't, because I *know*
it isn't. What about Kelly? She wasn't around when Ste
phen was sick. She didn't feel any of that stress, none of
it. What about my neighbor, who doesn't even want to
be in my house? She was the one who called and said
there was a green woman glowing in the upstairs win
dow. We didn't see it, but she did! And she didn't expe
rience any of the stress and strain of Stephen's illness."

"But I suppose she knows about the history of the
house."

"Well . . . yes, but she doesn't—"

"That's very important. You see, Carmen, death is
something that frightens all of us. Even those of us who
know that it should not. This house used to be entirely
dedicated to . . . death," he shrugged. "It seems per
fectly natural that anyone who knows of its history

would be afraid of it because of what it used to stand for."

With a miserable sigh, Carmen leaned forward and buried her face in her hands. "You don't believe me," she mumbled into her palms.

After remaining silent the whole time, Kelly spoke up and said, "Father, I don't mean any disrespect, but . . . please listen. Aunt Carmen's not crazy. There's something going on in this house that doesn't have anything to do with stress or strain or Stephen's cancer. There's something . . . well, I don't mean to tell you your business, or anything, and, like I said, I don't mean to be disrespectful but . . . there's something *evil* and *sick* in this house. Something that means to harm us. So please, *please* Father, don't ignore it."

Father Hartwell leaned his head way back and rubbed a finger back and forth thoughtfully just beneath his lower lip as he stared at the ceiling. Then he sat forward, folded his hands between his knees and asked, "Would you feel better if I blessed the house?"

Carmen lifted her face from her hands, trying to hold back the tears that were fighting to fall, and said, "Oh, please, Father, would you?"

"Certainly." He stood. "That would be no problem at all. I'll just go out to the car and get my bag."

While he was gone, Carmen leaned back on the sofa and said, "He doesn't believe me. He thinks I'm crazy."

"But it really doesn't matter as long as he's gonna bless the house, right?" Kelly said. "I mean, that's *gotta* help. And maybe . . . well, just maybe he'll see something. Or hear something, or *feel* something."

Carmen just shook her head, eyes looking weary, as Father Hartwell came back inside. They remained on the sofa as he blessed the living room by sprinkling holy water from a bottle and reciting the blessing, their heads bowed reverently. They still remained there as he went through the entire house, blessing each room, one after another.

As the father's muffled voice droned on in other parts of the house, Kelly put her hand on Carmen's and whispered, "Don't worry, Aunt Carm, this is probably gonna change everything. Really." Timidly, she added, "You've gotta have faith in God, that's all."

Carmen knew she was right. For her to remain doubtful and afraid was an insult to God. She had to have faith that the blessing would make a difference, that it would end the strange incidents that had plagued them.

But she could not stop thinking about Father Hartwell's obvious disbelief. If he were just going through with the blessing to patronize her, if he didn't really *mean* it, would that make a difference?

When Father Hartwell was finished, he returned to the living room and smiled at them. "Well, I'm finished. I hope it helps."

You hope *it helps*? Carmen thought. Her fear was realized: He'd done it just to appease her.

Father Hartwell held up a hand. "But if I might make a suggestion: You should consider some sort of counseling. I mean, all of you, your whole family. You've been through a great deal." He gave them a smile that was meant to appear comforting. "I think you might benefit from it."

Kelly squeezed Carmen's hand and looked away from the priest; Carmen bowed her head, hoping Father Hartwell wouldn't see the doubt in her eyes.

After the priest had left, Kelly said, "He didn't sound too believing, did he?"

Carmen shook her head.

"Yeah, well, he's a priest, right? So maybe it'll help anyway, y'know?"

Carmen didn't respond for a little while, then, almost imperceptibly, she shook her head very slowly. After see-

ng the doubt in Father Hartwell's eyes, the look of disbelief on his face, she suddenly realized how Stephen
must have felt—how *they* must have *made* him feel—the
whole time he was trying to tell them there was something wrong with the house.

21

Physical Attacks

The morning Father Hartwell was supposed to come Carmen had been too nervous to do the breakfast dishes and, instead, had stacked them neatly in the sink after giving them a cursory rinsing. After he left, she changed into a baggy shirt and jeans, went into the kitchen, and began to wash the dishes. Kelly had offered to help, but Carmen had said, "No, no, you stay here and watch TV or something." She wanted to be alone for a while; she wanted to think about the things she'd done and said to Stephen—the things they'd *all* done and said to him.

She was standing at the sink washing the dishes when she felt a pinch on her behind. She chuckled and, still holding a plate in her wet, soapy hand, turned around saying, "Stop it, Peter," as she looked down, expecting to see him. He wasn't there.

She stared at the empty space on the floor for a moment, then felt another pinch.

There was a third pinch and then she felt fingers—she *knew* they were fingers because she'd felt Al do the same thing before, but playfully—slide between her legs and press upward.

The plate she held slipped from her hand and shattered against the edge of the sink.

Kelly hurried into the kitchen, saying, "Aunt Carm! What's wrong?"

"I-I . . . uh, well it was—"

The hand pushed between her legs again and probed with strong fingers. Carmen grunted and jumped forward to get away from it.

"It's after *you* now, isn't it?" Kelly gasped. "Like it was after *me* last night."

"Just go back in the living room, Kelly. Please."

She hesitated a moment, then did as she was told, looking over her shoulder, concerned.

With suds still on her wet hands almost up to her elbows, Carmen left the kitchen and hurried down the hall to her bedroom, where she slammed the door hard and locked it, then leaned her back against it for a moment, trying to catch her breath.

Her heart pounded in her chest.

The back of her neck felt cold.

And even as she leaned back against the door, she felt the alien touch again.

Carmen threw herself forward with a muffled cry, not wanting Kelly to hear her, and landed on the bed, but the hand moved with her, holding on all the while, fat fingers groping.

She struggled to sit up, but suddenly there were more hands on her body, pressing her arms, shoulders, and legs to the mattress as one of the fingers entered her, entered her hard and roughly.

Carmen could not hold back her cry of pain. But it didn't end there.

Something longer and fatter than the finger, something that even throbbed, shoved itself into her rectum.

Carmen's entire body stiffened.

The thing moved in and out furiously, ripping at her.

"Oh, please," Carmen gasped.

There was a knock at the door. "Aunt Carmen? You okay?"

"Please Jesus! In the name of Jesus! *Stop*! In the name of Jesus!"

The bedroom door opened and suddenly, everything stopped. The hands let go, the fat, throbbing thing pulled out of her, and Carmen was left on the bed, shaking uncontrollably, sobbing.

Kelly hunkered down beside her and put an arm around her shoulders, asking, "Aunt Carmen, what's wrong, what happened?"

Carmen could not speak. She could not give Kelly an explanation. She simply shook her head as she tried to catch her breath and regain her ability to speak.

"I-I-I . . . don't know, Kelly, something attacked me. Something . . ." Her lips pursed and her hands clutched the pillow as she tried to find the right word. "Something, um . . . hurt me!" she hissed, her voice quivering with disbelief as she spoke.

When Kelly spoke, she sounded near tears: "Oh, God, I knew it, I *knew* that's what it was, oh God, it's still here, the blessing didn't help, oh God, Aunt Carm, what're we gonna do?"

Carmen realized that, more than anything at that moment, she wanted off that bed, and she pushed herself away from the mattress quickly. In an instant, she was standing beside Kelly.

"Well, for a little while anyway," Carmen said, "we're gonna get the hell out of here, you, me, and Peter. But first, um . . . I'd like to take a shower."

Carmen felt filthy—*vile*. It was a relief when she stepped beneath the hot water. She covered her body with soap lather and scrubbed herself hard with a washcloth, hoping to scrub away the dirty feeling of violation.

After scrubbing for several minutes, crying quietly, she

stepped forward to rinse off under the spray, but the shower curtain moved and, although she saw no one there, she knew she was no longer alone.

A foreign sound suddenly meshed with the hiss of the shower, meshed and then, after a moment, separated and formed words in a voice that was deep, rough and resonant:

"I wanna roll in bed with my two favorite playthings . . . you and Kelly. I wanna *fuck* you. I wanna fuck you until you *screeeaam*!"

Then the voice laughed a long, cruel laugh, and the attack began.

Hands clutched her shoulders from behind, spun her around and slammed her hard against the wet tile. She started to cry out, but her lips were smashed against the wall. The laughter continued as something slammed into her hard . . . pulled out . . . slammed in again . . . and again and again and again . . .

Hands squeezed her breasts hard, pinched her nipples until pain shot through her chest, up her neck and down her abdomen.

And yet there was no one there . . .

Carmen pulled her face away from the tile, sucked in a deep breath, along with the moist and humid spray of shower, and screamed as loud as she could.

But it continued: the pounding inside her, the painful crushing and pinching of her breasts . . .

Then the bathroom door opened and Kelly screamed, "Aunt Carmen I'm here what is it what's wrong what is it?"

It stopped.

Carmen found herself leaning against the wall, her body covered with lather that began to run down to the floor of the tub with the shower's spray. She pushed away from the wall, her hands slipping over the tile, turned and pulled away the curtain.

"It was here," she gasped, her voice hoarse. "It . . . it attacked me again, it sod—it did the same thing to me again."

Her tears were washed away by the shower and she folded her arms over her breasts as she sobbed.

"Just get out of there!" Kelly cried. "Please, just get out of there so we can leave!"

Carmen nodded. "I am. I will. I'll be out in a minute. Go get Peter for me, okay? Make sure he's all right."

She rinsed quickly, left the shower and began to dry off furiously, not caring about whether her hair was dry or not. With Kelly and Peter at her side, she dressed fast, gathered up a couple of Peter's toys and they left, with no idea where they were going. . . .

They drove around town for a while, then went to a nearby shopping mall, where they had ice cream, let Peter ride a small mechanical spaceship for a quarter, and did some window-shopping. They kept moving, kept their attention diverted, and did not think about what had happened at the house.

After a few hours of trying to lose themselves in the safe and anonymous crowd of shoppers, Carmen realized how late it was and decided that, as much as she dreaded returning to the house, she had to get back so Stephanie and Michael wouldn't come home from school to an empty house—or at least one that *appeared* empty.

They did some quick grocery shopping for dinner, then headed home.

When they got to the house, they climbed the porch and stood at the door . . . staring. With nervous clumsiness, Carmen took the keys from her purse, found the right one, slowly slipped it into the lock, turned it, and they entered.

There was nothing out of place. There was nothing unusual waiting for them.

Clutching a bag of groceries in one arm, Carmen turned to Kelly and said, "Whatta you say we just go ahead and start dinner, take our time, have some fun, and forget about everything?"

Kelly's eyes were wide as she looked around, taking cautious steps along the hall. She nodded her head and said, "Yeah. Okay."

And so they did. They unloaded the groceries in the kitchen and started dinner.

Stephanie got home first. They told her nothing, just kept her in sight.

When Michael came home, he asked if he could go to a friend's house down the road until dinner and Carmen gave him an enthusiastic yes; she was relieved to have him out of the house.

By the time Al came home, dinner was nearly done and nothing had happened. Carmen gave him a kiss when he came in and headed for the shower.

She felt guilty, just as guilty as if she'd been unfaithful to him. She felt she needed to tell him about what had happened, but how? What could she say? What would *he* say? Maybe he'd think she was crazy—like Stephen— and get angry and not want to get near her.

He might even leave her. After all, if he thought it was just her imagination, if he thought she was *imagining* such things—things like that—maybe he would think there was something wrong between them.

She decided she wouldn't tell him; at least, she would resist the urge to tell him as long as possible.

Dinner was quiet. There was little talk, just a lot of dinner noises: forks clanking against plates, chewing, drinking.

When it was over, Carmen and Kelly washed the dishes, whispering to one another about whether Carmen should tell Al or not, about what they were going to do.

Kelly suggested she tell him, because it was only inevitable that something would happen to him, too. What then? She insisted that he should know.

As much as Carmen didn't want to admit it, she thought Kelly was right.

After dinner, Al settled in his chair with a beer to watch television. When the dishes were done, Carmen went to him, hunkered down beside the chair and put a hand on his arm.

"Can we talk?" she asked quietly.

"Sure," he said, nodding.

"Um . . . in the bedroom?"

He frowned slightly. "You okay?"

"Well . . . let's talk first, all right?"

They went into the bedroom, sat on the edge of the bed and Carmen told him, in a nervous and halting voice, everything that had happened that day.

The expression on his face changed again and again as she spoke. It went from comical disbelief to serious consideration to anger and then to blank shock.

"You're serious, aren't you," he whispered after a while.

"Yes I'm serious. You think I would joke about something like this?"

"I . . . I don't know, I'm wondering . . . well, how long has this been going on?"

"It just happened today. Why? I mean, why would you ask a question like that?"

"Well, I just wondered if . . . I mean, I just thought that maybe . . ."

Suddenly, Al burst into tears and buried his face in his hands, his shoulders shaking with his sobs.

Carmen was shocked. She just stared at him for a moment, then leaned forward, put an arm around his shoulders and held him close.

"Al, what's wrong? What's the matter?"

Through his tears and sobs he said, "I-I was afraid to tell you that . . . th-things have been happening to me, too."

She clutched his shoulders. "What things?"

"Oh, j-just . . . music and voices and . . . just *things*! I've been telling myself it's nothing. I didn't want to think that . . . that . . . One night after I'd taken all the light bulbs out of their sockets downstairs, Michael woke me up and said his light was on even though there was no bulb in the socket and . . . well, I went downstairs and it was . . . *glowing*, Carmen, the light was *on*, but there was no bulb! There was nothing except . . . except *light* coming from that thing!"

"Why didn't you *tell* me, honey?"

"Because I didn't want to tell *myself* that I saw it. But there was . . . more. Music, coming from downstairs. Voices. Like a party. Late at night. And the bed . . . vibrating."

"You told me that was because of the refrigerator upstairs."

"I was lying. I just didn't want you to know. I knew better. It was vibrating. It wasn't from upstairs. There is, um . . . yes, there is something wrong. There's something wrong with this house, there's something *in* this house."

She waited a long moment, then leaned close to him, her arm around his shoulders, and whispered into his ear, "Stephen tried to tell us that and now . . . he's in a mental hospital."

Al shook his head. "No, no, I think it was more than that with Stephen. I really think there was something wrong with him. He changed. He became . . . *hostile*. It was something more than this, I really think that."

"Okay, maybe. But he *was* trying to tell us about the house."

He sucked his lips between his teeth and said through

more tears, "You don't think I know that? You don't think that's killing me?"

She nodded. "We both know it now. So what're we gonna do?"

"We can't afford to move, that's for sure. Not right now, anyway."

"Okay, so what're we gonna do?"

He shook his head, tears glistening on his cheeks. "I don't know, sweetheart. I just don't know."

22

A Prison Without Bars

As that winter passed, slowly and torturously, the events in the Snedeker household escalated and tensions increased. The mood inside the house seemed to grow darker along with the weather outside; it grew increasingly worse as the clouds darkened and it began to rain, worse still as snow began to fall and turn to thick, icy mud beside the roads.

Everyone in the family moved through the house expecting something horrible to happen; more often than not, they weren't disappointed. Things moved of their own volition. Everyone, at one time or another, heard voices. They saw shadows that weren't there. They spotted things rushing by them from the corners of their eyes. Small sections of the house were inexplicably colder than others.

Stephanie had moved back into her room with Kelly, and Peter had moved back into his room as well. So Michael was left alone in his room downstairs.

Very late one night, he came running up the stairs screaming for his parents. They awoke instantly and rushed into the hall, where they found him running toward them, arms spread and eyes round.

"Mom! Mom, he came back!" Michael shouted, throwing his arms around Carmen's waist.

"Sh-sh-sh, Michael, who came back?" she asked, holding him.

"That guy, that guy Stephen and me saw! He came to me tonight!"

"Oh, it was just a dream, sweetheart, that's all, just a dream."

Michael backed away from her, shaking his head, and insisted, "No, no, it wasn't just a dream, it was *more*. I mean, I was still in bed, but I was awake! And I couldn't move, I was *paralyzed*!"

Carmen and Al exchanged a long look and Al gave her a slight, but helpless, shrug.

"Would you like to sleep somewhere else tonight, honey?" Carmen asked Michael.

After a moment, he nodded. "Can I sleep on the couch?" he asked quietly.

"Sure you can. I'll get blankets and pillows from the hall closet." She turned to Al and whispered, "You go on back to bed, I'll be there in a minute."

Once she'd set up a bed for Michael in the living room, Carmen tucked him in and gave him a kiss.

"Mom? If he comes again . . . can I call you?"

"Sure you can, sweetheart. You just call and I'll be here."

Back in bed, Al stared up into the darkness as he whispered, "This is gonna keep up . . . and get worse, isn't it?"

"I don't know," she whispered back.

"What're we gonna do if it does?"

"I don't know."

He reached over and took her hand in his. It took them quite a while to get back to sleep.

* * *

After that night, Michael began sleeping on the living-room sofa regularly. Unlike Stephen, he heard no protests from his parents and no one in the house complained; in fact, they were very cooperative. One morning, while he was getting ready for school, Carmen offered to bring a few things up from his room and put them in the hall closet so he wouldn't have to go downstairs. He accepted her offer eagerly and told her what to get for him.

She waited until early that afternoon to go downstairs. Somehow, she just kept remembering there were other things to do around the house. It took a few hours for her to admit to herself that she just didn't want to go downstairs. She knew what was down there . . . funeral things . . . burial things . . . death things . . . things she didn't want to be near.

Besides that, many of the frightening events that had happened in the house had happened down there, things that Stephen had tried to tell them about, things they had ignored.

But she had promised. And *someone* had to go downstairs.

Finally, she did. She told herself she didn't have to go any farther than Michael's room, that all the really bad stuff was deeper in the basement and that she really didn't have anything to worry about.

But when she went downstairs, something happened to her for the first time; it was something that would happen to her again and again throughout the coming months.

When it happened, she was taking socks and underwear from the floor to be washed, clothes from the backs of chairs and from the closet for Michael to wear to school, and clean socks and underwear from dresser drawers.

Suddenly, she froze. There was a feeling in the air, as

if it were shifting, being stirred up . . . as if something were cutting through it rapidly, approaching fast.

Standing before Michael's dresser with socks and underwear in her hands, Carmen gasped as something enveloped her, something like a very dark shadow as thick as pudding; it engulfed her, swallowed her, embraced her entire body and held her in paralyzed terror for what seemed an eternity.

And then it was gone, and Carmen collapsed to the floor, curled into a fetal position and gasping for breath. When she had finally collected herself, she looked at the clock.

It had only been seconds . . . not an eternity.

She got up, gathered Michael's things quickly and hurried upstairs, still a little stooped and gasping.

"Aunt Carmen, what's the matter?" Kelly asked, rushing toward her in the hall.

In an instant, Carmen decided not to tell her. She straightened up, smiled a little and said, "Oh, I guess it's just those stairs. I haven't used them enough, I suppose, 'cause they wear me out."

"Oh. Jeez, you scared me."

"No, nothing . . . nothing."

As she caught her breath, she put Michael's things in the hall closet, relieved that Kelly had not caught her in the lie.

Over the next few days, Stephanie cried out twice in the night because she said the "shadow-blob" had moved through her room again. Kelly had been asleep at the time and had not seen it but, after the second time, Stephanie said she did not want to sleep in her room anymore.

Carmen didn't know what to do with her. She asked Kelly if she'd mind sharing a bed with Stephanie to make her feel better, and Kelly said that would be fine.

Al became more and more uncomfortable with going to work and leaving them alone, but he had no choice. He'd been feeling very weak and helpless lately. He was used to having at least *some* control over the events that surrounded his family. When Stephen became so ill, that confidence began to chip away. And now . . . this. He felt that everything around him—his entire household— was out of his hands. Something he couldn't see and did not understand had taken control.

Their home had become a sort of prison. They didn't have enough money to move at the moment. They couldn't just pick up everything and go get another place. They would be there for a while . . . with whatever was there with them.

The weeks passed and turned into months: long, slow months that stretched out beneath heavy clouds black as soot. The winter grew colder, more bitter.

The children cried out at night.

Voices spoke to all of them at times—from nowhere— at all hours of the day and night.

Sometimes the smell of rotting meat, at other times the smell of human feces, assaulted them in one part of the house or another, a smell so thick and eye-watering that they were certain that, should they look down at their feet, they would find themselves standing in a pile of rotten, decaying filth. But there was never anything on the floor around them and the smell only lasted an instant, a sickening stench wafting by in a breath, there and gone, almost tauntingly.

But there were, at times, flies. Real flies that were really there—or at least seemed to be—but never for very long.

One cold winter evening, a fuse blew and Al went downstairs into the basement to fix it. He had long since replaced the lightbulbs in all the sockets and, when he reached the bottom of the stairs, he turned on a light.

When he flicked the switch, the opaque glass globe covering the fixture remained black, giving out mere speckles of the light from the bulb. As Al frowned up at the light, the blackness that seemed to be smeared over the glass moved . . . squirmed . . .

As he listened in the silence, he could hear a faint hum coming from the blackness, a thing buzzing.

The blackness was made up of flies—hundreds, maybe even thousands of flies crawling over the globe and twitching in a pool around it on the ceiling, their wings humming as they crawled over one another in black, writhing heaps.

Al stared at them for a long moment, his jaw slack, eyes opening slowly from a squint to wide, gaping amazement, frozen in place, his finger still on the light switch.

His voice a mere breath, he whispered slowly, "Where . . . in the hell . . . did *you* come fr—"

All at once, the flies became airborne and flew in a swarm toward Al's face.

Al threw his arms up protectively and let out a strangled cry of horror through clenched teeth, closing his eyes tightly, so surprised that he was unable to turn and run back up the stairs. He expected to feel them over him, feel the small vibration of their wings, the tickling-twitching of their movements, but . . .

He felt nothing.

Slowly, very slowly, he lowered his arms and opened his eyes.

The flies were gone. They were nowhere in sight. He couldn't see them, and he couldn't hear them.

There was a noise then, deep and throaty, sounding at first like a groan, then becoming a low, evil chuckle. It came from nowhere . . . but from everywhere around him.

Al took a long, deep breath, set his jaw, crossed himself and—although it took some silent, internal fighting —he ignored what he'd thought he'd heard, opened the French doors and went into the next room, flipping on lights on his way to the fusebox. But he stopped a moment to take a careful look at the light overhead.

There were no flies this time.

He wound his way through the basement to the fusebox, opened it up and reached into his pocket for the fuse he'd brought from the kitchen drawer.

That was when the smell hit him.

First, it smelled like roses, a strong, sweet, flowery odor. Al froze, looked around slowly and allowed himself a slight smile. It was a good sign, the smell of roses; it was a sign of blessing, a sign of peace and safety . . . a sign from the Virgin Mary herself.

Al's nerves calmed, the tensed muscles in his body relaxed slowly. The scent of roses had made him feel much better. In fact, he could still smell it as he replaced the fuse.

And then, quite suddenly, the smell changed. For the worse.

Al recoiled as the air filled with the odor of spoiled meat. He slapped a hand over his nose and mouth as he leaned over to retch dryly. Coughing as he stood, he slammed the fusebox shut, turned and hurried back through the basement.

The odor was everywhere.

As he moved through it, the smell changed. It went from rotten meat to the smell of a vast open sewer—the smell of massive, uncontained shit. The odor filled his nostrils and clung there, clogged them like thick grease.

Al hurried through the basement, his hand over his face, but in the middle of the room that used to be Stephen's, he weakened and dropped to his knees; the thick, cloying smell was overpowering and literally pushed him to the floor, shedding tears and gagging.

He walked on his knees for several feet, trying to get to the stairs, but in a moment the smell was gone.

Still on his knees, Al froze. He removed his hand from his face slowly, lifted his head, looked around, sniffed the air.

It was gone.

Moving quickly, he stood, hurried to the stairs and, in a rush, left the basement.

The winter gradually began to recede. The snow began to melt and occasionally, patches of blue sky appeared between the dark clouds.

Al began to drink even more than usual. As the frightening events that took place in the house steadily grew worse, he felt weaker and more out of control, more helpless against . . . whatever it was that had decided to target them.

Carmen, on the other hand, held fast to her faith. She prayed more, she always kept her rosary with her, she wore a crucifix around her neck at all times. She refused to let the fact that Father Hartwell's blessing of the house apparently did no good whatsoever to sway her faith; she told herself that didn't matter and just kept praying, kept asking God to be with her family, to watch over her house and her family, to protect them from whatever evil, supernatural force was plaguing them.

Sometimes they had conversations late at night in bed.

"You're drinking a lot," Carmen whispered one night as the two of them cuddled together.

"Whatta you expect?" Al whispered back.

"Well, is it necessary?"

"Whatta you think? I mean, maybe that doesn't excuse it, but good Lord, I've been . . . I-I've been—"

"Okay. Yeah, I know, honey, things have been, uh . . ."

"Things have been fuckin' *scary*, is what they've been."

"But remember, we still have God on our side."

"So, where is He?"

"He's here, sweetheart. If He wasn't, maybe we would have been hurt. Maybe *we* wouldn't be here."

Al pulled away from her and said, "Yeah, I know, but . . ."

It was on a summer evening that Kelly went out on a date with a pleasant, tall, muscular young man who arrived to pick her up while Carmen was preparing dinner. Al invited him in and they chatted for a few minutes until Kelly was ready to go.

Michael had gone down the street to a friend's house for the night, and Stephanie and Peter were quietly occupying themselves on the living-room floor; none of the children spent time alone in their rooms anymore.

They ate dinner in silence, as they had been doing every night for some time, and they ate it in the living room before the television. In spite of the silence, though, the tension was not as thick as it had been lately. There was more of a feeling of calm in the house, as if things might be all right . . . at least, for the time being.

After dinner, they watched some more television, Al had a few more beers, Carmen sipped a cup of tea, and eventually everyone started heading for bed. The children were reluctant and Carmen kept waiting for them to ask if they could sleep with her and Al; she decided that if they did, she and Al couldn't very well say no because now they *knew* the kids had good reason to be afraid.

But they didn't ask. Peter was very sleepy, and shuffled, droopy-eyed, to his room. Stephanie asked if it was all right if she stayed awake in her room until Kelly got home. Carmen told her that would be fine. After all, it was Friday night and she didn't have to go to school the next day.

Al went to bed first and, after she'd given the kids their goodnight kisses, Carmen joined him.

"Is it just me, or do things seem better tonight?" she asked.

"Yeah. Maybe. A little. I guess." He was very reluctant to be too optimistic.

They cuddled beneath the covers, unable to sleep for a while because they were waiting for—actually expecting —something to happen. But their room remained quiet and calm and, eventually, the two of them dozed into a light sleep. . . .

Carmen awoke to a scream late in the night. It took a moment for her to understand what the screaming voice was saying.

"Aunt Carmen! Aunt Carmen please help me, my God, dear Jesus, please, please *help* me!"

Running footsteps thumped through the house.

Instinctively, Carmen reached over to her nightstand and grabbed her Bible, on top of which lay her rosary.

The bedroom door burst open and Carmen sat up. Kelly stood slightly silhouetted in the doorway wearing her usual long nightshirt.

"Aunt Carmen!" she cried. "*Aunt Carmen!*"

Carmen got out of bed, Bible and rosary tucked beneath her arm, and headed for the door, saying, "Kelly, what's wrong, honey, what's the matter?"

Al did not wake up.

Kelly threw her arms around Carmen's neck, much the same way she used to when she was just a small child and, while they were embracing, Carmen led her into the hall and pulled the bedroom door closed gently.

"What's wrong, honey?" she whispered.

"It's playing with me again, Aunt Carm, it's doing it *again!*" she hissed, pressing her face into Carmen's shoulder. "It was picking at my bra before I got undressed and then I reached for my rosary and the cross came off

—just came off—like it was *pulled* off—and then it started pulling at my blankets and touching me and, and, a-and—"

Carmen put her arm around Kelly and began to lead her down the hall, saying, "Okay, okay, just calm down, it's all right now. We'll go to your room and we'll, um . . . whatta you say we read the Bible together for a while?"

And that was what they did. Kelly curled up beneath the covers and Carmen sat on the side of the bed. By the light of the bedside lamp, with Stephanie still sound asleep on the cot a few feet away, Carmen began to read quietly from Psalms, hoping to soothe Kelly's fears.

It seemed to work for a little while. The room was quiet, the only sound being Carmen's soft, half-whispered voice as she read.

" 'Remember the word unto thy servant, upon which thou hast caused me to hope,' " she read. " 'This is my comfort in my affliction, for thy word hath quickened me.' "

Kelly's breath began to come slowly, rhythmically, her eyes were closed and her body relaxed.

Then she sat up suddenly, tossing away the covers, eyes wide, her body trembling, her lips quivering as she gasped, "Do you feel it? *Feel* it, Aunt Carm, it's coming, it's coming right now!"

Carmen stopped midsentence, her words stuck in her throat like chunks of glass, because she suddenly felt swollen with fear. For a long moment she couldn't breathe, as if all the oxygen were somehow being sucked out of the room by . . . *something*, and the air grew cold, and there was, without a doubt, a new presence in the room with them.

"It's here!" Kelly breathed. "My God, dear Jesus, it's *here*!"

Carmen looked around the room and reached for her

rosary, clutching it in her fist, her Bible closing between
her legs as she recited rapidly, "Our Father who art in
heaven hallowed be thy name"— Her voice grew louder
as she began to feel more and more suffocated, as if she
were being smothered by some invisible force—"thy
kingdom come thy will be done on earth as it is in
heaven give us this day our daily bread and forgive us
our trespasses as we forgive those who trespass against
us—" Her voice rose to a shout as the atmosphere in the
room became even more oppressive and the air filled
with the stench of untended garbage. "—and lead us not
into temptation but deliver us from evil amen Lord,
amen Jesus, please, God, *take it away*!"

Kelly heaved a sigh and tried to catch her breath as
she panted, "It's gone. It's gone, Aunt Carmen. It went
away."

Immediately, Carmen opened the Bible again, searching for Psalms. When she found it, she began to read in
a trembling voice, " 'Rejoice in the Lord, O ye righteous,
for praise is comely for the upright. Praise the Lord with
the harp, sing unto him with—"

"Do you feel that?" Kelly interrupted, sitting up
again, her voice more frantic than before. She threw herself at Carmen, wrapping her arms around her shoulders.

Suddenly, from the cot beside the bed, a small, shrill
and frightened voice cried, "Mommy! *Whatsamatter?*"

Carmen started to respond, but her breath was suddenly taken from her and she was pushed back on the
bed as something wet and slimy—but absolutely invisible
—brushed past her arm. She propped herself up on one
arm and watched as that invisible something slithered
beneath Kelly's nightshirt and then quite visibly clutched
at and fondled her breasts.

The bedside lamp, which was the room's only source

of light, began to flicker tenuously, threatening to black out.

"Oh God," Carmen groaned as Stephanie began to scream. Carmen immediately began to recite the Our Father again, this time very loudly. "Our Father who art in heaven! Hallowed be thy name!"

Kelly began to scream, "Oh Jesus, oh God!" as the thing began to move back and forth beneath her nightshirt, painfully squeezing her right breast, then her left, then her right, over and over again.

"Thy kingdom come! Thy will be done!"

Stephanie left the cot and huddled beside the bed, embracing Carmen's legs and still screaming.

"On earth! As it is in heaven!"

Kelly began to writhe on the bed as she screamed, slapping at the lumpy shape that continued to move beneath her nightshirt, in turn brutally squeezing her breasts and thrusting itself between her legs.

"Give us this day our d-daily br-br—" The rosary slipped from Carmen's hand and she choked on her words, slapping her hands over her mouth as she watched what was happening to her niece, helpless.

Stephanie began to sing in a ragged, tearful voice: "Jesus loves me, this I know . . . for the Bible tells me so . . . lit-tull ones to Him be-long . . . they are weak but He is strong—"

After setting her Bible aside, Carmen reached down with one hand and patted Stephanie's back, saying quietly, "Please calm down, honey, please, sweetheart, just calm down." With the other hand, she groped for her rosary and, when she found it, she began to recite the Hail Mary very rapidly as she slowly pulled her legs away from Stephanie and began to make her way to the door.

"Hail Mary full of grace the Lord is with thee blessed art thou amongst women and blessed is the fruit of thy womb Jesus Holy Mary Mother of God pray for us·sinners now and at the hour of our death amen, Haïl Mary full of grace the Lord is with thee blessed art—"

Before she got very far the second time, Stephanie began to cry, "Don't leave, please, Mommy, *don't leave*!"

Carmen stopped and said quickly, "Honey, I have to go call Father Hartwell, we need him right now, we *need* him, so please—"

The bedroom door opened and Al stood in the doorway wearing his robe, his eyes wide, mouth open, and he asked breathlessly, "What the hell's happening?" But it took only an instant for him to *see* what was happening. "Oh God," he breathed, "oh God oh Jesus what's happening, dear Jesus what's happening. . . ."

"Go get me the phone!" Carmen said urgently.

He was back in a moment with the cordless telephone and handed it to Carmen, keeping his distance from the bed, where Kelly was still under attack by the invisible arm that writhed and groped and clutched beneath her nightshirt.

With a trembling finger, Carmen punched in Father Hartwell's number. She hadn't even looked at a clock but knew it was late and assumed he'd be asleep.

He was. His voice was thick and groggy when he answered, "H'lo?"

"Father Hartwell?"

"Mm-hm. Yeah, that's me."

"This is Carmen Snedeker, Father, and we—well, there's something happening here th-that, um—"

"What's wrong, Carmen?" he asked.

She told him. The words spilled out of her in a rush as she explained what had been happening, what was happening at that moment, and she told him they needed his help desperately.

She waited for a long moment as silence came over the line. Then, Father Hartwell cleared his voice and said sleepily, "Well, Carmen, tell you what. You sit down with Kelly and do the Rosary with her. Do it over and over if you have to until she's calmed down and forgotten all this and can go to sleep."

Then he hung up.

Carmen kept the phone to her ear for a moment, her jaw slack with disbelief. Then she tossed it to the floor and leaned toward Kelly, holding her rosary tightly.

"Sweetheart, it's gonna be all right," she said loudly. "It'll be all right, Kelly." And then she began to do the Rosary as Father Hartwell had told her.

Until something tried to pull the rosary from her hands.

She stopped and stared at the string of beads which was taut, as if someone else was trying to pull it from her.

It won.

The rosary broke and beads scattered in every direction over the rug and over the wood floor, clicking against the wood and the walls.

Carmen stared at the mass of beads as they rolled over the floor.

"Hail Mary, full of grace," she began, her voice hoarse, "the Lord is with thee."

The thing beneath Kelly's nightshirt began to retreat.

"Blessed art thou amongst women, and blessed is the fruit of thy womb, Jesus."

It slithered out from under the shirt and disappeared.

"Holy Mary, Mother of God, pray for us sinners, now and at the hour of our death."

The smell of rotten garbage was gone.

Kelly stopped screaming, stopped squirming on the bed. She was still for a long while—everyone was—then she sat up slowly.

"Aunt Carmen," she rasped, "do we have to stay in here?"

"No, honey. No, we don't."

A bit later, Al and Kelly were seated at the dining-room table sipping tea that Carmen had made while Stephanie had a mug of hot cocoa.

Carmen went into the living room, turned on a light, and searched for the magazine she'd gotten from Fran. When she found it, she thumbed through the pages until she found the article about Ed and Lorraine Warren. Skimming through it, she found out where they lived—in Monroe—grabbed a pad and pencil and used the living-room telephone to call information.

Their number was listed and she wrote it down.

Then she returned to the dining room with the magazine and showed the article to Al. After he'd looked it over carefully, she said, "If our own priest isn't going to help us, we're going to have to go to *somebody*."

After frowning at the magazine for a while, Al asked, "How much do they charge?"

"I don't know."

"How do we know we can trust them? I mean it's a pretty weird thing to do with your lives, hunting down ghosts and demons."

"We'll just have to find out, won't we?"

A long moment passed, then he began to nod and said, "Okay, go ahead and call them."

Hands shaking nervously, Carmen hurried back into the living room and called the Warrens.

After a few rings, a very groggy woman answered. "H'lo?"

"Is this Lorraine Warren?"

"Mm-hm, it is. Who's calling, please?"

"Um, my name is Carmen Snedeker, and I read about you and your husband in a magazine, and I think my family needs your help because—" Suddenly, Carmen's words spilled out in a desperate rush as she explained to Mrs. Warren what had happened in their house that night and what had been happening for so many months. She even began to sob as she spoke, unable to hold back the tears.

"Sweetheart, sweetheart," Lorraine Warren said, sounding more awake now, "calm down and listen to me. I can't understand what you're saying, okay, hon? Just calm down a little."

Carmen tried, took a few deep breaths and went through some of it again. Lorraine listened silently, then, when Carmen was done, said, "Okay, honey, here's what you do. If this starts happening again tonight, have your husband hold up a cross or a rosary, whichever, and you say—shout it at the top of your lungs, if you want—'In the name of Jesus Christ, I command you to leave this place *now* and go back to the place from which you've come!' Do you understand that?"

Carmen nodded absent-mindedly, then realized what she was doing and said, "Yes, yes, I understand."

"But listen, that's only for tonight, okay? You do that tonight, keep doing the Rosary, *all* of that. Then, around nine in the morning, you give us a call. We'll come on over, okay?"

"Okay. I'll call you."

"You try to get some sleep, okay? If you have evil spirits in your home, you need to know they thrive on weakness. Not sleeping makes you weak, and they'll use that, believe me. And I'll say a prayer for you tonight."

"Yeah, okay. Th-thank you."

"God be with you, honey. Bye-bye."

Carmen hung up the telephone slowly and stared at it for a long while afterward. Nine o'clock tomorrow morning could not possibly come quickly enough. . . .

23

The Investigation Begins

The next morning, while everyone else tried to catch a little more sleep—except for Al, who had already awakened and called in sick for the day—Carmen paced by the telephone from eight until nine, when she promptly called the Warrens' number again.

Lorraine was much more alert this time, and Ed got on the other extension.

Carmen went back over the things she'd told Lorraine during the predawn hours, but she did so more quietly and calmly than before. When she was done, she asked, a bit too eagerly, "Do you think this could be happening because of . . . well, because maybe someone died here?"

Ed replied, "Well, from what you've said, it sounds very unlikely. No, doesn't sound like that kind of situation at all. But we'll have to look into it ourselves before we can know."

"Why do you ask, dear?" Lorraine wondered.

"Well . . . there's something about the house that, um, I didn't tell you before. It's a, um . . . see, it used to be a funeral home."

After a brief silence, Ed said, "Really? A funeral

home, huh?" They were quiet a moment, then: "What-taya think?"

Lorraine said, "Well, it's hard to say. We'd have to go see it first, look around."

"Yeah. Tell you what, Mrs. Snedeker, we'd like to come over to your house right away—this morning—and have a look around. Of course, if that's all right with you."

"All right? Oh, *please!*"

"Why don't you give us your address and tell us how to get there?" he asked.

Carmen did, trying to speak slowly so they could understand her.

"Well, it'll take us an hour or so to get there," he said when she was done, "so I want to tell you a few things before we go. First, you should all stay together—all of you—from now on. Don't split up, just in case there are more attacks before we come."

"And be sure to keep your rosary with you," Lorraine added. "Same for everyone, if you've got enough. And say the Hail Mary and the Our Father as often as you want."

"We'll get there as soon as we can, Mrs. Snedeker. If that's okay with you."

"That's fine. We're all looking forward to seeing you. We're . . . very scared."

"It's okay to be scared, love," Lorraine said. "Just remember you've got the power of God behind you."

They got her phone number in case they had a problem finding the house, then said goodbye.

When Carmen hung up, she felt a little better . . . but only a little.

The Warrens did not take very long, although it seemed like a long time to Al and Carmen. While they were waiting, they'd been talking about how they might keep everyone together once it came time to go to bed again. They decided to move mattresses out onto the living-room floor. Everyone could be close as they slept. Yes, it would be uncomfortable, but, just as the Warrens had said, it would be safer should anything else happen in the night.

When the Warrens arrived, Al and Carmen were still the only ones in the house who were awake. They became nervous when they saw the station wagon pull into the drive. What would these people be like? What if the Warrens didn't believe their story?

Al and Carmen watched through a window as the Warrens got out of their car.

They looked exactly like their pictures in the magazine. Lorraine was tall and carried a large gray bag slung over her shoulder. Ed was tall, too, large and imposing, with broad shoulders and a barrel chest that pressed against his dark-blue shirt. They both walked with authority, heads held high as they neared the house.

Al and Carmen met them at the door, invited them in, and led them to the living room, where they seated themselves on the sofa.

Al and Carmen expected small talk at first, superficial conversation to break the ice. That was not the case.

"Before we say anything more," Ed Warren said, holding up a large hand, "we'd like you to know that, if we sound as if we doubt what you're saying, that's not the case at all. We just have to make *sure*, in every way we possibly can, that the things you tell us about have been brought on by supernatural forces. So you need to understand that it's nothing personal—it's just our job. It's something we *have* to do."

"And another thing we have to do is record our conversation," Lorraine said as she removed a cassette recorder from her bag. She looked up at Carmen and smiled. "I hope you don't mind, honey. Do you?"

Carmen was so warmed by that smile that she smiled herself and sat right down in a chair facing the sofa. Al seemed more relaxed too and settled down in his recliner after turning it toward them.

"Mrs. Warren," Carmen said, "you can do whatever you have to, as long as you listen to us . . . and help us."

Lorraine leaned forward and patted Carmen's knee. "We're gonna do what we can, honey, believe me." Then she set the recorder on the coffee table and hit the button marked REC.

Ed leaned forward, locked his hands together, elbows on his knees, and said, "Now, why don't you tell us, from the beginning, in any way you'd like, exactly what's been going on in your house. Both of you."

Slowly, steadily and with great care, Al and Carmen gave the Warrens every detail, right from the beginning.

When they were finished, there was a long silence.

Neither of the Warrens had interrupted them to make comments or ask questions. Carmen and Al had simply told their story in their own words, taking turns and sometimes speaking together. Ed and Lorraine watched them carefully and listened with great intent.

"We'd like to ask you a few questions," Ed said finally. But he said it with a smile. "Uh, if you don't mind . . . does anyone in the family drink alcohol to excess?"

Al and Carmen looked at one another.

"Al has his beers in the evening," Carmen said, without taking her eyes from his.

Al gave her a tiny, minuscule shake of the head.

She said, "But not . . . not like you're saying. No. No, of course not."

"Anyone in the house take drugs?" Ed asked. "And I mean any kind of drugs, illegal drugs, prescription drugs, anything that might be . . . mind altering?"

There was another glance between them, but this one

was brief and disbelieving. Al began to shake his head as Carmen said, "No, no, *no*! I mean, we don't—well, we, uh, certainly haven't—"

"What about the boy?" Ed asked. "Stephen, I mean. What about him?"

The next look between Al and Carmen was long.

"We were never sure," Al said. "I mean, we didn't know. He was acting strangely, yeah, but . . . we never knew if it was because of *that*."

Ed nodded and said, "Okay, okay. How about supernatural interests? Has anyone in your family ever dealt, in any way or at any time, with a ouija board?"

Al and Carmen shook their heads simultaneously.

"No, no, not at *all*," Carmen said.

"Attended a séance? Consulted a medium of some sort?"

"No, absolutely not."

"Okay, okay," Ed said, "that's fine."

"Would you mind if I walked through your house?" Lorraine asked. "Alone, I mean. By myself."

"No, we wouldn't mind," Al said.

Carmen shook her head. "Of course not." Then she smiled and said, "It might be a mess, but—"

"Oh, that's okay, believe me," Lorraine laughed, waving Carmen's remark away with a hand as she stood. "That's not what I'm looking for."

"Lorraine is a light-trance medium," Ed said. "That means she can walk through a house and *feel* things that other people can't feel. In other words, if she goes through this house, she might get some idea as to what's wrong. She might get a lead on the source of our problem."

"Go right ahead," Al said.

"Please," Carmen said, "go anywhere you want."

Lorraine smiled at them both and nodded pleasantly. "Thank you. I'll be back in a little while."

They watched her turn and leave the room, watched her lift her right hand slightly and move it back and forth a bit, as if she were feeling her way through the dark.

Once Lorraine rounded the corner into the hall, Carmen perked up, turned to Ed and asked, "I'm sorry, I completely forgot—would you like coffee or tea?"

"That's very nice," Ed replied with a smile, "but why don't we wait till Lorraine gets back."

Lorraine's every nerve was alive and waiting. Her mind was open to anything, to whatever might be in the air, in this hallway or the next room or downstairs—to whatever might be waiting to tell her something.

She walked slowly through the dining room, deaf to the sounds of voices talking quietly in the living room. She went through the kitchen, pausing between each step, then into the hall, up and down the hall a couple times then, pausing at the top of the stairs for a moment —was that a tingle she felt, the slightest hum of . . . *something* not far ahead?—and then she went down into the basement.

It was darker down there—even then, before noon— and cooler, too, with an ever so slight dampness in the air. But the cold and damp were deeper than normal; they curled around Lorraine's ready mind, telling her that it was a psychic cold, and that whatever was wrong with the house was most likely in the basement.

She walked through Michael's room, hand still held out and moving slowly back and forth, a few inches in each direction. There were posters on the wall of sports figures, books on the nightstand, including a Bible, and baseball cards and car magazines on the dresser. She saw nothing harmful, nothing dangerous—nothing that might invite the kind of activity Al and Carmen had described.

She went through the French doors and into the next room.

Something changed.

She felt different.

A familiar nausea began to twist through her stomach. But, whatever it was, she hadn't reached it yet.

She passed through the room that had once been Stephen's, wincing at the feelings she got, the dark, threatening, *helpless* feelings. But they weren't telling her anything, only making her hurt, so she moved on.

Across the concrete runway—the bad feelings darkening—into the next room, where the chain hoist waited for boxed-up bodies that would never be lifted again, and the blood pit waited for bodily fluids that would never again be spilled down its sloped sides; then into the next room, the room in which, unknown to Lorraine, bodies had once been embalmed. It was there, in that small, dark, concrete-floored room, that it finally hit her, the thing she'd been looking for, embraced her with icy arms and held her, stiff and frozen, in a blurry and bone-cold vision:

. . . *dead bodies, some burned to black, stiff figures of charred flesh . . . boys and girls, men and women, laid out as if after a horrible fire or explosion, some kind of terrible catastrophe . . . but something worse, much worse, something much more horrible . . .*

. . . *hands—rough, male hands that reached down to fondle the dead bodies, to touch their most private parts in horrible ways . . . fingers closing over limp, dead male genitalia . . . entering the cold, dead private places of the women . . . roughly pulling and probing . . . and worse still . . .*

. . . *laughter . . . harsh, throaty laughter . . . the laughter of depraved enjoyment and excitement . . . the grunting of sick, malignant passion . . .*

It filled her mind, blinded her eyes so she could see

othing else but that horrible, sickening vision: those rightening images of perversion, things she'd never even nagined, things she never dreamed she'd ever see in her fetime.

But they were taking place before her wide, distant yes which, to anyone else, would appear to be staring at blank wall.

Her right hand was outstretched, fingers trembling. Her left hand was pressed to her chest as she struggled to reathe, taking her breaths in tiny, panicky gasps.

And then it left her, pulled away from her like hands hat had been closed tightly on her throat.

It pulled away and—

It was gone.

Lorraine found herself standing with her back pressed ard against the wall, her entire body tensed, every muscle in every part of her taut as piano wire. She forced erself to relax, lowered her right arm, felt the burning che of relaxation course through those tensed muscles. he closed her eyes, took some slow, deep breaths, and eaned weakly against the wall behind her.

Her eyes rang with the sound of blood rushing hrough her veins. Her heart thundered in her chest, ushed on by the rush of adrenaline that was still flooding through her body.

Something crawled over her feet.

She sucked in a deep and ragged gasp, her nails clawing over the wall.

Something pawed at her leg just below her knee.

Lorraine looked down.

It was a ferret, thin and wiggly, trying hard to get her ttention.

It looked up at her, made a quiet smacking noise with ts black lips, and rapidly swiped a paw over its face a ouple of times.

Relief swept through Lorraine. She smiled at the ani-

mal, then laughed at herself, at her fear. When sh
reached down to pet the ferret, it scurried out of th
room.

Her eyes were watery, her vision blurry, and sh
reached up with both hands to wipe the unspent tea
from her eyes. Then she headed upstairs.

Al and Carmen were still talking with Ed when Lor
raine returned and Michael, still groggy with sleep, ha
joined them. He had been sleeping in his parents' be
and had not slept long enough, but he was up.

Carmen stood as soon as Lorraine entered and aske
nervously, "Would you like some tea? Or maybe cof
fee?"

Lorraine nodded rather absently and said, in a hoars
voice, "Tea would be nice."

"Yeah, I'll have some tea, too," Ed said, standing. H
went to Lorraine and said quietly, "So, what happened?

She just shook her head slightly.

He took her arm. "You wanna talk alone?"

She nodded.

Ed turned to Al. "Is there someplace we can talk alon
for a minute?"

Al directed them to the master bedroom, where the
closed the door as he walked away.

"What do you think is wrong?" Carmen whispered i
the kitchen.

Al shrugged. "I don't know. They just wanted to tal
alone a minute."

"Well, that can't be too good . . . can it?" Carme
asked.

Al shrugged again as he left to go into the living roon
and keep Michael busy, just in case he, like Carmen, wa
beginning to worry about what was happening.

By the time the Warrens came out of the bedroom
their tea was ready and waiting for them in the livin

room. They sat on the sofa together and leaned forward as if they had something to say. And they did.

After Al and Carmen were seated—Michael was lying on the floor, sleepy-eyed, but listening—Ed Warren spoke.

"The news isn't good," he said quietly. "I think it's pretty clear what we're dealing with here. It is demonic in nature. It's very old, very cunning and absolutely, without a doubt, very, very evil."

Lorraine spoke up then, her voice reassuring. "But we can fight it. And we can win." Suddenly, she held up her index finger and closed her eyes. "I'm sorry. That's not quite accurate. We can fight it all we want. But only with the help of God will we win."

Ed sipped his tea, and set down his cup. "Let me explain to you exactly how this works," he said. "Manifestations like this always occur in a five-step progression. First there's encroachment. Then infestation, oppression, possession, and finally—if it's allowed to go that far—death." Obviously uncomfortable, he took another sip of tea, then leaned back on the sofa.

He continued: "First, there's the encroachment—or *permission*—stage. That is when a demon somehow gains access to a person or persons—a family, perhaps. Usually, it's voluntary. A person invites the demon in somehow, maybe by dabbling in the supernatural—such as by attending or holding a séance or using a ouija board—or by delving into satanic ritualism. Maybe even by doing something as apparently innocent as playing with tarot cards. Then again, sometimes the person *doesn't* invite it. Sometimes, someone else does something that draws demonic attention to that person. We think that might be the case with you. We think something might have happened in this house before you moved in—perhaps *long* before you moved in—that could be causing this activity."

Ed gave them a moment to absorb that information, shifted his position on the sofa, had another sip of tea, then went on.

"During the next stage, infestation, the demons will try, *literally*, to drive you crazy. They'll wreak havoc with your physical environment. They'll move things, break things, they'll pound walls and make frightening sounds. They'll show you things—visions, you might call them—or make you hear things that aren't really there, things that are absolutely terrifying. They'll try to make you feel like you're all alone in the world, that no one will believe you. They'll make you think you're losing your mind."

Ed took a deep breath, taking a good look at Al and Carmen to see how they were taking it. Then:

"And then, at some point, the oppression begins. This is when the demonic force shifts its attention from disrupting the environment to the people themselves. It will cause you great pain. It's been known to cause paralysis, blindness, mental or physical illness. It humiliates you. It can make you the victim of sick and disgusting sexual games.

"Then, when it's worn you down enough . . . when you're weak enough and sick enough . . . when you're constantly in terror and you've lost all hope . . . that's when it finally moves in. That's when possession begins."

Lorraine leaned forward and held up a hand. "But we can thank the good Lord that it hasn't gone that far in this case." She smiled. "And the power of our God is going to see to it that it doesn't."

"You could say that, from this moment on," Ed said, "we're going to be like prosecuting attorneys, Lorraine and I. Then we'll take our findings to someone in the church and hope that they decide in our favor, that they decide to *do* something about it."

"We'd like to come back this evening," Lorraine said.

"If it's all right with you, we'll bring some of our researchers with us and assign at least one of them to a twenty-four-hour vigil here at the house."

"Maybe one or two of them," Ed added. "We'd like someone to be here at all times to record the activity that goes on. I know that sounds difficult: you know, invading your privacy, and all. But it's a part of the process. And . . . well, honestly, I know all this sounds like an episode of *Twilight Zone* or something, but it's not. Apparently, at the moment, it's your *life*. We want to help you. But you're gonna have to let us."

Al and Carmen exchanged a long, silent look. Then Al said, "We need help. We need it bad. And we want you to do whatever you have to do."

24

The Researchers

When the Warrens returned that evening, the family was together in the living room. Michael and Stephanie had stayed home from school that day, much too tired and worried even to go in late.

The station wagon pulled into the driveway again and, behind it, a white hatchback. Ed and Lorraine got out of the wagon and were followed by four others, three men and a woman. Four more people got out of the hatchback and brought with them video cameras and recording equipment.

"Oh boy," Carmen whispered to Al as they watched through the window. "What're the neighbors gonna think?"

They met the Warrens at the door and Lorraine said jovially, "I'm really sorry, but we told you it was gonna be an invasion of privacy." Once inside, she said, "We've brought our researchers with us and some people to videotape every room in the house so we can have a record of the layout. We'll need to interview you again, on video, and get a complete record of your story."

"Well, then," Carmen said hesitantly, "I guess we should get started. . . ."

* * *

The house came alive with the sound of voices moving in and out of every room, men and women with video cameras perched on their shoulders, others holding up lights, some speaking quietly into small tape recorders, describing the house, giving their impressions.

While all this was going on, Ed and Lorraine interviewed Al and Carmen before a video camera, having them go over the entire story again, but slower this time and in more detail. When they had something to add, Stephanie, Michael, or Kelly would speak up.

It seemed to take forever, but by the time the sun disappeared and the crickets were chirping outside, they were done. Those who had come from the hatchback with their video and recording equipment agreed to meet with the Warrens the next day, thanked Al and Carmen for their patience and wished them well, then left, leaving them with the Warrens and the three male researchers whom they'd hardly had a chance to meet in all the confusion.

First, there was Chris McKenna, Ed and Lorraine's grandson. He was a pleasant, soft, gentle-looking man with blond hair and somewhat sad eyes. He'd been fascinated by his grandparents' work since he was a child.

John Zaffis was Ed and Lorraine's nephew, a tall, lean man with energy to spare; as they spoke, he seemed to find it difficult to sit still.

The last researcher was a man named Carl Yoblanski. He had attended a number of Ed and Lorraine's lectures and gone to their classes. Like John and Chris, he was a member of the New England Society for Psychic Research, the organization founded by the Warrens.

It was the researchers' job to maintain round-the-clock surveillance of the Snedeker household, to keep records of everything that happened, of their impressions, their feelings, and the feelings of others around them.

John asked politely if they could have some coffee and went to the kitchen to fix it.

They all sat in the living room and talked quietly for a while.

"I think it's important that you get to know one another," Ed said, "because, like it or not, this is the only way we can do this. The only other way would be to do nothing. I think it's best if everyone meets first, and tries to get to know one another."

It wasn't easy, of course, to become acquainted in such a short period of time. But Kelly and Chris hit it off right away. It wasn't long before they had one another laughing as if they'd been friends for a while.

Al and Carmen talked with the three men, too, and found them friendly and even apologetic about the situation. They told the Snedekers that whatever sleeping arrangements they wanted to make would be just fine.

"Well, as a matter of fact," Al said, "we were thinking of moving mattresses in here, on the living room floor, so we could all be together. Mr. Warren told us not to split up."

"That's a good idea," Lorraine added. "And I think it would be *especially* wise if no one went downstairs. That's . . . not a good place to be."

"That's why we thought we'd bring everyone up here," Carmen said, turning to the three men. "So if you don't mind pot luck when it comes to sleeping arrangements—"

"Not at all," Chris said.

John shook his head and smiled. "Whatever you want to do is fine with us."

Carl nodded silently with a smile to let them know he agreed. He was clearly new at this and a little nervous.

They talked a while longer as the night wore on, then Ed and Lorraine stood.

"We should be going," Ed said. He turned to the researchers and said, "You guys wanna get your things from our car now?"

The three men left to go to the car outside.

Ed looked at Al and Carmen and said, "Let us know how it goes after the first night. You have our number. I know that, sometimes, personality conflicts come up, and that makes things difficult. If that's the case, please tell us. But I hope you'll do your best to work with them. They're here to help. Together, we'll get to the bottom of it, then we'll consult the church."

Al and Carmen said goodnight to the Warrens, who left them with their new houseguests, the three men whose job it was to find out what was wrong.

25

Demons Under Scrutiny

The next several weeks were a living hell, not only for the Snedekers but for the researchers as well.

It was almost as if the forces that were moving invisibly through the house were not pleased by the fact that they were under close surveillance by three strangers. It was almost as if they were angry: More than ever before, those forces began to show their power with a vengeance.

One night, Al went to bed before Carmen. He lay down on one of the many mattresses spread over the living room floor.

Peter and Stephanie were already sound asleep in their respective corners, curled up beneath sheets and blankets, their heads resting on their pillows. John had been up for nearly twenty hours and was now snoring lightly on the floor in front of the sofa.

Carmen and Kelly were talking softly with Chris and Carl in the dining room when Al finally settled beneath the blankets. He'd had a bit too much to drink and felt sluggish and weary. It wasn't long before his eyelids were lowering heavily, and his breathing was becoming very slow.

Then he suddenly jerked awake and stared, wide-eyed, at the ceiling for a long moment. Then it began again, the process of going to sleep. . . .

He jerked awake again. This time, he rolled on his side and tried to get as comfortable as possible.

He began to drift away again . . . not quite asleep and not quite awake . . . and that was when it came to him. . . .

Spots of bluish-white light danced and spun behind his closed eyelids. They began to gather together as they drew closer and closer . . . larger and larger . . . and they began to form a picture . . .

Not quite asleep, Al turned on his back again and opened his eyes, thinking that perhaps he was experiencing some negative side effect of having had too much beer. That, however, was not the case.

When he opened his eyes, he expected to see the ceiling, but instead, the spinning and dancing lights that seemed to draw nearer and nearer did not go away. Even with his eyes open, he saw them against a deep-black backdrop—not against the ceiling that he knew was above him.

As he watched in awe, the lights drew closer and closer together, slowly forming a figure . . . a very familiar figure . . . one that swept rapidly toward his face . . . the figure of Christ on the cross . . . but this Christ was unlike any in the pictures . . . this one had a face that was horribly mutilated . . . twisted into a deformed, hideous mask of pain . . . eyes bulging from their sockets . . . swollen tongue protruding from the fat, cracked lips, which moved and began to speak:

"I can't help you, Allen . . . I can do nothing . . . I am dead . . . do you understand?"

The figure of Christ drew closer and closer.

"I . . . am . . . DEAD! I am no MORE!"

It drew closer and closer until Al could smell its putrid breath, until he thought he could feel that fat, protruding tongue on his face . . .

"I can't HEEAAR YOOUU, Al! I can't HEELLP YOOUU, Al! IIII'M . . . NOT . . . HEEEERE!"

Then the stinking, bleeding figure of the monstrous Christ fell on him, and—

Al sat up screaming again and again.

John sat up and scrambled toward Al.

"What's wrong?" he asked breathlessly. "What's wrong, Al, what's the matter?"

Al's arms reached upward toward the ceiling. "Jesus! It was Jesus! He came to me! He said He couldn't help! He said He was dead! He said He wasn't here!" Al gasped for breath and his whole body shook with panic.

John put a hand firmly on Al's shoulder. "It's okay, Al, it was just something the demon wanted you to see, that's all, just something to discourage you."

As John spoke, the others rushed in from the dining room and gathered around, concerned after hearing Al's screams.

"It's okay," John said. "This will happen. This is the kind of thing it's going to do. It wants to scare you. All of you. It wants you to let go of your faith. It wants to discourage you. But, believe me, you can't let it."

Al had calmed down quite a bit by then. He turned to John and said, "I'm okay, now. Really. I'm fine."

As John went to his notebook to make a record of the incident, Carmen sat down beside Al.

"You sure you're okay?" she whispered, putting an arm around him and holding him close.

"Yeah, I'm fine now. I just . . . I just hope that doesn't happen again. That was"—he shook his head and took a deep breath—"really horrible. Believe me."

"You want me to stay with you until you're asleep?"

"Would you mind?"

"Of course not, sweetheart, of course not."

So that was what Carmen did. She stroked his hair and spoke to him in a gentle voice until he was asleep, until it seemed that nothing more was going to be shown to him by whatever force was working in their house.

A couple of weeks later, Al and Carmen were seated on the porch steps together, enjoying the warm summer night. It was late and Kelly and the kids were asleep.

Inside, all three of the researchers were awake, talking quietly and watching over the others who were sleeping.

Al and Carmen spoke quietly, enjoying a rare moment of privacy.

"Things've been rough," Al said, putting his arm around her and holding her close.

"No shit," Carmen laughed, laying her head on his shoulder.

"We'll get past it," he said. Then he added quietly, "I hope."

"Oh, we will. I know. It's just everything that we apparently have to go through *before* we get past it that bothers me."

"Yeah, I know what you mean."

Over the preceding weeks, they had let their friends and relatives know—as gently as possible, but firmly enough to get the point across without giving them any ugly details—that it wouldn't be a good idea to drop in for a visit, at least not for a while. As a result, they got a number of telephone calls from their concerned friends and family asking what was wrong, if anyone was sick, if they were having some sort of marital problems.

Al and Carmen decided to tell a select few about what was going on. They told Al's family, Carmen's sister Vicki, and their neighbor Fran, who was the least surprised of all and not a bit skeptical. Carmen explained to her that she'd called the Warrens and that their researchers were staying in the house now.

They were enjoying a moment of privacy on the front porch, Al drinking a beer, Carmen sipping tea and smoking a cigarette. They said little, just sat close, vaguely hearing the voices of the researchers in the house, enjoying, for a while, the feeling of being alone and close to one another.

Suddenly, Carmen's cup of tea slipped from her hand. It shattered two steps down from them and hot tea splashed over their feet.

Al flinched at the sound, startled, but Carmen did not move, did not react at all.

"Carmen?" Al said quietly.

Next, the cigarette fell from her fingers and rolled down the steps, its red ember glowing a brighter red as it rolled farther from the glow of the porchlight and into the dark of the night.

Carmen fell back on the steps with a grunt, as though she had been pushed by invisible hands. Her legs jerked. Her mouth opened and her tongue protruded stiffly as her elbows locked and her fingers curled into stiff claws.

"Oh, dear Jesus, *Carm*!" Al cried, leaning toward her as he dropped the bottle of beer. It, too, shattered and foamy beer hissed down the steps.

With her eyes open impossibly wide, Carmen's throat began to blacken steadily, to swell slowly into a tremendous, bulging, balloon of flesh, like the throat of a croaking frog.

Al screamed, "Oh my God, get out here get out here *now*!"

The front door opened and Chris, John, and Carl burst out of the house as Carmen's rigid, trembling limbs relaxed, and she released a long, gurgling sigh. . . .

For a little while—just a very short while—Carmen could hear the voices around her. But they faded fast, moving away from her, far, far away from her, until she could no longer hear them . . . *She was someplace else, some dark, cold place, so dark that she could see nothing, so unreal and dreamlike that she could* feel *nothing.*

Everywhere she looked, Carmen saw only blackness, a blackness so thick and oppressive that it was almost tangible. There was nothing . . . nothing around her . . . nothing to see . . . nothing to touch . . . nothing.

And then she looked up.

Far, far above her was a circle of faint, sickening, reddish light, and she realized she was at the bottom of a very deep hole. As she stared at that circle of light high above her, two faces appeared.

One was male, the other female, both very pale, with black, stringy hair. Their mouths split into broad grins simultaneously, revealing narrow teeth gray with decay and separated by silver-thin gaps.

"You miserable cunt!*" the man shouted, and his phlegmy voice echoed in the darkness.*

"You stupid *bitch!" the woman spat.*

Carmen huddled in the darkness, cowering from their insults as they continued to spew profanity at her, to call her names and laugh at her fear.

"You think there's something you can do about us?" the man asked.

"You think you have a god more powerful than we are?" the woman laughed. "Your god's a weakling!"

"A pussy!"

"Your god's a cocksucking faggot and he's not going to help you now!"

"You belong to us! Your soul is ours!"

Their voices reverberated throughout the darkness that surrounded Carmen and their spittle rained down on her. Their words dug into her like filthy, jagged fangs.

Al and the three researchers hunched over Carmen, listening as she rasped and gurgled through her swollen, bruised-looking throat, "Ho-Ho-leeee M-Mary,

M-Mother of G-God, pr-pray for us sinners, n-now and
at the hour of our d-death, a-a-mmmmen. . . ."

As Al began to cry, they lifted Carm from the porch
steps and carried her into the house.

*The faces leering over the edge of the hole's opening con-
tinued to spit obscene insults and blasphemous curses down
at Carmen, continued to mock her God and her family, continued to remind her that they and their millions were far
too powerful for her, or anyone in her family, to resist or
overcome.*

*And then suddenly, horribly, those faces began to draw
closer and become larger and larger, their smiles growing
wider, bigger, and their grotesque, rotting teeth becoming
more and more detailed as Carmen was somehow lifted up
from the bottom of that deep and narrow pit, lifted closer
and closer to the opening above, to those faces, those hideous,
gaunt, pale faces with their sickening grins and their deepset,
corpselike eyes that watched as she rose higher and higher
until her feet were planted firmly on the ground with the
hole (she thought) directly behind her. But when she turned
slowly and looked down at the ground, there was nothing
there. Just hard, dry dirt veined with dark, wide, jagged
cracks that webbed out in all directions, like lightning bolts
that had been sewn together.*

*Her tormentors were nowhere to be seen. Apparently, they
had simply disappeared.*

*When she looked ahead of her, Carmen realized she was
on a road . . . a long road made up of dry cracked earth.
There was so little light, though, as if it were night . . .
and yet, not exactly as if it were night.*

*Carmen leaned her head back and looked up to see a sky
filled with malignant black clouds that were racing by at a
dizzying speed.*

*But there was a light coming from someplace . . . a sick,
cancerous light that illuminated whatever it was that lay on
either side of the road.*

Carmen did not look, though. She was afraid *to look. She
began to walk, slowly at first, limping a little from her fear
and the trembling exhaustion that coursed through her. Then
she picked up her pace, her feet crunching over the broken
road as she began to shed tears silently, tears that rolled hotly
down her cheeks as she wondered where she was and what
had become of her husband, her family, her house . . . as
she wondered what had become of* her.

*Ahead, the road narrowed to a needle point in the dis-
tance. It seemed to go on forever, as far as she could see and
farther, the jagged cracks fading to visual memory far, far
ahead in the corrupt darkness.*

*Her chest began to tighten with panic as she realized that
she was very, very far from home . . . just like Dorothy in*
The Wizard of Oz *. . . just like Alice in* Through the
Looking Glass *. . . she was in a frightening, foreign place,
and it was very* real *. . . and she had no idea how to get
back.*

*She continued walking, her shoulders aching with tension
and her chest beating with fear.*

Al and the three researchers lay Carmen down on one
of the mattresses in the living room.

"Jesus Christ, what's happening to her?" Al rasped,
his eyes welling with tears.

"She's under attack," John said.

"But shouldn't we call a doctor or an ambulance?" Al
asked. "I mean, my God, she looks like something's
wrong with her, like she's dying!"

"There *is* something wrong with her," Chris said,
leaning over her. "She's under attack by whatever demonic force is at work in this house. We've seen this
happen before."

"Yeah, Al, we have," John said reassuringly. "A doctor
would find nothing. In fact, it might be over by the time
we got her to one. Look, where's one of the rosaries?"

"Well, I think there's one, um—" Al looked around

until he spotted one on top of the television. He stumble
over the mattresses to the television and grabbed the ro
sary, then hurried back, holding it out to John.

"No, no," John said. "It's for *you*. Hold on to the ro
sary and do the Hail Mary and the Our Father."

"And keep doing them," Chris said firmly, "unti
we're done." Then he looked at John and Carl and said
"We're gonna have to do the invocation and just keep
doing it for as long as it takes."

They both nodded.

"Oh, dear Jesus, it's bad, isn't it?" Al whispered.

"Nothing God can't handle," Chris said reassuringly
And then, as Al started reciting the Hail Mary, the three
researchers began to say together, "In the name of Jesu
Christ! We command that you leave this place! To g
back to the place from which you've come! In the name
of Jesus Christ!"

Al knelt at Carmen's head as her throat continued t
grow darker and thicker, as the three men repeated the
invocation. He placed one hand on her shoulder and
gripped the rosary in the other as he said the Hail Mary
and the Our Father at nearly a shout, and Chris, John
and Carl continued to invoke the name of Christ.

*Carmen gasped for breath as she made her way down the
endless road. Finally, she began to look to her right and left
at the landscape that surrounded her.*

*The first thing she noticed were the crosses . . . enor-
mous crosses made of rugged wood, planted firmly in the
ground . . . upside down . . . in both directions as far as
she could see.*

*All around those crosses, writhing upward out of the
ground, were black, shapeless blobs that seemed to be trying,
unsuccessfully, to ooze up from the hard, cracked earth and
pull themselves free.*

*Jagged needles of light shot silently through the black
clouds that rushed by overhead, and suddenly, coming from*

nowhere in particular but from everywhere around her, a deep and gravelly voice—the sound, Carmen thought, of disease—spoke to her:

"They are souls, Carmen . . . lost souls that belong to us now . . . to me . . . just as you belong to me . . . just as you and everyone in your family belong to me . . ."

Carmen stopped on the road and screamed at the top of her lungs, praying to God that someone would hear her, that someone would find her and help her.

When Al heard Carmen making a small, strangled sound deep in her throat, he stopped in the middle of the Our Father and leaned toward her, placing a hand on the side of her head and whispering to her, "Carmen, honey, what is it? What's the matter?"

Chris, John, and Carl had been invoking Christ again and again and, suddenly, Chris spoke up and said, "She's not here, Al, she's not with us, just keep praying and keep—"

Upon hearing that, Al said with great determination into Carmen's ear, "Where are you, Carmen, honey, where *are* you?"

When she began to respond as best she could, the three researchers stopped their invocation and listened.

"Dark," she gurgled, spittle gathering at the corners of her mouth. "Dark place . . . in a . . . place . . . in a *dark* place," she said, forcing the words up from her chest and through her throat.

"Oh God where is she?" Al cried, looking up at the three men.

"It has her," John said, "and we have to get her back."

Immediately, they raised their voices as they continued their invocation, and, after a long moment, Al finished the Our Father and went into the Hail Mary.

Carmen continued to scream and dropped to her knees as she looked around at all the souls . . . all the black, trapped souls . . . feeling oppressed and smothered by their need to

*break free, by their desire to get away from whatever it was
that had brought each of them to this place . . .*

*The voice that seemed to come from everywhere, the
phlegmy, disgusting voice that seemed to come from the bottom of the very deepest pit in hell began to laugh. Its laughter was deep and throaty and filled with malignant, decadent
glee.*

*Carmen slapped her hands over her face and screamed
once again, unable to tolerate the laughter on top of the
claustrophobic feeling brought on by the black, tumorous
souls squirming up from the barren ground.*

*After a small eternity, the laughter began to fade and,
along with it, the feeling of oppression.*

*Slowly . . . ever so slowly . . . Carmen began to take
her hands away from her face.*

Her eyes opened to look blearily up at Al, whose concerned face hovered over her, his lips forming a straight,
tense line.

"Carm?" he whispered hoarsely. "Oh, dear Jesus,
Carm?"

"Al," she breathed, reaching up to take his hand. She
gripped it hard, as if he were being pulled away from
her.

She saw Chris and John and Carl kneeling beside her
suddenly, all of them smiling as John said, "Thank
God," and Carl said, "Amen," and Chris just grinned so
broadly that he looked as if he might burst into laughter
at any moment.

"You're back," Chris said finally.

"Yeah, I guess so," Carmen whispered.

Nearly two hours later, Carmen was sleeping restlessly
beside Al on the mattress. Chris, John, and Carl were
talking softly over coffee in the dining room.

Al was propped up on his side in pajama bottoms and
a robe, watching Carmen as she slept. His forehead was
creased with worry, fear, and confusion.

Carmen tossed back and forth as she slept, her sleeping eyes pressed together beneath a dark frown.

He prayed silently, never taking his eyes from her, relieved that Kelly and the kids weren't around to see what had happened.

And then, Carmen's body stiffened and her back arched as if she were in silent agony. Once again, her throat began to swell and darken, turning a purplish black.

Al sat up, clutching her shoulder, calling, "It's happening again, get out here, it's happening *again*, oh Jesus, Jesus *Christ!*"

Footsteps rushed across the hall and into the living room and the researchers hurried over the mattresses to Al and Carmen.

John had a crucifix in his hand and held it out before him as he said loudly, with authority, "In the name of Jesus Christ, I command you to leave this place—"

Chris and Carl quickly joined in, saying the words with him.

Carmen's head tilted back. Her eyes opened to reveal only glistening whites as she gurgled and choked and her arms and legs began to shake and convulse violently.

Al shot to his feet suddenly, fists at his sides, teeth clenched, and growled furiously, "Goddammit, I'm stronger than she is! Come to *me*, you son of a bitch, do it to *meeee*—"

All three men fell silent at once and turned to Al. Chris shouted, "Al, don't say that!" and Carl grabbed Al's arm and barked, "*Stop!*" as John dropped to his knees at Carmen's feet and continued the invocation alone, nearly shouting now, still holding the cross out toward Carmen as if it were a weapon.

But Al ignored them.

"Come to *me*, dammit!" he continued. "*I'll* fight you, you goddamned son of a bitch, you fucking—"

Al's words caught in his throat as sharply and suddenly as fishbones, lodging there as he began to make a strangled gurgling sound. His eyes grew wider and wider, the color drained from his face, leaving him a sick, pale color.

Then he was thrown down to the mattress as if by powerful but invisible arms and he landed with a strangled grunt.

"Oh dear God," Carl groaned.

Al landed on his hands and knees, head falling forward weakly.

Carmen's erratic movements began to calm down. The swelling and blackening of her throat began to go away as Al's condition seemed to worsen.

John continued to invoke the name of Christ at a fever pitch, his forehead sparkling with beads of perspiration.

As Chris and Carl watched, the hem of Al's bathrobe was thrown hard up over his head and the elastic waistband of his pajama bottoms was torn as they were pulled down violently, revealing his bare behind.

Al screamed, his voice so high and shrill it sounded like a woman's, and his whole body began to jerk as if something were ramming into it again and again and again. His screams continued, screams filled with pain, with horror.

Carmen began to stir. She opened her eyes and blinked several times as she sat up.

"What's wrong?" she asked, turning to Al. "Oh, my God, what's happening to him?"

John stopped the invocation and took a long breath. Then, his voice hoarse, he said, "He's being attacked . . . like you were . . . just a few seconds ago."

For a long moment, they all watched Al, stunned and helpless, knowing exactly what was happening to him.

"Oh God," Carmen gasped, beginning to cry. She moved toward Al and put an arm around his shoulders as he continued to scream shrilly again and again, a sound that was so foreign to Carmen coming from her muscular, rock-ribbed husband. She looked over her shoulder and shouted at the others, "Do something! That's what you're here for, dammit! *Do* something!"

But their prayers had no effect. When it was over, Carmen huddled beside him and held him close, "Oh, my God, honey, I'm sorry, I'm so sorry you had to go through that." Having experienced the same thing herself, Carmen knew exactly how humiliating it was, how helpless she'd felt while she was being violated; it made her heart ache to know that Al had been through the same humiliating experience.

Another night had passed in a house that had, somehow, developed a pipeline to hell.

Al and Carmen and Kelly were not the only ones to be attacked by the entity that had targeted their house, though for some reason, it showed little interest in the smaller children; during their stay, all three researchers were assaulted in one way or another. They were tormented in their sleep as well as pinched and stung and slapped again and again throughout the day and night. Objects continued to move around the house, apparently by themselves, almost as if they had lives of their own.

Early one evening, after Al had gotten home from work, everyone had dinner outside, picnic-style. When they came in, Carl was the first to notice that something odd was happening in the living room. He called for the other researchers and, naturally, everyone else in the house followed them in.

Each of the mattresses on the floor was breathing. The middle of each one bulged slowly, as if inhaling, then relaxed, leveling out.

Ed and Lorraine dropped in frequently and stayed for

a few hours, witnessing for themselves many of the incidents that the researchers had seen firsthand.

They saw some of the attacks; they witnessed the objects that moved around the house; they smelled the odors and saw the flashes of movement just out of their line of sight, movement seemingly caused by nothing.

During one of their visits, they heard a loud, metallic rattling sound that seemed to be coming from the master bedroom. Al was at work, the kids were outside, and Carl and John were resting in the living room, so Ed and Lorraine, Carmen, Kelly, and Chris went down the hall hesitantly and into the bedroom. Carmen and Kelly each held a rosary while Ed and Chris were carrying crucifixes.

In the bedroom, the sound was much louder and beneath their feet, the wooden floor was vibrating slightly. They all stopped just inside the room.

Finally, Lorraine stepped forward and put her hand lightly on the footboard of the bed.

"It's much worse here," she said quietly.

"Where's it coming from?" Ed asked, moving through the room slowly.

Lorraine lifted her right hand before her as she had during her first visit to the house and closed her eyes.

"Not in here," she whispered. "Somewhere else."

"Oh God," Carmen said, "it sounds like the pulley . . . the body lift downstairs. It's right below this room. In fact . . . it's right below the *bed*."

Suddenly, the sound made sense; the metallic rattling was the kind that might be made by a chain hoist, like the one in the cold, damp basement below.

They filed through the door at the back end of the bedroom that led down into the basement. When they were halfway down the stairs, the rattling stopped abruptly.

In the basement, they found the heavy chain swinging lightly, the links jingling very softly.

It was not the last time that happened, nor the last of the many strange occurrences Ed and Lorraine would witness.

During another visit, Lorraine was enveloped by another frightening vision, not unlike the one she'd had the first time she'd walked through the house.

She was standing at the top of the stairs near the bathroom, looking down into the bedroom below, about to descend into the basement—the part of the house that the Snedekers now refused to enter—when it began. It was so vivid and unexpected that, for a moment, she wasn't even aware that it was a vision—until she realized that she couldn't move, that she was paralyzed.

A man appeared at the bottom of the stairs. He did not step around the corner, he simply *appeared*, as if from the very air around him. He wore a filthy undershirt and a pair of baggy, too-long pants that had once been tan but were now so stained and soiled that they looked more brown than anything. The ragged hems bunched around his feet, which wore nothing but dirty white socks. His round, sagging belly pressed against the undershirt and hung over the waist of the pants, with faint shadow filling the massive indentation made by his navel. His hair was black and stringy and fell to his shoulders; on top, he was going bald and his pale scalp was visible through wisps of hair. Beneath his left arm was tucked a pair of brown workboots. With the stubby fingers of his fat hands, he was pulling up and fastening his filthy pants. His breath came in winded, wheezing gasps, as if he'd been exerting himself a great deal.

The man looked up and his watery, bloodshot eyes locked with Lorraine's, which were wide and frightened. He grinned, showing jagged, discolored teeth. His lips were fat and dry and cracked and his glistening tongue

slid out to moisten them as he began to make his slow
way up the stairs.

"Nice bodies," he said, his voice low and phlegmy, wet
and guttural. "Nice cold bodies. Cold, firm bodies."

He took step after step, closer and closer . . .

"Don't move when you touch 'em. Don't fight when
you hold 'em or lick 'em." He laughed.

. . . closer and closer, step after step . . .

"Fact, you can do anything you fuckin' *want* to 'em,"
he chuckled as he reached the top of the stairs. He
reached for Lorraine's hand, saying, "C'mon, I'll show.
You want, you can watch me. See? I'm ready again." He
laughed as he let the boots drop from beneath his arm
and reached down for his crotch.

Lorraine lowered her eyes and watched as he grabbed
the horrible bulge that had grown between his legs. The
zipper of his pants was still open and she caught a
glimpse of what looked like lumpy, purplish flesh, discolored with what appeared to be dirt, or maybe blood.

Closing her eyes and pushing herself backward away
from him, Lorraine cried out as her back slammed
against the bathroom door. When she opened her eyes
again, she was sitting on the floor and the man was gone.
Ed was kneeling at her side, anxiously whispering, "Lorraine, what is it, what's wrong?"

"Necroph . . . necro . . . horrible things, Ed . . .
horrible things happened in this house."

"Necrophilia?"

She nodded. "I saw something . . . a man . . . he
told me what he did . . . he wanted me to watch . . ."

Once Lorraine had calmed down and was able to
stand and talk coherently, they explained to the others
what she had seen and what it meant.

"That sort of thing," Ed said, "necrophilia, I mean—
sex with dead bodies, the kind of thing that, according to
what Lorraine saw, happened here at one time—is evil

t draws demonic activity. The location of such things an become a target for demonic attention."

"It's not necessarily a definitive explanation," Lorraine aid hoarsely, a glass of icewater in her hand, "but it ertainly goes along with the vision I was shown when I irst came here. I really believe that is what happened ere . . . and I believe it's what brought about the trou-le you're having now."

"So what do we do?" Carmen asked quietly. "How an we stop it?"

Ed and Lorraine looked at one another, silent for a noment. They had no doubt that what was happening in he house was very, very real. They knew what the next tep was, but they didn't know what the result of taking t would be and were reluctant to raise the Snedekers' opes.

"Next," Ed said, "we contact the church."

"We've already done that," Al said, a little angrily. "It lidn't get us anywhere!"

"I know," Ed replied. "Now *we're* going to contact hem. We'll tell them what we've found, what we've seen nd what we believe to be the problem. The only thing is . . and I'm not saying this is going to happen, ut . . ."

"*What?*" Al snapped impatiently.

"We might get the same response you did."

26

Attention from the Church

He pressed the doorbell, then stepped back from the door and put on a smile, holding his black bag at his side.

Carmen opened the door and his smile opened into a grin. He held out his hand and said, "You must be Mrs. Snedeker. I'm Father Tom. I talked with the Warrens and they told me about your problem."

"Oh, Father, I'm so glad you're here," she said, her voice sounding a bit desperate as she welcomed him into the house.

He felt it immediately, a dark, oppressive aura that seemed to be everywhere. But he kept his smile on, not wanting to alarm Mrs. Snedeker.

"So, what did the Warrens tell you?" Mrs. Snedeker asked as they stood in the hall.

"They said you had some very unpleasant supernatural activity taking place in your house that they felt was demonic in nature, and that you needed the help of the church."

That wasn't all they'd said, but he didn't tell her that. There was a good deal he didn't tell her.

He didn't tell her that, along with being a priest, he'd

een schooled in demonology and was just as familiar
with the subject as the Warrens. He didn't tell her that,
after what the Warrens had told him, he'd known immediately how urgently his help was needed in the
Snedeker home. And, of course, he didn't tell her that,
upon stepping into the house, he could feel just how bad,
just how advanced, the problem was, and that he knew it
would only get worse without immediate spiritual attention.

Carmen took him into the dining room and introduced him to Kelly and Peter. She explained that the
researchers, Chris and John (Carl had gone), were resting
in the living room and needed some sleep. She made him
some tea, then asked him what he'd like to do.

"Well, how about if I just go through the house, bless
it, sprinkle holy water in each room and see what I find?
Then, if you don't mind, I'd like to come back in a day
or so with another priest and perhaps say a Mass."

"That sounds fine," Carmen said. "Is there anything
you need from me?"

"Absolutely nothing. You've been more than kind."
He gave her a big smile as he stood and leaned down for
his bag on the floor. "Do you mind if I just take myself
through the house?"

"Oh, sure, that's fine," Carmen said, a little nervously.
"Go right ahead. But it's . . . well, it's not the house it
used to be. All the mattresses are in the living room so
we can sleep together in there, and—"

"Please, don't feel you have to apologize or explain. I
understand, really." He gave them another smile and a
nod, then left the dining room and started down the hall,
opening his bag.

As soon as he was out of their sight, his smile fell
away. It had been an effort to maintain ever since entering the house; the air itself felt alive with malignancy.
Carmen Snedeker and her niece Kelly both showed the

toll of living in such an atmosphere. They looked disheveled, puffy, depressed, and every movement was heavy and labored; their eyes were bloodshot and watery and their speech, even when anxious, was just slow and halting enough to give away their situation. He said a silent prayer for them as he went down the hall.

Father Tom went into the bedroom first, then the bathroom, then partway through the hall again, sprinkling holy water and blessing each room, each section of the house. Then . . .

. . . to the stairs.

He felt it even on the very top step and prayed for strength as he made his way down, knowing that something evil awaited him in the basement. The Warrens had warned him, but as he neared the bottom step, he realized their warning had not been strong enough. Something was gripping his stomach, twisting until he felt he might soon vomit.

Finally, he stood at the bottom of the stairs and slowly, with hands trembling slightly, went about blessing the first room, then the next, where the feeling was even stronger. The corridor seemed stronger still, darker . . . almost smothering.

He continued blessing each room in the basement, until he realized he was crying, and had been for some time, his cheeks wet with tears. He stood in the room that had once been a morgue, surrounded by walls once stained with the blood of the dead, and went through the blessing, his words finally crumbling into babbles as he realized that something was happening.

Something dark and yet transparent, a shapeless mass that moved fluidly, flowed and waved as it oozed out of the far wall and advanced toward Father Tom.

He sprinkled more holy water and held up a crucifix as he backed out of the room, stumbling into the next

oom, and then he turned and crossed the corridor and
urried up the stairs.

As he stood facing the bathroom, he paused to catch
is breath, to calm down and wipe the tears from his
heeks with the hanky from his back pocket, praying to
God to help him hide his fear from Carmen Snedeker
nd the others, who had already been through what was
learly more than enough.

He went into the living room, where the researchers
vere sleeping, blessed it quietly, then moved carefully
ver the mattresses to get to the other bedrooms.

When he was done, he returned to the dining room
nd smiled at Carmen and Kelly.

"If it's okay with you, I would definitely like to return
s soon as possible with another priest to celebrate the
Mass. Perhaps tonight, or tomorrow morning?"

"Sure," Carmen said hoarsely. "But . . . why'd you
hange your mind? Is something wrong?"

"Oh, no, no. I've just . . . been thinking about my
chedule, is all. Thank you for your patience and hospi-
ality. I really should be going now."

Carmen stood and followed him to the door, then
vhispered, "Do you think everything, um . . . every-
hing's gonna be all right, Father? I mean . . . are *we*
onna be all right?"

He gave her his best, most comforting smile and put a
and gently on her shoulder, saying, " 'All things work
ogether for good to them that love God.' "

Carmen smiled then, looking as if that had made her
eel better. The priest opened the door and said, "I'll see
ou again soon."

He started down the sidewalk and, when he heard the
ront door close, he was surprised to find himself still
rembling from the assault his senses had undergone in-
de the Snedeker household.

Father Tom returned that very evening with another priest, who identified himself as Father Frank.

Al met them at the door, shook their hands as he introduced himself and led them into the living room.

Everyone was there: Carmen and the three children, Kelly, and the two remaining researchers, Chris and John.

As they stood just inside the living-room doorway, Father Tom introduced Father Frank to the family and said, "We would like to conduct a Mass this evening. If it's all right with all of you, of course."

No one objected. Michael reached over and turned off the television as everyone stood, some on mattresses, some on the floor.

"What would you like us to do?" Al asked.

"Well, if we could have a table?" Father Tom turned and looked at the coffee table that had been pushed against the wall and out of the way of the mattresses.

"Oh, no problem," Al said, and John helped him move the table onto the mattresses and in front of the two priests.

"Now," Father Frank said, sounding a bit shy, "if all of you could gather before us . . . if you don't mind standing on mattresses, that is."

"We're used to it, by now," Chris chuckled.

They all did as the priest had asked.

In a few moments, Father Tom and Father Frank began the Mass, delivering it in Latin.

During the Mass, something began to happen, something silent and very wrong—something that should not have been happening during a Mass.

Carmen and Kelly were the first ones to notice it. They would not learn until later that they were the *only* ones to notice it. But they did see, simultaneously—the exact same thing.

The shadowy cloud moved into the room, flowing liq

uidly and silently. First, it oozed around Father Tom, then around Father Frank, until it held both of them in a diseased shadow.

Although they let on to no one else what they were seeing, Carmen and Kelly each felt their heartbeats speed up, their breathing grow short and their throats become dry as they watched the undulating darkness surround the priests silently, mockingly, without the priests' reacting at all. It was as if the entity were simply making fun of their harmless little ritual.

In a little while, Kelly began to feel something moving about her legs. She was wearing a pair of khaki hiking shorts and a white cotton blouse. She felt what seemed to be small hands on her bare legs, like the hands of a small child that wanted to be picked up. The tiny hands patted at her bare flesh, tugged at the hem of her shorts, their palms moist and cold, stubby fingers pleading with their movements.

. . . pick me up, please . . . carry me . . . hold me . . . please hold me close to you—close to your little tits so I can suck them, so I can suck the fuckers dry, you cunt, you horny little cunt with your pussy lips so wet and your hole open so wide for something to—

Kelly flinched at the words that screamed through her mind as hot as fire, and her eyes blinked several times and began to water. She tried to focus her attention on the Mass, tried hard, tried not to cry out, which was her first impulse.

The Mass continued without any interruption and seemingly without event.

But as Kelly was experiencing the tiny hands on her legs and the voice in her head, Carmen felt what seemed to be stiff fingers poking her all over her body, invisible fingers that continued to prod and poke relentlessly, as if a child were walking around and around her, a spoiled, angry child, a brat that wanted something it couldn't

have and was angry. But Carmen did not move. She
focused her attention on the Mass and silently prayed for
strength.

And as Kelly was being touched and spoken to, and
Carmen was being poked and prodded by an invisible
finger, Chris began to feel something, too. It felt like a
hand and it was groping in the area of his crotch. At
first, it seemed to be on the outside of his pants, scraping
the material around his zipper as if trying to find its way
in. Then, as if it needn't have done that in the first place,
it eased through the material of his pants, through his
undershorts, and he felt thin, icy cold fingers wrap
around his penis.

At first, those fingers took turns applying pressure and
rubbing just a bit, like the fingers of a lover trying to
turn him on, trying to prime him for lovemaking; but
these fingers were too bony, too cold, like the fingers of a
corpse . . . a long-dead corpse.

But the gentle movements soon gave way to harsh
squeezing. The hand began to pull hard—*too* hard—
until it became difficult for him to keep from crying out.
But he managed somehow. He kept his attention on the
Mass and prayed silently, asking God for strength, until
it finally stopped.

For the next week, the Snedeker house was the center of
what could only be described as an angry retaliation by
the demonic forces that, until the Mass, had gone un-
checked and had had free rein.

Late one night, while Chris was sitting up at the dining-room table, thumbing through a magazine and listening for any trouble that might arise, Kelly's sleep was
interrupted by what she, at first, thought to be a dream.

She was shaken violently as her nightshirt was pulled
up until the hem was gathered around her neck. Fright-

eningly cold hands began to grope her breasts, to squeeze and knead roughly.

Sticklike fingers pinched her, playfully at first, then harder and harder until the pinching began to hurt, until it became terribly painful—until it became *unbearable* and Kelly tried to scream, hoping the nightmare would end.

But she had no voice, and it did not end.

Instead, she felt something other than the hands, the fingers. She felt something solid brush over one breast, then the other, something as cold as steel, something with a razor-sharp edge.

She realized suddenly that it was a blade—the blade of a knife held by one of the hands that had been groping her a moment before.

The sharp edge brushed lightly up and down one of her erect nipples. And then, so smoothly that, for a moment, she did not even realize it, the knife began to cut . . . to slice back and forth . . . back and forth . . .

Kelly could feel the blade enter her flesh, feel it move from side to side beneath her nipple, which she *knew* must be peeling away.

She opened her eyes, opened them wide, so wide that it hurt the muscles around them, but she could not see.

And then she realized that it was not a dream at all . . . and that she was blind.

She tried to scream . . . could not find her voice . . . then could only sigh . . . only whisper . . . only murmur . . . and then, with all the strength she possessed, she screamed at the top of her lungs, screamed her throat ragged, screamed until she had no breath left in her.

Then she gasped for air and screamed again, this time crying, "*It's cutting me! I'm blind!*"

Everyone around her awoke immediately—including

Peter who awoke crying—and Chris ran stumblingly across the hall and into the living room.

Kelly sat up, throwing aside her sheet and blanket and clutching at her breasts, screaming again and again, her eyes wide.

Chris flicked on the light and looked directly into Kelly's eyes. It was obvious to him immediately that she was seeing nothing—that she was blind.

Then it ended as abruptly as it had begun.

Kelly fell back on her pillow and relaxed, groaning as she rubbed her eyes a moment, then looked at all the concerned faces that hovered over her.

Chris knelt at her side after grabbing the tape recorder and John joined him.

"Tell us what happened," Chris said breathlessly.

She did, slowly and with a lot of stuttering and stammering.

When she was done, the two investigators looked at one another.

"They're attacking the eyes," Chris whispered.

"That means we'll have to act fast," John responded quietly. "They're angry. . . ."

Late one night, while everyone else tried to sleep on the mattresses in the living room, Chris and John sat up at the dining-room table. Chris dozed, his head resting on his folded arms, while John browsed distractedly through that day's paper. He was scanning the comics when he first heard the sound: footsteps . . . coming slowly up the stairs.

John let the paper fall to the table, reached over and shook Chris's arm. He didn't budge. He shook it harder and hissed, "Chris, wake *up*!" He stopped, suddenly realizing what was happening. He'd experienced it before. Sometimes, a demonic presence puts some of the people in a house into a deep trance while leaving others con-

ious to witness some sort of manifestation. John stood,
ot behind Chris and lifted his shoulders from the table;
hen he let go, Chris dropped back onto the table like
ead weight.

"Oh God," John breathed as the footsteps continued to
scend, now joined by a new sound: a voice, murmuring
d whispering, growing closer and closer as it came up
e stairs slowly . . .

John's denim jacket was hanging on the back of the
air he'd been sitting in and he reached down, fumbled
its pocket until he found the small flashlight he kept
ith him.

Suddenly, the room—the whole house, it seemed—
rew as cold as a meatlocker, and John pulled the jacket
om the chair, slipping it on as he left the dining room.

In the dark hall, he shone the thin beam of light
ward the top of the staircase at the other end. He saw
othing yet, but could still hear the footsteps—and the
ice, forming words now:

"Do . . . you . . . know? Do . . . you?"

John crossed the hall quickly, his chest tight with fear
ow, his free hand in the other pocket of his jacket hold-
g the crucifix he kept there as he prayed silently.

He shone the light into the living room, sweeping it
ver the still forms on the floor.

"Anybody awake?" he asked, his voice cracking.
ouder, he said: "Anybody hear me?"

"Do you know . . . what they did?" the voice asked,
uder now, the words clear. It was neither male nor
male and it gurgled wetly.

John smelled something unpleasant . . . something
tten.

When he spoke again, he saw his breath form a cloud
efore his face. "C'mon, wake *up*, somebody! *Wake up*!"

No one moved. No one even stirred.

"Oh God," John mumbled as he backed out of the

living room, knowing that they weren't going to wal
up, that they *couldn't.*

Once in the hall again, he turned slowly to his righ
removing the crucifix from his pocket as the slow foo
steps reached the top of the stairs. He turned the lig
down the hall and sucked in a ragged gasp that caught
his constricted throat.

The beam landed on bare flesh, mottled with whi
and purple; it was loose, flabby flesh that jiggled an
swayed as the thing that stood at the top of the stai
with its back to John slowly began to turn.

For a long moment, John could not move, could on
stare with his jaw slack and his eyes gaping and his arn
and legs trembling.

It was a woman. She was stooped and pear shape
with tubelike breasts, nipples laced with stretch marl
and spread thinly over the entire rounded end of each
the breasts, which dangled back and forth over he
broad, jiggling belly as she hobbled forward slowly dow
the hall toward John. Her belly almost hung over th
patch of mangy pubic hair between her fat, lump
thighs. Her long hair—dark with gray streaks—hung
greasy, matted strings. Her fingernails and toenails we
thick, black chunks that curled downward over her fir
gers and toes and her eyes rolled loosely in their socket
The beam from John's flashlight moved jerkily over fles
spotted with large clots of bruiselike purple. She had n
teeth and her lips pulled back over gums as she spoke

"Do . . . you . . . you . . . *know* . . . what the
did . . . to us down there? Do you *knooowww*?"

He'd been holding his breath, but now began
breathe again and held up the cross, saying weakly, h
breath puffing in the dark, "Hail Mary . . . full
grace . . . the Lord is with thee . . . blessed art tho
amongst women . . ."

What am I doing? he wondered silently. *I've done this before, I know what I'm supposed to be doing!*

"Do you *knooowww* . . . what they *did* . . . to our *bodies?*" the corpse rasped, coming closer and closer, the stench of rotting flesh growing more overwhelming as it neared. "Do you *know* the things they did to us?"

He stiffened his arm, holding the cross out farther as he shouted, "In the name of Jesus Christ I command you to leave this place and go back to the place from which you've come!"

"And do you know what *else?*" it asked, ignoring his words as the loose, flabby lips spread into a broad grin, baring pink-and-purple gums and a waggling tongue. "Do you *knooowww* . . . what *else?* We *loved* it!" the corpse hissed, beginning to laugh, a wet, cackling laugh. "We *loved* the *groping* and the *fucking* and the *sucking*—"

"In the name of Jesus Christ I command you to leave this place—"

"—and the *tonguing* and the *fingering* and the *humping*—"

"—and go back to the place from which you've come!"

"—do you hear me you godless, cocksucking asshole? *We loooved it!*"

And suddenly, the corpse stopped hobbling and began to rush down the hall impossibly quickly, but now, suddenly, as if John had blinked and missed the transformation, it was no longer a corpse.

It had sprouted wings, great leathery, batlike wings edged with tufts of gray fur, and the head was no longer that of a long-dead woman but was reptilian and pointed, with no lips, and with tiny glistening eyes. It thrust itself toward him rapidly as the body—now covered with scaled, wrinkled skin that hung in loose, jiggling folds and sporting an enormous, fat erection that tapered to a conelike point—swayed back and forth, running on its clawed, reptilian feet.

John screamed so loudly that he felt as if his eyes might pop from their sockets: "*In the name of-of-of—*"

But he was unable to get any further because the creature was on him and he felt its hot, sickening breath on his face as its powerful arms turned him around and threw him to the floor facedown, and then it was on top of him, its foul-smelling wings embracing him from behind like the arms of a lover.

John began to scream.

Then he lost consciousness. . . .

When he awoke later—he had no idea how *much* later —he was still lying on the cold wood floor of the hall. He began to crawl toward the dining room immediately, trying to call out but unable to do little more than murmur. His flashlight was still on the floor, its narrow beam shining over the wood.

Chris darted out of the dining room. "John! What happened?"

It was a while before John could tell him.

A single night did not pass without eventually erupting into screams—sometimes one scream, sometimes more at the same time—at least once, but usually more often.

No one slept an entire night through, and the researchers hardly slept at all, a fact that was made obvious by their puffy, bloodshot eyes and their sometimes slurred speech and sluggish movements.

Ed and Lorraine came by almost every day and prayed with them. But they could tell that the demonic force in the house was gaining strength and that it wouldn't be long before they could do nothing to stop it. They made frequent calls to Father Tom to see how long the Snedekers would have to wait before the church took some action, and each time, Father Tom told them the same thing: "I'm doing the very best I can."

What he didn't tell them was that, since their visit to the Snedekers' house, both he and Father Frank had been the victims of a number of attacks similar to those going on in the house every day and night. But he really *was* doing his best to get the church's permission to conduct an exorcism in the Snedeker home.

In fact, everyone continued to do their best.

But the assaults continued, day after day, night after night . . . the voices and the smells . . . objects moving around by themselves . . . physical attacks . . . the stinging and prodding and touching . . . the sexual attacks . . . until everyone in the house began to think they were losing their minds.

And then, finally, help came.

27

Father Conlan

Permission for an exorcism was finally granted by the Catholic church and a priest experienced in performing the ancient ritual was chosen for the job.

Father Timothy Conlan was a broad-shouldered, muscular man who stood six feet three inches tall. He maintained the exact same physical fitness regimen he had followed when he was in the Marine Corps.

When he was asked to perform the exorcism of the Snedekers' home, Father Conlan immediately began a week-long preparation—training, of sorts—that consisted of three days of constant, private prayer, followed by three more days of fasting and study. When he did eat, he stuck mostly to fruits and vegetables, and increased his exercise program.

He knew that his physical, mental, and, most important, his spiritual resources would be needed for the coming battle. Because that was exactly what it would be: a vicious, all-out battle. He'd been through several exorcisms before this one and was well aware of the danger to an exorcist during a confrontation with pure, naked evil.

He knew the risks he was taking—profane and humiliating assault and a hideous death—but he also knew that only the Lord could save him . . . if his mind was clear and his faith in God was strong. So he worked hard to prepare, using prayer the way an athlete might use exercise, using the Bible study the way a boxer might use weights.

Because Father Conlan knew that, once the exorcism began, it could not be called off . . . no matter how much he might want it to stop.

Meanwhile, as the day of the exorcism drew nearer, Al and Carmen Snedeker began to grow concerned.

Very early one morning, just before dawn, after both of them had awakened and were unable to go to sleep, they sat at the dining-room table facing one another over tea.

The children and Kelly were still asleep, as was John. Chris was in the bathroom taking a shower.

"Do you really think it's gonna do any good?" Al whispered groggily.

"Well . . . guess we don't have much choice, do we?"

"Yeah, but what about the other things? The blessings. The Mass. They just seemed to make it angrier. What's an exorcism gonna do?"

"If it gets worse, I guess we could always move."

"With what? How? We can't afford to move!" he hissed. "We're barely gettin' by now, Carmen. We're still suffering from all those medical bills. If our insurance had been better, yeah, sure, we could probably move now. But our insurance stinks. We're still paying off most of those damned bills."

"Please, Al, don't talk that way. It had to be done. Poor Stephen was . . . he didn't get cancer on purpose, you know."

Al bowed his head and sighed, "Yeah, I know. Dammit. Poor kid. Hope he's doin' okay."

They had visited him regularly at first, calling him often. But after a while, he started refusing their calls. Then he said he didn't want to see them and one of the doctors told them it might be best if they stayed away for a little while; Stephen was going through some intensive therapy, he explained, and that could be very taxing, but extremely beneficial.

"We could always call it off," Carmen said. "The exorcism, I mean."

"Oh, yeah, and how would that look? Like we were a bunch of fakes who'd changed their minds under pressure, that's how it would look. No. We'll go through with it."

"And if things get worse afterward?"

"Well . . ." He shrugged. "I guess we'll just have to deal with that if it happens, huh?"

Before the day of the exorcism, Father Conlan asked Al and Carmen to remove Michael and Stephanie and Peter from the house so that when he arrived, only Al and Carmen, Kelly, Ed and Lorraine, and the two remaining researchers, Chris and John, were there to meet him.

Father Conlan came to the house wearing street clothes—a pair of black slacks, a powder-blue shirt and a gray sportcoat—and carried a small black suitcase, only slightly larger than a briefcase, as he headed up the walk toward the door.

It was just a little after noon on a warm, bright, and sunny day. But when Father Conlan walked into the house, winter surrounded him.

It was much colder than a house should have been in the summer. It was darker in there than it should have been, too, in spite of the fact that the drapes were open and the blinds were up.

There was a charge in the air, far worse than static electricity, a malignant energy that made every inch of Father Conlan's body tingle sickeningly.

He knew immediately that he was dealing with something much worse and much stronger than he'd anticipated, something that had been in this place far too long and had managed to take root, like an ugly, strangling vine.

"We're not sure what you need us to do, Father," Carmen said as they stood in the hall, "but we're willing to do whatever you ask."

"That's very kind of you," Father Conlan said, giving her a warm smile as he touched her arm. "For one thing, we need a sort of makeshift altar."

"Will a coffee table do?"

"It will do perfectly. For another thing, I think everyone present who is of the Catholic faith should confess their sins and be given absolution."

"I think everyone here is Catholic."

"Then that's fine. I am going to change my clothes, then we'll begin."

"Um, Father, if you don't mind my asking . . . why did you come like this?"

"Well, I thought it would be better for you. You've had enough priests come to your house lately and, this way, your neighbors won't ask a lot of embarrassing questions."

It had not even occurred to Carmen, but she smiled appreciatively and said, "Thank you."

"Where can I change my clothes?"

She directed him to the master bedroom at the end of the hall, where he closed the door behind him.

When Father Conlan came out of the bedroom, he was wearing a white robe and a purple collar.

The altar was set up on the coffee table in the living room, which still had mattresses spread over the floor.

Private confessions were made to Father Conlan by each person present and absolution was given. Once the confessions were made, Father Conlan blessed the house for the third time.

Then everyone gathered in front of the makeshift altar in the living room.

"First," Father Conlan said, "I would like to say a Mass to cleanse us all . . . and the house as well."

Everyone agreed immediately and, a few moments later, Father Conlan began the Mass.

Once again, as during the previous Mass, those present began to have silent struggles with the presence in the house. Carmen began to feel a cold hand lightly moving over her body, fingers probing and prodding in intimate places. She squirmed and shifted her weight from one foot to another, but remained focused on the Mass and fought to ignore it.

A finger began to poke Kelly in the eyes, first the left, then the right, again and again, then both eyes at once, until she finally closed them tightly and bowed her head in what appeared to be an act of reverence, rather than self-protection.

Al began to hear a voice. It did not come from anywhere around him, but from *inside* him, in his head. It was, however, just as loud and just as clear as if the speaker were growling angrily in his face:

"What fucking good do you think *this* will do, Allen? You think this God will help you now? *Why?* He hasn't helped you before this, has He? Well . . . *has He?*"

Al took a deep breath, locked his eyes on Father Conlan, and after a while, the voice went away.

But Al's discomfort did not.

Ed Warren began to experience a curious feeling in his chest. It came and went, but it was a familiar one. It was a tight, constricting feeling, not unlike what he'd felt in 1985 when he'd suffered from a heart attack.

Lorraine was experiencing white flashes behind her eyes, as if there were a sluggish strobe light inside her head. Within each of those bright white flashes was a picture: a naked corpse on a table . . . rough hands on bluish-white breasts . . . a living male body atop the corpse, face locked in wide-mouthed passion . . .

And deep in Lorraine's head, she heard the sound of distant, echoing laughter . . . cruel, mocking laughter. . . .

And then the Mass was over.

Father Conlan faced them and sighed, smiling.

"Now," he said, "I would like to begin the exorcism. But first, I'd like to say a few things."

Everyone was attentive. The demonic harassment had stopped.

"First of all," Father Conlan said, "this may go on for some time. For hours, perhaps. And I want to assure you,"—he chuckled—"no one's head is going to spin around. If you saw that movie, I know what you must be thinking. This may not be easy. We might very well meet with some retaliation, but it won't be like *that*. It could, however, get unpleasant. It could get rough. I just want you to be prepared."

"How long did you say it could take?" Carmen asked timidly.

"Hours. It could take hours. It just depends on what happens."

Everyone nodded slightly.

"So," Father Conlan said quietly. "Are you ready to begin?"

"Yes," Al and Carmen said simultaneously.

Then Carmen added, "Please."

28

The Exorcism

The moment the exorcism began, Ed Warren noticed a
violation of protocol that made him realize that the situation was even more serious than he had suspected. Even
more than that, it made him realize that the church *knew*
how serious it was, and that they had sent someone who
would act accordingly.

The ritual being used by Father Conlan was the *Ritu-
ale Romanus*, the Roman Exorcism Ritual, which was
performed in Latin and which, in forty-two years of research in psychic and supernatural phenomena, Ed had
never, *ever* seen a priest use in the exorcism of a house. It
was often used for the exorcism of a person of the Catholic faith whom the church had decided was, indeed, possessed by a demon, but it was *never* used to exorcise a
house.

As the exorcism went on, Ed began to feel, once again,
the constriction in his chest that he'd felt during the
Mass. His heart began to pound against his ribs so hard
that he could feel it in his throat. He took a deep breath
and tried to ignore the sensation as the exorcism continued.

Carmen began to feel the hand again, but this time it

was much rougher than before. Her exhaustion was overwhelming. She thought she might not win this battle after all.

This time, Kelly felt more than just a finger poking her eyes. This time, it was poking her all over her body, poking mercilessly, poking everywhere, poking *hard* . . . but she knew why: If she were to cry out, she would bring the exorcism to a screeching halt . . . and she knew she did not want to do that.

So she simply prayed silently and stiffened her back, determined not to pay attention to the things that were being done to her.

The voice that had growled inside Al's head during the Mass returned during the exorcism. It returned with a vengeance, *screaming* this time, saying, "You stupid sonofabitch *asshole*! You think this'll *do* something, you spineless fucking *weakling*? You think this'll *help*, you cocksucking wimp, you ass-licking weakling?"

He closed his eyes for a moment, telling himself, *If you just ignore it, it'll go away and this will all be over.*

The exorcism continued.

Knickknacks on shelves in cabinets began to rattle.

Pictures hanging on the wall began to tremble, their frames clattering against the wall.

Four hours into the exorcism, Ed Warren's left arm began to ache; it began to throb as his chest grew tighter and tighter.

Beads of sweat began to break out on his forehead and upper lip and trickled slowly down his face as his breath gradually grew short and his heartbeat began to pound in his head.

Ed grabbed Lorraine's hand, clutched it tightly and leaned toward her, whispering in her ear, "I can't believe what's happening to me."

She felt the trembling in his hand, which was very

uncharacteristic for Ed, and when she saw the sweat pouring down his face, she became very concerned.

"What is it?" she whispered, turning to him, trying hard not to interrupt the ceremony.

Ed put a hand to his chest. "I think . . . it's m-my heart," he whispered as the pain in his arm increased and his chest felt as if a steel band were tightening around it, pulling tighter and tighter.

"I'm gonna have to get outta here," Ed wheezed, squeezing Lorraine's hand even tighter as he tried to catch his breath.

She began to lead him from the living room to the hallway, but something happened that brought them to a sudden halt.

The entire house tilted so that Ed and Lorraine were suddenly climbing *up* the floor rather than walking across it.

Everyone in the room cried out, suddenly clutching one another for balance.

Father Conlan leaned down and gripped the table, but did not miss a beat; he continued the ritual, his voice louder than before, his eyes wider and his jaw set firmly with determination.

Lorraine was not deterred by what she knew to be nothing more than a very convincing illusion, and she continued to lead Ed out of the room, across the hall and into the dining room, where he dropped heavily into a chair, folded his arms on the tabletop and lowered his head weakly.

Father Conlan continued as the others regained their balance when the house seemed to level out.

But it was not through with them.

As the ritual went on, what felt like waves moved fluidly through the floor, making all of them stumble again and again.

Tendrils of smoke rose from the carpet, tendrils that

stretched upward like arms and formed hands at the ends . . . groping, clawing hands . . . hands that clutched at their legs as they rose . . . hands they could *feel* . . . hands with sharp claws that scraped over their clothes, trying to slice through, trying to get to their skin, to slice through their flesh as well. And then, as suddenly as they had come, they were gone.

The ritual continued.

Perspiration was visible on Father Conlan's face and his hands were beginning to tremble. The strain showed in his eyes and on his unsteady lips.

Suddenly, voices began to fill the room, low, hoarse and guttural voices that were heard by them all and that began to close in on them from every direction . . . wet, gurgling voices that brought with them a smell . . . a vile, hideous stench . . . the reek of rotting, decaying flesh.

"We *looooved* it . . ."

"The fucking and the sucking . . ."

"All that groping and fondling . . ."

"It was wonderful . . ."

Then they began to appear, oozing out of the walls and through the furniture like fluid in the shape of human bodies . . . both male and female . . . naked and bruised, their bodies puffy and mottled with white and blue and purple . . . their eyes rolled back in their heads so that only glaring whites were visible . . . some with their arms swaying limply at their sides as they moved in, others with an arm—or both arms—outstretched as they shuffled, the voices continuing:

". . . no god that can stop it . . ."

". . . don't *want* it to stop . . ."

". . . enjoyed it, *all* of it . . ."

". . . all that licking on our skin, all that feeling and touching . . ."

". . . fucking and sucking . . ."

". . . groping and licking . . ."

Father Conlan raised his voice to a near shout, standing straighter than before, his voice growing even louder as he ended the ritual at a fever pitch, shouting the Latin words hoarsely.

They were gone.

The horrible stench had left the room.

Father Conlan was dripping with sweat. He faced those in the room for a long moment, trying to catch his breath. Although he was in top physical condition, he looked as though he had been brought to the very precipice of his endurance.

He turned from the makeshift altar, left the room and went into the dining room, holding a vial of holy water in one hand.

Father Conlan stood over Ed Warren, looking down at him with great concern. "How is he?" he asked Lorraine, who sat beside Ed with her arm around his shoulders.

"Well . . . I'm not really sure," she whispered hoarsely. "He's had a heart attack before, you know. If he doesn't come out of this soon, we're gonna have to call an ambulance."

Father Conlan sprinkled Ed with holy water, waved his hand through the air in the shape of the cross and murmured something in Latin. Then he leaned forward and asked quietly, "Are you all right, Ed?"

Ed lifted his head from the coffee table and coughed, "Y-yeah, I think so."

"Good. So am I." He stood and said, very loudly, "By the power of Jesus Christ, we are *both* all right."

Almost as if a heavy blanket had suddenly been lifted from the house, the feeling of oppression, the dark and smothering atmosphere that had permeated the house for so long, was, in that moment, gone.

It was so noticeable that those still standing in the

ving room gasped with shock when they felt the
hange.

The house seemed brighter, as if the sun, for the first
me in a long while, was finally able to penetrate the
indowpanes and illuminate the inside of the house.

Ed Warren pushed his chair away from the dining-
oom table and stood slowly, carefully, with Lorraine's
rm still around his broad shoulders.

He turned to Father Conlan, gave him a weak smile
nd said, "I think it worked, Father. I think it worked."

29

A Few Months Later

They were moving. Finally.

Kelly and Trish had gone back to Alabama to be with their mother. Stephen was out of the hospital, but had refused to come back to the house. He was staying with his aunt until they were moved out. Even then, he guaranteed nothing; he was still very cautious with them and once they'd moved out, they would have to take their relationship from there and try to patch up all the holes.

The important thing at the moment was that they were, finally and at last, moving out of the house in which their lives had been such a hell.

Epilogue

The Snedekers did leave the house on Meridian and never went back. In fact, merely driving close by made their skin crawl and their palms sweat.

They moved to another house in another Connecticut town, where they went about the slow process of recovering from their ordeal. They still live in Connecticut as of this writing.

And, as of this writing, the white, two-level Colonial still stands on Meridian, as does the twisted, dancing, corpselike tree in the front yard. Tenants have come and gone since the Snedekers left and the house is currently occupied.

Not long after leaving, the Snedekers heard whispers about the new tenants having some strange experiences in the house. They heard that the new tenants were asking questions about the previous occupants, curious to learn if they knew anything about what was happening there.

Carmen felt sorry for them. She feared for them . . . prayed for them. One evening, she timidly suggested to Al that they contact the occupants of their former house and try to help them.

Al turned to her suddenly and lost some of the color in his face as his eyes widened.

"Are you kidding?" he asked, barely able to speak in a whisper. "I . . . I don't even want to *talk* to anybody who lives in that house, not even over the phone. If . . . well, if they don't like it there, they'll leave."

"But what if they're like us?" Carmen asked. "What if they *can't*? What if they don't have any choice?"

He looked away from her and turned to the television. "Then . . . we'll just have to pray for them, I guess."

But Al was right. The new occupants of the house did leave.

They were, however, followed by another family . . .

. . . and another . . .

. . . and still another . . .

Sometimes Truth is More Startling than Fiction!

— True Crime Stories —

You've read it in the newspapers, you've seen it on TV—now get the story behind the headlines of the most sensational crimes of the decade!

☐ **IN BROAD DAYLIGHT**
by Harry M. MacClean
20509-3..................$4.95

☐ **PERFECT VICTIM**
by Christine McGuire and Carla Norton
20442-9..................$5.50

☐ **SAVAGE GRACE**
by Natalie Robins and M.L. Aronson
17576-3..................$5.99

☐ **SAY YOU LOVE SATAN**
by David St. Clair
17574-7..................$4.95

☐ **EXIT THE RAINMAKER**
by Jonathan Coleman
20752-5..................$4.95

☐ **MOBBED UP**
by James Neff
20755-X $5.99

☐ **MISSY'S MURDER**
by Karen Kingsbury
20771-1..................$4.99

☐ **FINAL VOWS**
by Karen Kingsbury
21198-0..................$4.99

☐ **SOLDIER OF FORTUNE MURDERS**
by Ben Green
21401-7..................$4.99

☐ **MILWAUKEE MASSACRE**
by Robert Dvorchak and Lisa Holewa
21286-3..................$4.99

☐ **DEADLY PRETENDER**
by Karen Kingsbury
21507-2..................$4.99

At your local bookstore or use this handy page for ordering:
DELL READERS SERVICE, DEPT. DTC
2451 South Wolf Road, Des Plaines, IL. 60018

D e l l

Please send me the above title(s). I am enclosing $_____.
(Please add $2.50 per order to cover shipping and handling). Send check or money order—no cash or C.O.D.s please.

Ms./Mrs./Mr. _____

Address _____

City/State _____ Zip _____

DTC-4/94

Prices and availability subject to change without notice. Please allow four to six weeks for delivery.